JAMES BOND:
Inspirations of a Legend

JAMES BOND
INSPIRATIONS OF A LEGEND

WILLIAM MAST

LUMINARE PRESS

WWW.LUMINAREPRESS.COM

Cover Design: Claire Flint Last

Luminare Press
442 Charnelton St.
Eugene, OR 97401
www.luminarepress.com

ISBN: 978-1-64388-181-2
LOC: 2019913259

To Stan + Marianne –
I hope that you enjoy
reading about the real
spies who inspired
Ian Fleming to create
his fictional character.
Best regards,
Will Mast.
(2020)

TABLE OF CONTENTS

Preface

In April 2011, *The Guardian* reported that Ian Fleming surpassed Agatha Christie as the British top earning crime writer at +£100M.[1] In 2008, *The Times* ranked Ian Fleming fourteenth out of the greatest fifty British writers since 1945.[2] In April 2012, Amazon Publishing acquired a North American ten-year license to the entire James Bond novel collection for both print and e-book formats.[3] Since 1953, more than one hundred million James Bond books have been sold, and more than half the people on the planet have seen at least one of the films in the Bond franchise—the longest-running film franchise in the world.

Such enormous recognition, interest, and success have sparked curiosity over the years about the real-life individuals who served as inspirations for the James Bond character. Bond fans have pondered such questions as:

Was there a real British spy who signed his letters as OO7?

Did a real British spy named Bond exist in England?

Did a real Bond inspiration mission contribute to saving the world?

Did Fleming's personal attitude toward cold-blooded murder affect Bond's ability to use his license to kill?

The answer to all of these questions is yes. During the 1980s numerous biographies and books that portrayed specific individuals as James Bond inspirations were published. Other new books continued to emerge in the new millennium, as a result of the 1997 and 2000 versions of the United Kingdom *Freedom of Information Act* that facilitated the release of millions of documents on the Internet that further answer these and other related questions. More information regarding real-life Bond inspirations became obtainable when the United States released tens of millions of Cold War documents in January 2009.

With new information continuing to be released, I searched for but found no single book in print that correlated James Bond real-life inspirations with associated story elements from Fleming's Bond novels, short stories, or screenplay/films on which he worked before his death.

Armed with these findings, I wanted to write a book that could present how Ian Fleming evolved James Bond from an assassin who killed for Crown and Country while involved in indiscreet sexual experiences, to a rational thinker who chose to avoid indiscriminate future assassinations and support a more monogamous romantic life at the end of his career.

However, all the information in this book deals with espionage—a topic that is inherently paradoxical. How can anyone differentiate the truth about individuals who work in the world of secrets, lies, and deceits? Their lives are dedicated to investigating intelligence only to manipulate specific facts or circumstances that result in altered interpretations of the truth.

Therefore, what follows are comparisons of twenty-four James Bond inspiration events or behaviors (that were either known of or known by Ian Fleming) with fifty-two corresponding story passages found throughout all twelve Bond novels, five of the nine short stories, one television script, and four of the first five film screenplays released to the public before or shortly after his death.

Supported research draws respectfully from the Bond novels, short stories, films, researched websites, and newly released documents, as well as older books about Bond inspirations and espionage from the Elizabethan era to present day. Each chapter contains "Notes on Sources" and "Sources for Further Reading" that allow the e-book reader to jump to related websites that explore various topics of interest.

In the world of espionage, "a 'legend' is a fake biography of a spy used to provide him or her with a cover."[4] However, my hope is that the reader will discern that Bond is more than a fictional character but rather the embodiment of the ideal spy—a compilation of some of the best (and worst) traits of the most intriguing real-life spies in British history.

James Bond: Inspirations of a Legend fills this gap with each Bond inspiration presented in one or more of Fleming's Bond stories where he is described as an assassin, field spy, intelligence gatherer, diplomat, cryptographer, business/corporate spy, naval commander, double (XX) agent, expert marksman, celebrity spy, war hero, womanizer, food and beverage connoisseur, world traveler, expert car-driver/pilot/scuba diver/sailor, author, mystic scholar, moralist who kills or refuses to kill in cold blood, and ultimate public servant to the Crown & Country.

Introduction

ALTHOUGH IAN FLEMING NEVER SPECIFIED AN EXACT BIRTH-YEAR
for James Bond, the fictional character is believed to have been born
on November 11, 1917, 1920, or 1924.[1]

In chapter 21 of Fleming's eleventh novel, *You Only Live Twice*
(1964), M sends an obituary that includes the following information
to *The Times* for James Bond who, as a result of an official mission
to Japan, is presumed dead.[2]

---

*The obituary reads that James' father, Andrew Bond, was a Scot from
Glencoe and his mother, Monique Delacroix, a Swiss from Canton
de Vaud. His father worked for Vickers Armaments, a company that
produced a wide range of military equipment, including the first
British submarine and an aircraft that flew the first non-stop Atlantic
crossing in 1919.*

*James' early life was spent abroad where he learned to speak
fluent French and German. In 1931, both his parents died in a
climbing accident at Aiguilles Rouges, Chamonix, Switzerland.
James was eleven years old.*

*He was then homeschooled by his aunt Miss Charmian Bond
in Pett Bottom near Canterbury, Kent. At age twelve, following his
father's lifelong desire, James passed satisfactorily into Eton College.
Unfortunately, his grades were undistinguished, and he received an
early dismissal due to alleged ungentlemanly conduct with one of
the school's maids. Alternately, James was sent to his father's alma
mater, Fettes College, where he excelled in sports —representing the*

William Mast

school twice as a lightweight boxer. There, he also founded the first judo class in the British public school system.

In 1941, with help from an old Vickers friend of his father, James entered what was to become the Ministry of Defense. There, due to the confidential sensitivity of his work, he was appointed to the rank of Lieutenant in the Royal Navy Volunteer Reserve (RNVR) and rose to the final rank of Commander. After the war, Commander Bond continued working for the Ministry where he rose to the rank of Principal Officer in the Civil Service. For his outstanding service, he was awarded the Companion Most Distinguished Order of Saint Michael and Saint George (CMG) in 1954.

In a potential violation of the national Official Secrets Act, which prohibited individuals from divulging information pertinent to national security, a colleague published a number of James' exploits after the war. Fortunately, since the published missions revealed no actual government secret activities, official charges against the works were dismissed.

James was briefly married in 1962 to Teresa, the only daughter of Marc-Ange Draco, of Marseilles. Her tragic death shortly after the ceremony was reported in the press.

JAMES BOND, IN FLEMING'S EYES, WAS AN "UNINTERESTING MAN to whom things happened."[3] The following seventeen chapters present twenty-four James Bond inspirations that Fleming used to create his fictional spy as an undercover espionage agent who defied authority, made his own mission decisions in the field, worked as a diplomat/business/corporate spy, studied cryptography, rose to the level of a naval commander, became a highly sought Double O assassin, engaged in double (XX) agent operations, used assorted gadgets in the field, became a committed gambler, enjoyed being a food and drink connoisseur, excelled as an expert car-driver/pilot/scuba diver/sailor/world traveler, avoided being a decorated hero or celebrity spy, evolved from a womanizer to a committed male partner, questioned the morality of murdering people for his country, and always remained a faithful public servant to the Crown & Country.

The timeline starts in the 16th century with an individual known as 007, continues until June 1966 with the last James Bond print appearance in the *Octopussy and The Living Daylights* short story collection, and ends with the first five of the 50+ years of Bond films.

CHAPTER 1

John Dee (1527 – 1608 or 1609)

DR. JOHN DEE
Codename: 007

M ade popular by his self-proclaimed codename 007, Dr. John Dee[1] is the oldest Bond inspiration. Working as an "intelligencer"[2] or practitioner of mystical insight for Queen Elizabeth I, he used his knowledge of mathematics, science, astrology, alchemy, Cabala, Rosicrucianism, and magic to develop and decipher cryptographic codes for covert messages.

Much of Dee's work is believed to have contributed to the Nazi Occultism that was practiced by Adolph Hitler and Heinrich Himmler (Head of the SS) during World War II. And it was during that time that Ian Fleming, while working for the Department of Naval Intelligence (DNI), studied these topics to help second-guess political and military decisions made by the Nazi military leaders. As a result, it is likely that Ian Fleming incorporated these esoteric fields of study into his James Bond books.

Given Fleming's penchant for historical research, it is believed that James Bond's codename comes from this real-life 007. Fleming was an investigative reporter. He collected rare books, read history, and investigated stories for newspapers, magazines, and his own fictional stories that led him to find inspirations for his spy stories. But John Dee was not a spy in the true sense of the word.

Known as Dr. John Dee, the 16th-century conjurer never worked for MI6. He never personally battled spies yet is credited with sinking the Spanish Armada by foreseeing "that devastating storms would destroy the Spanish Fleet."[3] As a magician and conjurer, he was believed to do the devil's work. Unlike the fictional 007, John had a long, pointed white beard and wore a flowing robe, which made him look more like a cross between a gnome and Gandalf from *The Lord of the Rings* than a superspy.

John's position for Queen Elizabeth necessitated the creation of his "glyph"[4]—a style of writing that presents visual elements to convey secret meanings. His communication with Elizabeth needed to be confidential. Therefore, all of John's official court correspondence to the Queen was labeled with two circles (OO) covered by the number seven (7), which looks like a roof. This cryptographic symbol indicated that all of his communication was "for her eyes only." Putting the eyes under an extended Cabalistic lucky number seven, John visually represented his ability to protect the Queen under his roof. He later used this same cipher to communicate with the Queen's British Secret Service creators, Chief Advisor William Cecil and Spymaster Francis Walsingham.

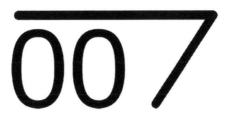

Fleming must have been familiar with the glyph and its associated meaning, as evidenced by the second Bond short story "For Your Eyes Only" (1960) and the twelfth Bond film of the same name released in 1981. It is also in the same codename that M uses for top-secret files.

It's October in London when Bond is called into M's office. The Indian summer brings the smell of freshly mown grass from Regent's Park into the room. "He [is] mildly intrigued because M had addressed him as James and not by his number – 007."[5] Such an address usually means that Bond is going to be given an assignment of a personal nature that extends beyond normal protocol.

With an intense look M explains that the Havelocks—a couple at whose wedding he was best man—were found, by their daughter, "full of bullets"[6] in their Jamaican home. An ex-Gestapo Nazi named von Hammerstein, who had formerly headed Batista's Counter Intelligence, ordered the couple killed because they had refused to sell him their property. Now hiding out in Echo Lake, Vermont with three of his henchmen, he continues putting pressure on their daughter to sell him the land and home.

Bond said, "These people can't be hung, sir. But they ought to be killed."[7] And with those words, M opens his drawer and pulls out a rubber stamp and red ink pad. He carefully inks, aligns, and tamps the stamp on the top right-hand corner of the grey docket folder. He turns the folder around and pushes it toward Bond. "The red sanserif letters, still damp, said: FOR YOUR EYES ONLY."[8] Acknowledging that his mission is to murder four individuals in cold blood, Bond walks out of the room and begins to mentally and physically prepare for the assignment.

BEYOND JOHN'S OO7 GLYPH, THE DOUBLE ZERO (OO) CODE WAS later used by the British Admiralty during World War II. After the war Fleming told an interviewer, "all the top-secret signals had the double-O prefix."[9] He further divulged that it was later changed for security reasons. However, to make James Bond's job more interesting, he kept the numbers in order to provide him with a license to kill.

John Dee was born on July 13, 1527, as the only child of affluent Protestant "mercer" (textile merchant) Roland Dee and his wife Jane. At the age of fifteen, John entered St. John's College in Cambridge to study mathematics, astronomy, philosophy, Latin, and Greek. During this time, mathematics was associated with magic and conjuration. Ignoring the negative correlations, John pursued his passion and immersed himself in the scientific study of numbers.

During this time, it was well known that the Earth was the center of the universe and the sun, moon, and planets revolved around it in concentric circles. Using this knowledge, astrologers, scientists, and mathematicians, such as John, were able to create astrological charts to foretell future events.

While attending St John's, John was involved in a production of the Aristophanes play *Peace (Pax)*. The opening scene required the protagonist Trygaeus to reach Zeus in his heavenly home. In order to create this effect, John painstakingly designed a flying beetle. Much like the Broadway production of *Spiderman: Turn off the Dark* (2010), he used advanced mathematics and technology to build a realistic looking scarab that allowed the actor playing the beetle to fly. The

William Mast

work was so effective the audience believed it moved through black magic. As a result, John became known as a magician and conjurer—a reputation that earned him caution, fear, and respect.

He graduated in 1546 and entered Trinity College at the age of nineteen, receiving a Master of Arts degree in 1548. After graduation, he traveled to Louvain, Brussels to study new concepts of triangulation land surveying techniques. As an emerging intellectual, he declined five court positions throughout Europe before agreeing, in July 1551, to lecture on Euclid at various schools of mathematics in Paris.

During his travels, he began amassing a library that would eventually contain approximately 4,000 rare books, manuscripts, and scientific instruments for his center for learning in Mortlake, which became the "largest philosophical and scientific library collection in Elizabethan England,"[10] attracting numerous scholars from England and Europe.

After returning home, John experienced the reign and death of Edward IV, and the coronation of the Catholic Queen Mary I. On August 23, 1553, three prisoners from the Tower of London came before Queen Mary's Privy Council for examination. One was John's Protestant father Roland, who was accused of ransacking government merchandise while traveling through London. Although he was released, Roland was a ruined man with no future means of support.

On May 28, 1555, John was arrested. Due to his reputation, he was charged with using mathematics, magic, witchcraft, and conjuration to create enchantments to kill the Catholic Queen. He was further linked to Mary's sister, Elizabeth, who refused to renounce her Protestant religion. By June 1st, he was incarcerated and his library sealed. As a devout Christian, John denounced both Protestants and Catholics believing that their sects, as well as the Pope and the Bible, were based on erroneous information. Instead he devoutly believed that religion can only be found in nature, mathematics, and learning. Due to an inability to find any evidence of a crime, John was released.

When Elizabeth succeeded her half-sister Mary, an official relationship developed between John and the Queen. As her newly appointed intelligencer for political applications, his first duty was to foresee the most appropriate day for her coronation. After creating and consulting Elizabeth's astrological birth chart, John chose January 15, 1559.

Aspects of John and Queen Elizabeth's relationship are apparent in the second Bond novel *Live and Let Die* (1954), which presents elements of magic, mysticism, and voodoo to assist the tarot reader Solitaire to foresee future events for Mr. Big.

----------◆----------

Bond and the CIA agent Felix Leiter travel to a Harlem club called 'The Boneyard.'[11] After they are led to a table with a reserved card, they sit and order scotch-and-sodas and chicken sandwiches. As the general patron dancing dies down, the MC introduces the stripper Sumatra to "a frenzy of applause."[12] Gyrating her body slowly for a time, she picks up her pace and plucks a strategically placed sequin star from one breast, then the other, leaving her topless. To the screams of the crowd, she dances wearing only a strip of lace around her lower waist that she tears away, revealing "a single black G-string."[13] With the crowd screaming for her to complete the dance, the MC announces that it can only be finished in absolute darkness.

As the lights are extinguished, the floor underneath Bond's table is lowered through a trapdoor. A second floor quickly moves above their heads, leaving them trapped in a small, soundproof room. Bond is separated from Leiter and taken to Mr. Big. Already aware of Bond's 00 status, Mr. Big asks, "Whom have you been sent over to kill here, Mister Bond? Not me by any chance."[14]

Bond chooses a story he could support and which would cover the facts. He explains that he is looking for the English "Edward IV Rose Nobles"[15] coins that are being sold in Harlem. After Bond casually sits in a nearby chair, a broad strap quickly surrounds his body, two short straps restrain his arms, and two others move around his ankles. He's trapped once again.

Then, one of the most beautiful women Bond has ever seen enters the room and closes the door. "She stood just inside the room and stood looking at Bond, taking him in slowly inch by inch."[16] It's Solitaire, whom Mr. Big introduces as his "inquisitor."[17] He explains, "Torture is messy and inconclusive. People tell you what will ease the pain. With this girl it is not necessary to use clumsy methods. She can divine the truth in people."[18] Asking Bond to repeat his mission in her presence, she turns her cards. After a dead silence she coldly states, "He speaks the truth."[19]

With his life now saved, Mr. Big has a henchman break James' little finger on his left hand as punishment for the intrusion. Then, as he is moved through a corridor, Bond manages to break out of an arm-lock and throw the thug down a stairwell. Now in possession of the thug's gun, Bond opens the door to a waiting car and shoots a standing gunman in the belly. He sends a second bullet through the head of the driver. Bond throws out the driver, commandeers the car, and screeches out of the garage amidst a trail of bullets from the injured gunman.

AND, SO BEGINS THE STORY OF MR. BIG'S "INQUISITOR" FORESEEING future events and truths in a similar fashion to John Dee in his role as Elizabeth's "intelligencer."

To enhance his studies in magic, conjuration, and mathematics, John left England to study Cabala for the next five years. Cabala uses mathematics, Hebrew, and mysticism to study letters and symbols that can be used to define the secrets of the universe, which, according to Cabalistic doctrine, is ruled by an estimated 301,655,172 angels who live at the top of the universe. Without realizing that his research would later become the foundation for the field of cryptography, John began a desperate search for angels.

Over the next few years, he studied the books *Steganographia* and *Polygraphia*, written by the founding father of modern cryptography, Johannes Trithemius. From his studies, John found correlations among theology, history, occultism, mathematical cryptographic codes, and Cabala mysticism with magical forces that rule nature. Unlike superstition (which John considered a foolish practice of fortunetellers), these books were full of ciphers that he believed could solve Europe's political problems and be used for secret service covert communication.

As a result, John worked with William Cecil and Francis Walsingham to establish a British espionage communication network that "came to rely heavily on codes."[20] Similarly, in *Live and Let Die*, Ian Fleming creates "'Language,' the secret Voodoo speech only used by the initiates"[21] to communicate encrypted messages with Mr. Big.

Uncertain how the Queen would respond to the Cabalistic interpretation of mathematics, cryptography, and mysticism, John shared his work with Elizabeth on June 14, 1564. Intrigued, she became his student and studied the enigmatic use of codes.

With Elizabeth's desire to pursue world exploration and domination of the seas, John foresaw a need to build a British navy capable of competing with Spain. In addition to their eighteen navigable ships, he advised that sixty 160- and 200-ton tall ships, plus twenty additional 20- and 50-ton ships, be built.

On May 4, 1493, Pope Alexander VI issued a papal bull dividing the New World between Spain and Portugal. However, John and England defiantly refuted the decree. In *Brytanici Imperii Limites*, John claimed that the British crossed the Atlantic in 1170, giving them rights to all islands and seacoasts in Florida—and all areas northward. Due to England's new naval strength and predicted colonization of North America, John is credited with creating the term "British Empire."

In February 1578, the fifty-year-old John married twenty-two-year-old Jane Fromands, who would create a future problem with John's ability to decipher the angels' language. On March 8, 1582, Edward Kelley presented himself to the couple as a "skryer"—a spirit medium who can contact angels. Through his séances, John met the archangel Michael and, with the help of Kelley, copied information dictated by angels in angelic Enochian language[22]—a mystical language of fewer than 1,000 words that John would later apply in the field of cryptography.

During one of their séances, Kelley reported that he and John were commanded to exchange each other's wives for a night. As a result, Jane became pregnant. Due to John and Kelley's declining personal relationship, after six years of collaborative work, the number of séances gradually diminished until they ended in 1588.

On December 15, 1589, John returned to Mortlake. In his absence, his cottage and library had been ransacked. Most of his books, scientific instruments, and furniture were gone. At the age of sixty-two, John found himself in debt placing the losses at well over £1,000.

England had changed. Astrological prophecies were now ridiculed and the idea that man can communicate with angels was believed to be absurd. Out of respect for his former work, the Queen gave John a position of authority at Manchester College to keep him out of London and the Court until her death in 1603.

On July 17, 1607, John resurrected his research and séances with an old friend and skryer, Bartholomew Hickman. During one of these séances, the angel Raphael visited John and told him that he would soon receive the knowledge and understanding that he had sought for so many years. However, first, he had to take a long journey. In preparation, John buried his books in locked chests around the fields of Mortlake.

The exact date of John's death is unknown. His diary records it as March 26, 1609. In 1642, Robert Jones, a confectioner, purchased a locked cedar wood chest at an Addle Street shopping stall near the bank of the Thames River. Twenty years later he found a secret drawer that when opened revealed a number of John's books and writings. Elias Ashmole, an expert in alchemy, occult, and astrology, interpreted them in 1672. As other chests were later found in the fields of Mortlake, the scholar Meric Casaubon copied the deteriorating documents that detailed John's spiritual conversations with angels.

John ultimately produced eighteen books, of which only a few survived. They contain an unknown language comprised of an alphabet list of words, rules of writing and pronunciation. The codes remained a mystery until German linguist Thomas Ernst and Jim Reeds of the AT&T Mathematical & Cryptography Research Department cracked them in the 1990s, finding them to contain true mathematical codes and not magical incantations. As a result of their findings, John is credited as being a major contributor to the field of cryptography.

John is also considered a founder of the Rosicrucian[23] movement of modern mysticism—a secret brotherhood that studies and interprets ancient esoteric wisdom for contemporary prophecies. And, just as the Nazi occultists tried to predict the outcomes of specific military strategies and movements, members of this organization try to use this ancient wisdom to provide insight into the physical, natural, and/or spiritual realms to predict outcomes of various problems.

As a result, one may conclude that Fleming used John's writings as well as his knowledge of Nazi occultism in his second Bond novel, *Live and Let Die*, where he integrated cryptography, Cabala, Rosicrucianism, mysticism, and voodoo through Solitaire's tarot card readings and premonitions. It may be further accepted that Fleming used John Dee's glyph with the Queen's eyes under John's roof to inspire the title of the eighth Bond book, *For Your Eyes Only*. And, John's contributions to Queen Elizabeth's official British espionage agency may have influenced Fleming's tenth Bond novel, *On Her Majesty's Secret Service*. Finally, the recorded use of 00 numbers assigned to British covert operations may have, in part, inspired Bond's "license to kill" credentials in Fleming's first novel *Casino Royale*.

CHAPTER 2
FOUR BONDS
James I, II, III & John

"The name is Bond – James Bond." This introduction is infamous in popular culture, print, and cinema history. An appropriate name for a protagonist is of critical importance, as it not only creates a signature for the individual but also molds a memorable image of the character in a person's mind. For Bond, this image may be of a ruthless killer, a heavy drinker, an ephemeral lover, and, of course, a superspy. However, Ian Fleming knew four Bonds, and their stories could also serve as credible sources for the fictional character's name.

Ornithologist James Bond taken at National Academy of Natural Sciences Philadelphia (1974) Courtesy of Jerry Freilich

James Bond #1
Occupation: Ornithologist

IN FALL OF 1960, JAMES AND MARY BOND RECEIVED THE FIRST press cuttings of a *Sunday Times* review of James Bond's forthcoming reprinted book *Birds of the West Indies,* which is where they discovered that Jim was being mistaken for the fictional spy in Ian Fleming's novels. At a Philadelphia photo processing shop, Mrs. Bond was informed that her husband was being interviewed by *Playboy* magazine. The couple remained perplexed about the connection until they received a February 1961 *Rogue* article verifying that Ian Fleming had "lifted the author's name"[1] from *Birds of the West Indies* for his fictional Secret Service agent. As a result, life for the real James Bond,[2] an ornithologist, was turned upside-down.

Born in Philadelphia on January 4, 1900, James Bond attended St Paul's School in Concord New Hampshire. After his mother's death, James traveled back to England with his father where he attended Harrow and Cambridge University, obtaining a B.A. degree in 1922.

When he returned to the United States in 1925, he signed on to an expedition in the Amazon sponsored by the Academy of Natural Sciences. With a developing interest in ornithology, he became an expert in Caribbean birds and in 1936 wrote his first book titled *Birds of the West Indies*. This was followed by *Field Guide of the Birds of the West Indies* (1947), *Check-List of Birds of the West Indies* (1956), and the second version of *Birds of the West Indies* (1961). Jim's major contribution was his finding that selected Caribbean birds originate from North America while others originate from South America. Those distinctions of ancestry and location became known as "Bond's Line."

Jim was awarded the Institute of Jamaica's Musgrave Medal in 1952, the Brewster Medal from the American Ornithologists Union in 1954, and the Leidy Medal from the Academy of Natural Sciences in 1975. He spent much of his career as the Curator of Birds at the Academy of Sciences in Philadelphia.

He passed away in Chestnut Hospital in Philadelphia on February 14, 1989, at the age of eighty-nine.

As an avid bird watcher, Ian Fleming, like many other bird watchers, had a copy of *Birds of the West Indies* on a shelf at his Jamaican *Goldeneye* home, where it is commonly believed that he first thought of his fictional spy's name.

During an interview with *Reader's Digest* Ian Fleming stated, "I wanted the simplest, dullest, plainest-sounding name I could find, 'James Bond' was much better than something more interesting like 'Peregrine Carruthers.' Exotic things would happen to and around him, but he would be a neutral figure- an anonymous, blunt instrument wielded by a government department."[3]

Fleming tried numerous times to explain that his protagonist was specifically named after James Bond the ornithologist. In an October 5, 1962 *New Yorker* magazine interview Fleming said,

"When I wrote my first book in 1953 ... One of the bibles of my youth was Birds of the West Indies by James Bond, a well-known ornithologist, and when I was casting about for a name for my protagonist, I thought, My God, that's the dullest name I ever heard so I appropriated it. Now the dullest name in the world has become an exciting one and Mrs. Bond once wrote me a letter thanking me for using it."[4]

In reality, nothing could be further from the truth. In a letter to Fleming dated February 1, 1961, Mary Wickham Bond wrote:

"Dear Mr. Fleming,
It was inevitable that we should catch up with you! First, the review in the London Sunday Times of my husband's new Birds of the West Indies revealed the existence of James Bond, British Agent [JBBA].

Second, our friend Charles Chaplin of Haverport, Pa., and friend of your brother Peter, gave us a copy of Dr. No, which explained the rest. I read further stories about JBBA and became convinced that that you must have been following JB authenticus around the West Indies, and picking up some of his adventures. It came to him as a surprise when we discovered in an interview published in Rogue magazine that you had brazenly taken the name of a real human being for your rascal! And after reading

Dr. No, my JB thought that you'd been to Dirty Dick's in Nassau and talked with Old Farrington and got from him the story about the "Priscilla" and a wild trip about Jim's collecting parrots on Abaco. That was the time he spent several nights in a cave full of bats to get away from the mosquitoes.

As a rule truth is stranger than fiction but your JBBA proves this isn't necessarily so! Just don't let 007 marry – certainly not until he's 55!

This is a hurried letter because we're getting off to Yucatan and Cozumel this afternoon, thence back to Nassau where we'll spend a few days with the Chaplins.

I tell my JB he could sue you for defamation of character but he regards the whole thing as a joke.
Sincerely yours,
Mary Wickham Bond"[5]

During this time Fleming was sued for illegal ownership of story elements in a screenplay of his new 1961 novel *Thunderball*. In an attempt to be sensitive to the fictional use of the ornithologist's name, Fleming responded on June 20, 1961, as follows:

"Dear Mrs. James Bond,
I don't know where to begin to ask your forgiveness for my tardy response to your letter of February 1st...

I will confess at once that your husband has every reason to sue me in every possible position and for practically every kind of libel in the book, for which I now confess the damnable truth...

I was determined that my secret agent should be as anonymous a personality as possible. Even his name should be the very reverse of the kind of "Peregrine Carruthers" whom one meets in this type of fiction.

At that time one of my bibles was, and still is, Birds of the West Indies by James Bond, and it struck me that this name, brief, unromantic and yet very masculine, was just what I needed and so James Bond II was born, and started off on the career that, I must confess has been meteoric...

So there is my dreadful confession together with limitless apologies and thanks for the fun and fame I have had from the most extraordinary chance choice of so many years ago.

In return I can only offer your James Bond unlimited use of the name Ian Fleming for any purpose he may think fit. Perhaps one day he will discover some particularly horrible species of bird which he would like to christen in an insulting fashion. That might be a way of getting his own back!...
Yours sincerely,
Ian Fleming"[6]

Surprisingly, the Bonds never seem to get their "own back," although the situation of sharing names with the fictional superspy did lead to compromising situations. Upon returning to Jamaica, James was questioned on declaring such items as cigarettes, liquor, or firearms. Also, as the couple left their small hotel in St. Lucia, upon hearing Jim say that he hoped to return at a later date, a chambermaid whispered to him, "I hope *you* will- James Bond!" These rather awkward circumstances for the married couple were accepted politely as oddly interesting and humorous.

The inevitable day when the real Bonds met Fleming for the first and only time came on February 5, 1964. Jim and Mary traveled to the Jamaican north shore in an effort to study a few primitive islands when they decided to take Ian up on his invitation. After arriving at *Goldeneye* and giving their names to Violet the house-keeper, pandemonium broke loose. With Violet's arms flailing as she screamed that the real Bonds had arrived, Ian hurriedly emerged from the living room and offered a quick friendly handshake. Explaining that the Canadian Broadcasting Corporation (CBC) was there to record an interview, Ian insisted that the reporters include Jim, who was then filmed with him at various locations around the house. When Ian returned to the interview, the Bonds went swimming before they sat down to a large lunch of seafood, strawberries, and conversation.

During their socializing, Mrs. Bond allayed any fears of a libel case by her husband and revealed to Ian's surprise that Jim was an American. Fleming's exhaustion from his CBC interview was obvious. With his energy depleted, he excused himself for an hour to relax before completing the last segment of the CBC interview. However, before leaving Ian reappeared with a first edition copy of his new book *You Only Live Twice* where he had written on the fly page:

> *"To the real James Bond from the thief of his identity, Ian Fleming Feb. 5, 1964 (a great day!)"*[7]

Always remembering that wonderful day, Mary and James Bond were saddened to see Walter Cronkite report on August 12, 1964, that Ian had died. In April they received a transcript of the CBC interview, and after his death they were sent a framed photograph of their trip to *Goldeneye*, making this story the most cited when explaining how 007 got his name.

In the twentieth Bond film *Die Another Day* (2002), Pierce Bronson disguised himself as a field guide, *Birds of the West Indies* book-carrying ornithologist in Havana, Cuba, where he also introduced himself as such to Halle Berry, who played Jinx in the film. However, it is in the sixth Bond novel *Dr. No* (1958) that Fleming created a cover for Bond to impersonate a person interested in birds, making this his only fictional ornithologist reference.

In search of information about a missing Regional Control Jamaican Commander Strangeways, Bond reaches Crab Key in the darkness of night. After hiding his boat, he falls asleep and then awakens in the morning to find a beautiful naked girl on the beach studying shells that she has just brought ashore. Emerging from the trees, he intro-

duces himself to Honeychile Rider as an Englishman "interested in birds."[8] He claims to be searching for the roseate spoonbill—a fish-eating bird, regarding which Dr. No later states, "I was entertained with the idea of converting bird dung into gold"[9] by collecting and selling their guano for fertilizer.

After the mysterious nemesis captures Bond and Honeychile, Dr. No attempts to kill Bond through a series of torturous trials, leaving Honeychile to suffer a slower death by being tied to rocks while crabs eat her alive. After passing all of the trials, Bond is ultimately reunited with Honeychile, who knew that crabs wouldn't eat human flesh that remains still. In retaliation, Bond kills Dr. No by burying him under a mound of guano.

———————◆———————

REMEMBERING HER FIRST LETTER TO FLEMING, MARY BOND expressed the belief that her husband's few nights in a cave with bats were inspirational to Ian's future development of his Bond fictional character. As the Bonds visited Fleming so near to his death, it may be concluded that the film producers' decision to introduce the ornithologist character in *Die Another Day* was one that the author would welcome.

Agatha Christie plaque – Torre Abbey (2008)
Courtesy of Violetriga & derivative work: Flanker

James Bond #2
Occupation: Opportunistic Sleuth

IN 1934, AGATHA CHRISTIE[10] PUBLISHED TWELVE SHORT STORIES in a book collection called *The Listerdale Mystery* through William Collins and Sons, UK. The protagonist in a story titled "The Rajah's Emerald" is none other than a young James Bond who travels on a seashore holiday with Grace, a female friend whom he has courted for the last three years. Showing discretion in their relationship, they stay at different hotels. James, possessing little money, stays at a small hotel, one and a half miles away from the beach while Grace, who has recently earned more money, stays at the elegant Esplanade beachfront hotel. Also, in attendance at the Esplanade are the three Sopworth sisters and their brother Claud, who is a source of potential affection for Grace.

When attending a swimming gathering with Grace and her four friends, James is not allowed to use the Esplanade changing huts and must use one of the long-lined public tents to put on his swimsuit. Attempting to save time, he uses another private hut hoping not to be caught.

After their swim he returns, changes into another pair of trousers, and leaves the premises—only to find a stolen emerald in the pocket. Returning to the hut to exchange pants, he is arrested by a man believed to be a Scotland Yard detective. To James' surprise, the detective's badge is one from a bicycle club where he is a member. As a result, James modifies his story to avoid being suspected of any further crime for which he is being set-up.

He states that the gem is at his lodging and then takes the detective past a police station. There he secretly places the emerald in the detective's pocket, calls out to the police, and has the man detained for stealing the stone.

When the owner of the changing hut arrives at the station to claim his stone, he discovers that the thief is his newly hired valet. The man is arrested, the jewel is returned to its owner, and James is proclaimed a hero. Deducing that the imposter detective was the thief and having him captured moves James from suspected thief to super sleuth. All ends well as the young James is invited to lunch at the owner's villa to the envy of his girlfriend and her friends.

It is well known that Agatha Christie and Ian Fleming were acquainted. It is also highly probable that Ian read "The Rajah's Emerald." Could it be that Fleming repaid his friend for use of the James Bond name when he described her as a successful gambler in his tenth Bond novel *On Her Majesty's Secret Service* (1963).

Bond has successfully completed OPERATION THUNDERBALL, where he prevented England from having to pay a £100M ransom by recovering two atomic bombs. Now, having spent the past twelve months searching the world for the head of SPECTRE—Ernst Stavro Blofeld, who masterminded the plot—Bond finds himself in at the Hotel Splendide in Royale, France.

After checking in, he enters Casino Royale and sits at a baccarat table near "a rather Agatha Christie-style little Englishwoman"[11] who appears to be winning. During the course of the evening, "the little old English lady"[12] pulls away from the pack and "bancoe[s] him at the tenth turn,"[13] leaving him with "three kings, making zero."[14] Bond has obviously met his match.

WRITERS OFTEN GET IDEAS FOR THEIR STORIES FROM OTHER writers, and Ian Fleming was no exception. Known for using friends' names for characters in his novels, the use of Christie's name and description may have been an intentional gesture to publicly thank her for not suing him for the use of her super sleuth's name for his superspy.

Of professional interest, in April 2011 Ian Fleming (1908-1964) edged out Agatha Christie (1890-1976) as the top-earning British crime writer. The record sales are based on book sales, box office returns, license fees, and company accounts. Christie falls slightly behind with £100M, including the continuing royalties from the longest running play in the world, *The Mousetrap*. The £100M+ honor for Fleming includes a new record of 100 million Bond books sold throughout the world.

In contrast, this outcome could have been reversed if Ian Fleming had had to pay for the book and film rights to use Agatha Christie's James Bond name for his own protagonist.

Promotional photograph of Barry Nelson from the
television game show To Tell the Truth (1962)

James Bond #3
Codename: Card Sense Jimmy Bond

AFTER PUBLISHING THE FIRST JAMES BOND NOVEL *CASINO ROYALE* in 1953, Ian Fleming was committed to using the James Bond name for his protagonist. He was also anxious to sell his work to a film studio —and an opportunity arose with the United States CBS television series *Climax*[15]. This one-hour, made-for-TV show directed by William H. Brown was produced from a modified three-act script based on the original novel. The production company paid $1,000 to air the live broadcast on October 21, 1954.

The show stared Barry Nelson[16] playing an American James Bond, a.k.a. "Card Sense Jimmy Bond,"[17] a secret agent working for "Combined Intelligence" in Washington D.C. Using reversed Anglo-American roles, his British counterpart was played by Michael Pate who portrayed Clarence (named Felix in the novel) Leiter, a member of the British Secret Service attached to the French Station F working in conjunction with the Deuxieme Bureau.

The show followed the original storyline of the espionage agencies cooperating to financially destroy their nemesis, Le Chiffre, through a game of baccarat. However, unlike the novel, wherein

James is captured, tortured by Le Chiffre, and saved from death by a SMERSH agent due to an absence of a contract to kill him, in the television show James is captured in his hotel room and tortured by Le Chiffre, who inflicts excruciating pain on James' toes with a pair of pliers.

Peter Lorre played the part of Le Chiffre. Linda Christian played Valerie Mathis (named Vesper in the novel), who enters the story as Jimmy's old love interest. This Americanization of the characters had minimal effect on the theme or plot (apart from insulting Great Britain).

Jimmy and Leiter drank scotch & soda, a popular American drink of the day, with the cane gun used in a similar fashion found in the novel to threaten Jimmy's life.

In the casino, Le Chiffre is seen with two gunmen—one who appears to be a cripple. "A chunky Malacca cane with a rubber tip hung on the rail beside him. He must have had permission to bring the cane into the Casino with him,"[18] as such items are normally forbidden to avoid potential acts of violence.

At one point during the baccarat game, Bond is cleaned out. Fortunately, Felix Leiter sends him thirty-two million francs in an envelope. While the table is being prepared for a final game between Bond and Le Chiffre for the bank of thirty-two million francs, the gunman stands directly behind Bond and presses something hard into the base of his spine. He hears "softly, urgently, just behind his right ear: 'This is a gun monsieur. It is absolutely silent. It can blow the base of your spine off without a sound. You will appear to have fainted. I shall be gone. Withdraw your bet before I count ten. If you call for help I shall fire.'"[19] Before the man can pull the trigger, Bond thrusts the chair back violently and wrenches the gun from the man while he falls to the floor. The man disappears, Bond rises from the ground, and the cane gun is given to Felix Leiter as a supposed friend of its owner.

William Mast

ALTHOUGH THE AMERICAN SHOW WAS PRESENTED IN A REASON-able facsimile to Fleming's work, Peter Lorre did not die at the end of the live-recorded broadcast as expected, either due to insufficient time or his own stubbornness. Another insult was the fact that the show set precedence for later Bond stories and films to call James "Jimmy" or "Jimbo." And finally, for the modern spy story and film enthusiast, Robert Ludlum chose to copy the initials J.B. for his recent novels and feature films series, featuring the modern American superspy Jason Bourne.

John Bond
Occupation: Spy for Sir Francis Drake

WORKING AS A SPY FOR QUEEN ELIZABETH I, JOHN BOND SERVED as a henchman for Sir Francis Drake. In 1583, Phillip II, King of Spain engraved a medal with the words "Non Sufficit Orbis" (The World Is Not Enough). He also had the words placed on a banner in his royal coat of arms. In 1586 when Drake raided the governor's mansion in Santo Domingo, he found the medal. Disgusted with the King's insatiable desire for power, he took it home to Queen Elizabeth as evidence of Philips' ambition to invade England and make it part of his empire. It is believed that this was the inspiration for what would become John's family motto.

Ironically, John's family motto "Non Sufficit Orbis" (The World Is Not Enough) also just happens to be the same as the motto of the fictional James Bond family introduced in Fleming's tenth Bond novel *On Her Majesty's Secret Service* (1963).[20] It was also the name of the nineteenth Bond film *The World is not Enough* (1999) starring Pierce Bronson, and the fifth Bond novel by Raymond Benson (published in 1999).

In Fleming's *On Her Majesty's Secret Service* novel, Bond travels to the College of Arms on Queen Victoria Street to gather information on a Coat of Arms for Ernst Blofeld.

While assisting Bond at the College of Arms, the heraldry officer, Griffin Or mistakenly believes that Bond is searching for his own ancestry coat of arms and states, "we have some ten different families of Bonds. The important one ended with Sir Thomas Bond, a most distinguished gentleman."[21] Explaining that his father was Scottish and his mother Swiss, Griffon excitedly interrupts saying that "The World is not Enough"[22] is a charming motto for which he may have the right of ownership. Bond replies, "It is an excellent motto which I shall certainly adopt."[23]

WILLIAM BOND, THE CURRENT HEAD OF THE JOHN BOND FAMILY, found his ancestor's diary in the family archives. The journal was written by Denis Bond, the son of John Bond, and has remained unavailable for public viewing.

It is probable that Ian Fleming was familiar with the motto because he went to school near the estate. He may have even been aware of the family, as they were well known in the area. The John Bond home in Dorset on the Isle of Purbeck was only a few miles from the Durnford House prep school where Ian attended. The Dorset historian and author, Rodney Legg, stated, "Fleming once said that everything I write has precedent in truth, and I think it is true of the Bond motto."[24] For the author to have dreamed up the motto for use in one of his books is highly unlikely.

CHAPTER 3

R. H. Bruce Lockhart in Malaya (1908)
Courtesy of Negeri Sembilan in Panta

SIR ROBERT HAMILTON (R.H.) BRUCE LOCKHART

Diplomat Spy

Robert H. Bruce Lockhart[1] was a British diplomat spy during World War I and the Russian Revolution. Like Bond, Bruce had salacious female relationships in the field and difficulty following direct orders during complex field assignments. When his superiors questioned his allegiance to Great Britain, he disregarded their misguided opinions and proved his actions to be professional, ethical, and in appropriate service to his country.

Robert Hamilton Bruce Lockhart was born on September 2, 1887, in Anstruther, Fife Scotland to Robert Bruce and Florence Lockhart. At twelve years old, Bruce received a scholarship at Fettes College where he spent five years playing sports rather than distinguishing himself as a scholar. Graduating VIth Form with no honors, limited abilities, and minimal future aspirations, he was sent to Berlin to learn German and later to Paris where he mastered French.

In 1908, he followed his uncle to Malaya filled with wild tales of becoming a rich rubber planter where one day he shot a cobra through the head with a single bullet, earning the reputation as a person to be fearfully respected.

During his time in Malaya, Bruce was invited to a "rong-geng"—a singing and dancing competition for local "istana" (aspiring young females). As the women sang and danced in a group, the attending young men would become sensually aroused.

Enthralled with the experience, Bruce decided to arrange his own rong-geng. Hearing of two girls in a neighboring state reputed to be possibly the most beautiful in the area, he sent invitations for the following weekend, built a small grandstand at his compound, and had a maximum capacity audience attend the event.

Then, she arrived. Her beauty was staggering. Dressed in a batik skirt and red silk coat, a sarong "of blue and red squares was drawn over her head, exposing only the tiniest oval of a face and eyes."[2] From the moment she began to dance, Bruce could see no one but her. Her name was Amai. She was twenty-three years old, married, soon to be divorced, and expected to marry the Sultan's cousin.

Despite warnings to avoid this unattainable woman, after the rong-geng "Every day at five o'clock Amai walked from her house to the 'istana.'"[3] Every day at five o'clock, Bruce would stand silently near the corner of the path that Amai would travel. Six weeks later, on one occasion after her divorce, she passed Bruce while wearing a crimson sarong over her head paused, looked into his eyes, and exposed a lotus blossom in her hair before quickening her pace.

Totally unprepared for the event, Bruce went home immediately to arrange a meeting through the local "biden" (court medicine woman). Against her better judgment, she arranged a rendezvous for the following night. With a pistol in hand, he went to the location and waited for Amai. When she arrived, he made her follow him to his bungalow where he intended she would never leave.

After days filled with visits from the Sultan's representatives, local police, irate villagers, and Amai's nephew who tried to placate all of the increasingly furious parties, Bruce fell ill with a terrible case of malaria. He was believed by some to have been poisoned by his Chinese cook. After receiving high concentrations of quinine from a local government doctor, Bruce's health continued to decline. And when he was almost unable to walk his uncle arrived, wrapped him in a blanket, took him to a ship bound for Scotland, and saved him from the possibility of being killed by the locals.

Like Bruce, James found a woman he couldn't live without. Her name was Contessa Teresa (Tracy) di Vicenzo (Draco) Bond. As the only woman to ever become Bond's wife, Tracy had a tumultuous relationship with Bond that evolved into love and marriage in the tenth Bond novel *On Her Majesty's Secret Service* (1963).

During the late afternoon on a chilly September day, Bond is sitting on a Royale-les-Eaux concrete barrier, spying on a woman. She is someone he met 24 hours earlier in an impromptu car race to the Royale casino/hotel where that evening he saved her from the embarrassment of not being able to pay a large sum of money she lost at the baccarat table. As repayment, she gave herself to Bond by saying, "Do anything you like... Take me."[4]

Now observing her from a distance on the beach, "He had an instinct that she was in some sort of danger. Or was it just that there was the smell of danger in the air? He didn't know."[5] Bond found himself near two other male observers. With the sun reaching the water, the girl rose to her feet and walked toward the waterline with the intent of swimming out to sea and her eventual death.

Following in her footsteps, "Bond quicken[s] his step until he [is] only ten paces behind her."[6] She turns slowly and, with tears in her eyes, asks what he wants from her. He is suddenly confronted with the two men he saw earlier, who then remove the Walther PPK from his trouser leather holster and escort him and the woman to a nearby boat.

They are taken to Marc-Ange Draco, head of the largest Corsican crime syndicate in Europe, who is familiar with Bond's British Secret Service position as well as his experiences with Tracy at the card table and in the bedroom. He explains that as a young man Tracy's mother, "had come to Corsica to look for bandits... She explained to me later that she must have been possessed by a subconscious desire"[7] to remain in a lustful relationship with him while traveling with stolen goods from cave to cave until he married her.

Tracy became their only child, who in her early teens adopted her mother's wild ways. Tracy married Count Giulio di Vicenzo who stole her money and deserted her with their young child, who later died a terrible death from spinal meningitis.

After the tragedy, Tracy traveled around Europe in her little red car, lost all her money and jewels, permitted Bond to pay her baccarat casino debt, have sex with her, fell in love with him, asked for her father's forgiveness, and requested repayment of Bond's lost money. Realizing that Bond prevented his daughter's suicide, Draco states, "I wish you to pay court to my daughter and marry her. On the day of the marriage, I will give you a personal dowry of one million pounds in gold."[8]

Refusing the gift, Bond offers to be with her after she receives professional help at a clinic. And, instead of the money, he requests help from the mafia boss to find the location of his nemesis, the villain Ernst Stavro Blofeld.

After finding Blofeld in a Swiss mountaintop hideout, Bond discovers that the criminal is brainwashing British women to use biological warfare to destroy the UK agricultural economy. After escaping Blofeld's hideout with incriminating evidence, Bond skis down the mountain, unexpectedly finds Tracy at an ice skating rink where they successfully escape Blofeld's men, and completes his mission by reporting the criminal plot to his superiors.

William Mast

On the following day, "Bond suddenly thought, Hell! I'll never find another girl like this one... She's adventurous, brave, resourceful."[9] As a loner, she would fit into his life and never leave him because she needs both his love and attention. And realizing that they could have children, to his surprise he says, "Tracy. I love you. Will you marry me?"[10]

While traveling to Kitzbühel, Austria for their honeymoon, Blofeld and his assistant Irma Bunt drive up to the couple's car and shoot Tracy in the head.

--------◆--------

LIKE BRUCE, BOND HAD THE LOVE OF HIS LIFE TAKEN AWAY IN A sudden event, leaving him with only the memory of her. However, unlike Bond, Bruce would soon find conventional love and marriage while unknowingly falling in love with an undercover Russian KGB agent.

In 1910, at the age of twenty-three, Bruce took the Foreign Office General Consular Service Examination; he placed first out of sixty candidates in the French and German language exams, earning him one of four open vacancies. After a short probation period in the Consular Department, Bruce was appointed the British Vice-Consul in Moscow.

Prior to leaving, he met a beautiful twenty-year-old Australian girl at a family farewell party. They were engaged within ten days and married the following year during Bruce's first leave from Russia.

After he arrived in Russia, Bruce was fluent in Russian within six months and interpreting all meetings and communication for the Consulate-General, Charles Clive Bayley. In early August 1914 Germany declared war against Russia, France, and Belgium, and Great Britain declared war against Germany on August 4. World War I had officially begun. Eleven months later on July 30, 1915, twenty-eight-year-old Bruce was appointed Consulate-General to Russia.

Over the next three years Bruce watched Tsar Nicholas II assume supreme command of the Russian army, lose numerous battles with Germany, and abdicate his throne. He further observed the Russian bourgeoisie lose their lives while the proletariat claimed and distributed their lands and possessions to the people.

Prime Minister Mr. Lloyd George wanted to establish unofficial relations with Trotsky, Lenin, the Bolsheviks, and Germany to benefit Great Britain. Bruce was assigned the diplomatic mission. He observed the signing of the Treaty of Brest-Litovsk peace agreement between Germany and Russia on March 3, 1918, only to see it dissolved before the end of the year, resulting in a war between the two countries. Consequently, Bruce found himself supporting the return of Russian rule to the Russian people.

With the Germans attacking and seizing control of St. Petersburg, Bruce received a cryptically worded telegraph message from his wife informing him that the Foreign Office didn't agree with his support for the Bolsheviks and as a result, he was viewed as a rogue agent. In a new telegraph, Bruce was reminded of the three rules for all diplomats: 1) to make himself an acceptable person to the country where he was stationed; 2) to interpret their government policies to his government and; 3) to interpret policies of his own government to his stationed government. Bruce was found to acceptably perform only the first two duties. To add further complications to his already complex assignment, while in St. Petersburg Bruce became romantically and politically intertwined with an undercover Russian KGB spy named Moura Budberg.

When ordered to return to Moscow in May 1918, Bruce first met Sidney Reilly (another Bond inspiration) who, dressed as a British officer, was refused entrance through the Kremlin gates to see Lenin with a message from Lloyd George. Furious with his insolence, Bruce reprimanded the new secret agent and threatened to have him sent home.

With the goal of developing a future direction for the government, on July 4, 1918, the Fifth All-Russian Congress took place in the Moscow Opera House, bringing together the Left Social-Revolutionaries and Bolsheviks. Bruce, Sidney Reilly, other official diplomats, and press were permitted to observe from the large Imperial Box.

Two days later when the group reconvened with the Bolsheviks absent, calamity struck when a hand grenade exploded in the building. All sections were surrounded and nobody was allowed to leave. Sidney Reilly began tearing politically sensitive documents and shoving them into the linings of his seat, while others were cut into smaller pieces and swallowed. The Social-Revolutionaries still in attendance were arrested and all diplomats and press were refused travel passes, as it was believed that they would instigate counter-revolutionary activities.

Forced to remain in the city, the Tsar and his family were shot on July 17th and their bodies disposed of down a coal mine shaft. Shortly afterward Bruce received a message that Moura was soon to arrive in Moscow.

On August 30th, a recently released female Jewish Socialist-Revolutionary prisoner named Fanya Kaplan shot Vladimir Lenin at point-blank range as he was leaving the Hammer & Sickle factory in Moscow. One bullet safely passed through his coat, another lodged in his neck, and a third entered his lung. Disturbed by the news, Bruce retired early only to be awakened in the middle of the night by the Cheka (Secret Service). He was allowed to dress while other agents searched his flat for compromising documents. He was then sent to the famous Loubianka No. 11 that served as the Cheka headquarters.

Bruce was placed in a room containing a wooden table and two chairs where an old friend named Yacov Peters, Vice-President of the Cheka, politely interrogated him. Bruce protested that he was a guest of the government with full diplomatic privileges. Peters only said, "It will be better for you if you speak the truth."[11] He was first questioned about Kaplan, who he claimed to have never met. Then other questions came about the location of Reilly.

During the conversation Bruce happened to grab his lapels, only to feel a notebook containing cryptic information. Bruce writes in his autobiography that, "The note-book was unintelligible to anyone except myself. But it contained figures, and, if it fell into Bolshevik hands they would find some means of rendering it compromising."[12] The figures could be used to represent Bolshevik troop movements or monies he spent on a counter-revolution. Realizing that he might be searched any moment, "I asked permission of our four sentries to go to the lavatory. It was granted, but the affair was not so simple."[13] Two gunmen, who oversaw his every movement, accompanied him. With no paper available and the walls smeared with human excrement, "As calmly as I could, I took out my note-book, tore out the offending pages and used them in the manner in which the circumstances dictated. I pulled the plug. It worked, and I was saved."[14]

Later a woman believed to be Kaplan was brought in to identify Bruce. After failing the test, she was taken out and shot. Newspaper reports referred to Lenin's attempted assassination as the Lockhart Plot. Bruce had been accused of arranging the murders of Lenin and Trotsky, after which British agents would bomb the railways to dismantle the city and allow the populous to starve in the streets. With the disappearance of Reilly, Bruce realized that the Lockhart Plot was really the Reilly Plot with Reilly operating as a rogue agent.

For the next month, Bruce remained in solitary confinement at Loubianka No. 11 where he slept on the floor and remained guarded twenty-four hours a day. As a diplomat, he was never tortured but was routinely cross-examined in an effort to find evidence useful to the Bolsheviks. Once Lenin's life was out of danger in early September, Bruce was put on trial for his life at the Kremlin, where no political prisoner was known to have ever left alive. Of particular comfort were his visits from Maura, who was allowed to bring him food, books, clean clothes, and tobacco.

During a visit, Maura passed Bruce a note in a book by Thomas Carlyle that was appropriately titled The French Revolution. It read,

"Say nothing – all will be well."[15] Then Peters came to tell him that he was to be set free in two days. Acknowledging that little damaging evidence had been collected to support their case, he asked if Bruce was interested in remaining with Maura and living in Russia.

However, there was more at stake than Bruce's personal life. The British government arranged an official exchange of Bruce for the Soviet Government's representative in Britain, Maxim Litvinoff, at the Russian frontier. In preparation, Bruce went to the train station where he saw forty to fifty French and British colleagues who had just arrived directly from prison. Few words were spoken and the exchange proceeded with little complication.

Bruce left Moura on the platform and returned to his diplomatic and personal life with his wife. However, the lovers did meet again. After receiving numerous love letters from Moura, Bruce met her in August 1924 in Vienna. Although she tried to make him believe that her affection for him remained the same, Bruce admitted that his former feelings had dissolved over time. Despite their differing emotions, they remained in contact for years through their mutual friends Sidney Reilly and Maxim Gorki. Later, it was revealed to Bruce's son that his father's lover had actually been a Soviet agent. Research into Moura's various amorous relationships revealed that she engaged in covert espionage activities as part of her romantic affairs until her death in 1974.

During World War II, Bruce became Director-General of the Political Warfare Executive, where he worked on propaganda development for the government. There he came in contact with both Ian and Peter Fleming. In 1943, he received Knight Commander of the Order of St. Michael and St. George (KCMG). After the war, he wrote and presented weekly BBC Radio broadcasts to the people of Czechoslovakia. On February 27, 1970, Sir Robert Bruce Lockhart passed away peacefully in his home at the age of eighty-two.

With apparent knowledge of Bruce's diplomatic missions, Ian Fleming made his secret agent accept two separate missions in two different Bond novels where he would work undercover as a diplomat spy. In Fleming's second novel *Live and Let Die* (1954), Bond is sent to negotiate and monitor a collaborative FBI, CIA, and MI6 mission to destroy a SMERSH gold smuggling operation.

"From the moment the BOAC Stratocruiser taxie[s] up to the International Air Terminal at Idlewild, James Bond [is] treated like royalty… As he walk[s] across the tarmac in the bitter January wind he [sees] his own name going across the network: BOND, JAMES. BRITISH DIPLOMATIC PASSPORT 0094567… FBI: POSITIVE AWAIT CHECK… FBI TO IDLEWILD: BOND OKAY OKAY."[16] Realizing that he just publicly passed through both FBI and CIA security, Bond worries that his loss of anonymity may lead to his recognition as a spy with possible future attempts on his life.

Within minutes, he finds himself in a limousine, taken to the St. Regis hotel in New York City, and delivered to the top floor suite where he discovers his old CIA friend Felix Leiter and Captain Dexter from the FBI. Negotiating their three-organization mission responsibilities to destroy a SMERSH pirate gold coin black market smuggling and sales operation, they determine that all U.S. operations will be overseen by the FBI, all Jamaican operations will be overseen by MI6, and the overall mission will be orchestrated by Felix Leiter from the CIA. Although complicated, the three organizations work well together and make the mission a success by killing the criminal Mr. Big and ending his illegal enterprise.

AND, IN FLEMING'S ELEVENTH NOVEL *YOU ONLY LIVE TWICE* (1964), Bond is sent to the Japanese Secret Intelligence Service to request permission for MI6 to receive their codenamed MAGIC 44 cryptographic transmissions from the Soviet Union, granting Great Britain access to invaluable intelligence.

Offered a promotion to the Diplomatic Section, M offers Bond an assignment to negotiate the mutual sharing of acquired Soviet Union espionage intelligence transmissions with the Japanese SIS. M says, "there won't be any strong arm stuff... none of the gun-play you pride yourself on so much. It'll just be a question of your wits and nothing else. But if you bring it off, which I very much doubt, you will just about double our intelligence about the Soviet Union."[17]

Arriving in Japan, Bond offers any reasonable price for the cryptographic intelligence to the head of the Japanese SIS, Tiger Tanaka. Instead, Tiger wants Bond to kill a man who is destroying the lives of numerous Japanese by coercing them to commit suicide. He says, "You are to enter this Castle of Death and slay the Dragon within."[18] Instead of a diplomatic solution, Bond accepts and completes a successful mission to assassinate this man who turns out to be Ernst Blofeld—the man who murdered his wife.

IN BOTH NOVELS BOND IS GIVEN THE OPPORTUNITY TO SERVE AS a diplomat spy but ultimately reverts to his field assassin behaviors. In *Live and Let Die*, Bond sets a limpet mine under the hull of a ship that blows up, resulting in Mr. Big being eaten by sharks and barracudas, while in *You Only Live Twice* Bond strangles his nemesis Ernst Blofeld to death.

In contrast, Bruce's missions left the murder to field assassin spies like Sidney Reilly, while he claimed full diplomat privileges and immunity from prosecution. In all his Bond stories, Fleming always separated the diplomat assignments from the assassin Double O missions.

In conclusion, few diplomat spies were as knowledgeable of Russian political and cultural life as Bruce. Sharing his experiences with Ian, gave the author operational information about the differences between traditional diplomats and field assassins. Bruce's stories may have further inspired Fleming to create a superspy who is not afraid to follow his own instincts in the field while trying to maintain allegiance to his superiors and country.

CHAPTER 4

*German passport photo of Sidney Reilly
as alias George Bergmann (1918)*

SIDNEY REILLY

Codename: S.T.1 & Ace of Spades

As a career spy, Sidney Reilly[1] traveled undercover at will. Fluent in seven languages, even when believed captured and killed he managed to remain in hiding only to return stronger than ever. Working as a double and possibly triple agent for Britain, Russia, and Japan, he reaped financial success to support his gambling habit.

Like Bond, Sidney loved women. He was recorded to have had a total of eleven wives—eight of whom were Russian women he exploited to help with his espionage missions. Aware of his polygamous life, the head of the British Secret Service is believed to have personally attended his third marriage celebration.

In one biography of Sidney's life, author Michael Kettle writes, "Sidney Reilly was the most successful spy ever employed by the British Secret Service."[2] However, with so many disputed and uncorroborated facts it's hard to find the simplest reliable information related to his birth, young life, early accomplishments, marriages, spy missions, double or triple X services, government and political allegiances, and circumstances of his death. Yet, without any doubt, the highly unreliable records may represent a perfect spy.

From many contradictory records on or near March 24, 1874, we can conclude that Sigmund Georgievich Rosenblum was born to Pauline and either Grigory Rosenblum or Grigory's first cousin Dr. Mikhail Rosenblum in Odessa, (Ukraine) Russia. As Jews were discriminated at that time, Georgi was believed to have been reared as a Catholic. It is possible that as an illegitimate adolescent son, Georgi unknowingly befriended his father Mikhail when he treated his mother for a deadly disease that ultimately killed her.

Believed to have developed a satisfactory background in chemistry to gain membership in the Chemical Society in 1896, nineteen-year-old Georgi became a member of a revolution conspiracy organization called "The League of Enlightenment." Upon learning that he was traveling to Russia, a league member asked him to sew a letter into his coat and deliver it to a person in Odessa. Georgi naively accepted the mission and, on his arrival, was arrested for treason and thrown into prison. After weeks of solitary confinement, Georgi was released to his family and made aware of his true parentage.

In a fit of anger, Georgi sent a letter to his biological father that read, "May your soul rot in hell of loneliness,"[3] and he faked his suicide by writing to his half-sister Elana, "You can look for me under the ice of Odessa New Harbour."[4] After severing his family ties, Georgi left Russia and traveled to Brazil where he spent three years working at the docks, kitchens, plantations, and brothels. In 1895, he saved the lives of three British Military Intelligence officers from hostile natives. As a crack shot, Georgi was able to fight off the advancing attackers. Then as they traveled through the Amazon jungle, one traveler fell ill and died. After helping the remaining two to safely reach Rio, the officers brought him to England as a prospective new agent.

Due to Georgi's mastery of languages, superb marksmanship, courage, and mastery of persuasion techniques, George Mansfield Smith-Cumming (C), the first head of MI6, saw a young man with potential. During his first successful mission to ascertain interest in Russian oil well development in northern Persia, Georgi met the beautiful twenty-three-year-old, red-haired Margaret Thomas, who became his first mistress. Since Margaret was married to a sixty-year-old British minister, Georgi followed the couple around Europe, bedding the woman at night unbeknownst to her husband. Then after returning to England, he is believed to have poisoned the man on March 13, 1898; by using his knowledge of chemistry, Georgi was able to make it appear as if the man had died of natural causes. On August 22nd, the two alleged conspirators married.

Desiring to enhance his extravagant lifestyle, Georgi returned to C for more spy contracts. Rejecting his Jewish past, he started using his wife's second name of Reilly and added the Irish name of Sidney to sound anti-British. C created a new passport for his young agent and, in 1899, Sidney Reilly was born.

By 1902, Sidney had performed more financially successful missions in Persia for the William Knox D'Arcy Oil Exploration Company. When Sidney returned to England, Margaret, who had started drinking heavily, broke off their relationship, leaving him with only a few hundred pounds to his name

In need of money, Sidney went undercover to steal armaments plans from a factory in Germany. Joining the factory fire brigade, he obtained access to secured areas. Then, one-night Sidney overpowered two security guards, stole the plans, and ripped them into three parts. He mailed the documents to three different locations, escaped from Germany, and succeeded in getting all of the plans and himself back to England.

While traveling home, Sidney happened to meet his half-sister Elana in Paris. Now an accomplished pianist, she was engaged to a Polish officer whom she didn't love. Unwilling to follow through with the marriage, she jumped out of her top floor hotel room window. In a note left for Georgi, she confessed a desire to end her own life instead of living in a loveless marriage. Remorseful about faking his own suicide, he returned to London, received a generous payment from C for his work in Germany, and avoided finding Margaret.

In 1905, Sidney was given a follow-up assignment. With the Royal Navy in desperate need of oil for their new fleet of ships, the mission was to resurrect earlier plans to obtain oil supplies from Persia. However, D'Arcy was now negotiating with the French. Disguised as a French priest, Sidney traveled to Nice and privately met with D'Arcy, where he doubled the French offer. It was accepted, resulting in a newly formed oil company. With the British government holding a fifty-one percent interest and D'Arcy accepting an enormous profit, that company is still known today as British Petroleum Company Ltd.—more commonly called B.P. Unfortunately, this time Sidney received little money for his work.

Frustrated, he quit espionage, traveled to the United States, and entered into a partnership called Rosenblum & Long, Manufacturers of Patent Medicines. After four years of financial insolvency, his partner stole the remaining £600, leaving Sidney penniless.

In 1909, Sidney went to Frankfurt, Germany where he met a man named Jones who he helped to steal plans for a new, highly advanced airplane magneto. Jones turned out to be a Secret Intelligence Service (SIS) agent working for C. After the successful operation, he talked Sidney into rejoining MI6.

For his next mission, he was sent to St. Petersburg to obtain intelligence on German military and naval operations. The year was 1911, and Russia had created a five-year plan to rebuild their navy, which had been destroyed during the Russian-Japanese war. Blohm & Voss (B&V), a naval construction company located in Hamburg, won the contract to rebuild the Russian fleet using the latest German technology designs. Sidney created a cover as a partner with an intermediary agency called Mendrochovich & Lubersky that collected all the plans from B&V to ensure safe delivery to the Russian Ministry of Marine. Prior to each delivery, Sidney made a new cast of the B&V envelope seal. He then broke the seal, using a special steam press and placed the blueprints between sheets of glass to make Photostat copies, before repackaging the items for final delivery. The operation worked as planned with England receiving free copies of every German warship and Sidney receiving enormous profits for his work.

When Sidney returned home, he again found Margaret drinking heavily. Keeping her at his local residence, he met Nadine Massino, the wife of a Naval Assistant to the Minister of Marine. Sidney and Nadine agreed to marry, and he offered Margaret forty-eight hours to accept £10,000 to divorce him. She refused at first, but after realizing that his alternate plan was to kill her, she fled with her life. Nadine's husband was more cordial. He accepted a large sum of money and allowed Sidney to hire a representative named Sasha Grammatikoff to handle the divorce proceedings.

Plans proceeded smoothly with the unfortunate complication that Margaret was still legally married to Sidney. Since he couldn't find her, Sidney conspired with an accomplice named Boris Souvorin to spread a story that Margaret had been killed in a Red Cross ambulance crash on a mountain road in Bulgaria. The story was published in Souvorin's newspaper *Novoe Vremya*. Sidney hoped that Margaret would get the message that remaining lost would permit her to remain alive.

The circumstances of Sidney's dual romantic life (and potential polygamy) are inspirational to the conditions surrounding Bond's first love in Fleming's first novel *Casino Royale* (1953).

After beating Le Chiffre at baccarat and then being tortured by him, Bond is taken to a hospital to recover from his wounds. He is nursed back to health by the attractive MI6 agent Vesper Lynd, with whom he falls in love. "He [finds] her companionship easy and unexacting. There [is] something enigmatic about her which [is] a constant stimulus."⁵

Three weeks into his recovery, the couple travels to a small seaside hotel. Advancing their relationship, Bond decides, "That day he would ask Vesper to marry him. He was quite certain. It was only a question of choosing the right moment."⁶ On hearing his intentions, she begins to sob. Bond says, "Tell me what's hurting you."⁷ Later as he kisses her goodnight, he tastes tears on her cheek.

The following morning Vesper is found dead from an overdose of sleeping pills. In a letter she leaves behind she writes, "I love you with all my heart and while you read these words I hope you still love me because now, with these words, this is the last moment your love will last. So good-bye, my sweet love, while we still love each other. Good-bye, my darling."⁸

She then confesses in the letter that she is a double agent for the Russians and was compelled to feed them with intelligence in order to keep her Polish lover alive. Unable to accept the circumstances, Bond can only see her as a traitor and see himself as a secret agent who must destroy SMERSH.

Armed with his new personal mission, Bond calls London to report that Vesper Lynd was a double agent working for SMERSH and that, 'Yes, dammit, I said "was." The bitch is dead now.'⁹

VESPER CHOSE TO KILL HERSELF RATHER THAN PUT JAMES' LIFE in jeopardy and possibly enter into a polygamous relationship with her Polish lover. Sidney similarly became reluctant to marry Nadine, who had since joined him in New York, out of fear that Margaret would re-emerge into his life. However, Nadine was insistent and in 1916 the couple married in the New York Greek Orthodox Cathedral, marking the beginning of Sidney's life as a clandestine bigamist.

Desiring to actively engage in the war, Sidney joined the Royal

Canadian Flying Corps (RCFC). Given the rank of captain, in 1917 he was sent back to C who lined up missions in Germany. Parachuting behind enemy lines, his fluency in multiple languages allowed him to seamlessly collect intelligence from both Germany and Russia. It was believed that he even enlisted in the German army, where he quickly rose from a private to a commissioned officer.

After the war, Sidney's records were destroyed. Few reports of his missions remained, except for one. In 1917, Sidney discovered the Imperial High Command preparing to attack British shipping routes with U-boats. He reported their movements, thereby saving British ships and lives that eventually helped win the war.

In April 1918, Lloyd George sent Sidney to Russia to monitor the developing revolution. Using the codename S.T.1, Sidney was ordered to organize the downfall of the Bolsheviks—even if it meant circumventing the pro-Bolshevik support being offered by another 007 inspiration, Bruce Lockhart. Following orders, Sidney paid money to various anti-Bolshevik organizations with the intention of capturing Stalin and Lenin whom he planned to defame by parading them naked and chained through the streets of Moscow—a plan that never came to fruition.

In Moscow, he began a sexual relationship with Dagmara Grammatikova, a dancer from the Moscow Arts Theatre, and her two female roommates. Together, they began helping him with his missions, allowing Sydney to continue his gambling lifestyle while maintaining a stable of mistresses for his personal pleasure. Using a total of 8,400,000 roubles that he kept at Dagmara's flat, Sidney paid counter-revolutionaries for engaging in plots to unhinge the new government.

His work continued until all hell broke loose. Lenin survived[10] an assassination attempt on August 30th, and by three-thirty a.m. on the following day, Lockhart had been arrested. Sidney and his agents immediately went underground. During his interrogation by Cheka (Russian Secret Service), Lockhart was questioned about Sidney's location. Believing that it was Bruce who had instigated counter-revolutionary organizations to kill Lenin and overthrow the Bolshevik government, the investigation became known as the "Lockhart Plot".

Concurrently, eight young and beautiful women all claiming to be Sidney's wife were arrested by Cheka and imprisoned with Lockhart, who witnessed their constant jealousy and fighting. Apparently, in 1918 only a simple marriage agreement was necessary to take a wife, and Sidney seemed willing to accommodate all interested parties. But more importantly, Dagmara had not yet been arrested. Cheka agents came to her flat on a general inspection and were unable to find the remaining roubles hidden in her knickers. She also pled no knowledge of Sidney's actions or whereabouts.

If captured he would be shot with Lockhart, so Sidney decided to make his way back to London. After he spent 60,000 roubles to be smuggled out of the country, Sidney arrived in London on November 8, 1918, and was awarded the Military Cross (MC) on January 22, 1919.

Fortunately, Lockhart was released later in exchange for the Soviet government's representative in Britain, Maxim Litvinoff. The Bolsheviks prosecuted a mock trial they called "The Lockhart Plot" and found *in absentia* Lockhart and Sidney guilty of treason with a sentence of death if they ever returned to Russia. Sidney's mistresses were found innocent, as they were deemed to be under his persuasive powers.

Unlike Sidney who became a domestic bigamist for love and an international bigamist to advance his career as a spy, in the tenth Bond novel *On Her Majesty's Secret Service* (1963) James mourns the loss of his first love, finds another, and loses her as a result of his chosen profession.

--------●--------

Having returned to the casino in Royale every year since his first major mission to battle Le Chiffre, Bond takes a moment to remember "the small granite cross in the little churchyard"[11] that he visits during every trip. The stone simply reads "Vesper Lynd. RIP." Although she committed suicide when she thought that they would both be killed by SMERSH, Bond simply can't forget her.

However, it doesn't take long for Bond to find Contessa Teresa (Tracy) di Vicenzo (Draco), who is willing to live and die as the spy's wife despite the hazards of her position. Just hours after their wedding, Tracy is shot by Ernst Blofeld and Irma Bunt as they leave for their honeymoon in James' car, leaving Bond despondent and revengeful to kill his SPECTRE archenemy.

FLEMING LEAVES BOND WITH TWO FEMALE RELATIONSHIPS THAT get destroyed by his profession. One woman commits suicide rather than face an unacceptable future career as a double agent who would eventually ruin the lives of her two lovers, and a second is killed by a nemesis assassin, making it impossible for James to achieve a sustainable marriage. In contrast, Sidney's multiple female relationships allowed him to live a thriving life as a bigamist for both personal and business reasons.

Under the circumstances, Cumming proposed that Sidney take a leave of absence from the service. He returned to New York, only to find that Nadine had been unfaithful to him. Upon returning to England, he found Margaret going to the Foreign Office to reclaim her husband. C was perplexed, trying to determine an accurate number of Sidney's wives. After a private meeting between Cumming and Sidney, the subject was never spoken of again, and Margaret returned to Brussels under unknown circumstances.

Adding insult to injury, Sidney began a relationship with a London prostitute nicknamed "Plugger." Like the numerous women highlighted in the Bond books and films, her name was a sexual innuendo. Then, he met Caryll Houselander, an impoverished, red-haired eighteen-year-old Catholic student at the St. John's Wood Art School who immediately fell under his charms. Sidney helped finance her studies while keeping her as his mistress when in London.

With his continuing desire to overthrow the Bolshevik government, Winston Churchill recommended Sidney assist Boris Savinkoff (former Minister of War in Russia) to lead a counter-revolutionary revolt and reorganize the government under Boris' Social-Revolutionary leadership. While working in their new Paris headquarters, forty-seven-year-old Sidney fell in love with a twenty-three-year-old French actress who he refused to marry due to his bigamy problem. After she got pregnant, Sidney paid for the abortion before she finally left him.

Realizing that he finally needed to divorce Nadine, he contacted Sasha Grammatikoff, who finalized their divorce papers. Later Nadine married Gustov Nobel of the Nobel Prize family, and after World War II she died in Switzerland, never having known about Sidney's first wife.

But Sidney was never without female companionship for long. In December 1922 on a trip to Berlin, Sidney met the young, charming, South American actress Nelly "Pepita" Bobadilla. She was the widow of playwright Charles Haddon-Chambers, who had helped start her career on the London stage. After one week, Sidney and Pepita were engaged. On May 18, 1923, they married at the Covent Garden Registry Office. In attendance at the Savoy Hotel reception was Cumming, who never divulged knowledge of Sidney's bigamy.

Hearing of the marriage, Caryll, now twenty-one years old, returned to the Catholic Church with a broken heart and dedicated much of her life to healing severely mentally ill patients. She never loved or tried to marry a man again.

In July 1923, Sidney and Pepita traveled to New York to retrieve $500,000 owed to him from the Baldwin Locomotive Company. The company stalled their payment until the summer of 1924 when Sidney was summoned back to Paris to see Savinkoff. Due to the sensitivity of his trip, he made certain financial arrangements to support Pepita in case of his death. It was almost as if he sensed the impending danger.

On August 29, 1924, Savinkoff decided to give up his revolutionary activities, returned to Russia, and surrendered to the Bolsheviks. He was immediately condemned to death, which was then reduced to a ten-year commuted sentence, after which he was acquitted and finally set free. It was believed that he had sold out the counter-revolutionary supporters and wanted to return to his beloved Russia, regardless of the political climate. In May 1925, Savainkoff jumped out of a window to his death. Sidney believed that he had been thrown out of the window to hide torture marks he received from Cheka interrogations.

The counter-revolutionary organization operating in Russia and its contiguous countries was called "The Trust." The Trust was expected to lead a revolt to take back their country and end the reign of terror. Sidney decided to work with the group and defeat the Bolsheviks. In a farewell letter to Pepita, Sidney wrote,

> "25th Sept. 1925
> Friday
> My most beloved, my sweetheart,
> It is absolutely necessary that I should go for three days to Petrograd and Moscow. I am leaving tonight and will be back here on Tuesday morning. I want you to know that I would not have undertaken this trip unless it was absolutely essential and if I was not convinced that there is practically no risk attached to it. I am writing this letter only for the most improbable case of a mischance befalling me. Should this happen, then you must not take any steps…If by any chance I should be arrested in Russia, it could only be on some minor insignificant charge and my new friends are powerful enough to obtain my prompt liberation…
>
> Naturally none of these people must get any inkling where I am and what has happened to me. – Remember that every move etc. may give me away to the Bolshies.

My dearest darling, I am doing what I must do. I am doing it with the absolute inner assurance, that if you were with me, you would approve.

You are in my thoughts always and your love will protect me. God bless you ever and ever. I love you beyond all words."[12]

From the content of the letter, it can be assumed that Sidney believed that he could get away with killing his Russian enemies, or that he wanted to return home but didn't want to reveal himself as a double or multiple agent.

After he left for his meeting with the Trust, nobody heard from him again. The *Reilly: Ace of Spades*[13] BBC miniseries fictionalizes how Sidney planned to overtake the Bolsheviks. It turned out that The Trust was a cover for the Bolsheviks to get Russian sympathizers like Sidney to return to home. In April 1927, Edward Opperput, a senior official in The Trust, confessed that Sidney was a member of the GPU (State Political Directorate). He stated that he knew of Sidney's arrest and placement in the Butyrsky prison two days after his arrival in Moscow. He further stated that a fake shooting at the Finnish border was staged to make the world believe that he had been shot accidentally as a suspected smuggler. However, Opperput claimed that in actuality Sidney was treated well, given his favorite whiskey, and allowed to go on drives.

The greatest fear was that he was one of the 250,000 executions or 1,300,000 incarcerations by the GPU. Their interrogations and tortures were horrible. The individual was placed in a straitjacket and tied to a bed with no blanket, food, or the ability to go to the bathroom. A gag was placed in the mouth, a stopper in the rectum, and beatings were periodically given with rubber poles. When given the opportunity, many prisoners preferred to kill themselves by setting fire to their mattresses rather than face the interrogators.

In Sidney's case, it was believed that he had cracked, divulging enormous amounts of information in the hope of saving his life. He was unable to receive support from the British government. Since

Savinkoff was dead, he was a totally independent agent. For Sidney, there was no alternative left but to sacrifice everything to keep his life.

Inconsistent reports were presented regarding his death. One reported that he had been killed in September 1925 at the Finnish border. Another posted his execution date as November 5, 1925. Yet another, reported in the Russian newspaper *Izvestia* in September 1927, was that he had been killed in June of the same year along with a group of Russian nobles. Melor Sturua, a former *Izvesta* correspondent in London and Washington, stated that the KGB and other related espionage agencies destroyed or lost all official records of Sidney Reilly.

However, there is still belief and evidence that Sidney willingly returned to Russia and worked to advance its cause for the remainder of his natural life. It's believed that he first became a Marxist when he was arrested by the Tsar's police for smuggling inappropriate documents into Russia at the age of nineteen. He then became disenchanted with democracy when he failed to retrieve his money from the Baldwin Locomotive Company. His bigamy problems burdened his financially insolvent life. And when pressured by the British Secret Service to meet The Trust and help destroy the Bolshevik government, he found an opportunity to return home. It is possible that from his experiences in espionage, and problems with capitalism, he ultimately believed that communism was superior to democracy and had no alternative but to once again fake his death and work behind the scenes to promote espionage activities for his motherland while living with Dagmara Grammatikova.

Robin Bruce Lockhart, son of the 007 inspiration Bruce Lockhart, believes that "Reilly lived on for at least twenty years after his return to Russia in 1925,"[14] during which time he trained highly intelligent and educated individuals to become "agents of influence." It was the job of these agents to covertly enter political organizations to spread Soviet propaganda and gather intelligence, bringing the field to a new level of sophistication. Lockhart further concluded that Sidney died sometime after 1945 at the age of seventy-one. Yet, another credible source reported, "Four GPU officers took him in the woods north-east of Moscow on the evening of Nov. 5, 1925" where one "put several bullets into Reilly,"[15] with another firing a shot that killed him.

Sidney appeared to be heavily influenced by money and love. His work for D'Arcy in Persia and Mendrochovich & Lubensky in Germany brought him wealth that was gambled away and lost to his numerous wives. His work for MI6 missions paid little, which made working for alternative governments more profitable. In love, he was most significantly influenced by his relationships with Margaret Thomas, Nadine Massino, Pepita Bobadilla, and Dagmara Grammatikova.

In a response to Robin Bruce Lockhart, when congratulated on his publication of *Casino Royale*, Ian Fleming stated, "James Bond is just a piece of nonsense I dreamed up. He's not Sidney Reilly, you know!"[16]

Yugoslav Leader Marsal Tito talking with Brigadier General Fitzroy Maclean (1944)

SIR FITZROY MACLEAN
Diplomat Spy & Field Agent

S ir Fitzroy Maclean[1] worked as a diplomat spy and field agent for the British Foreign Office and MI6. Early in his professional life, he befriended Ian Fleming with whom he shared his perceptions of the Russian culture. Often followed by the NKVD (Russian Secret Service), his extensive travels throughout their country afforded him insights normally unavailable to the British government. Following a brief career as a diplomat spy in Russia, he worked as a field agent in Northern Africa and Persia where he contributed to the destruction of numerous enemy military installations, and in Yugoslavia where he oversaw resistance operations and the establishment of a post-World War II government. From these abundant experiences, Fitzroy was a bountiful resource of knowledge about espionage missions for Ian Fleming.

Fitzroy Maclean was born in Egypt to Charles and Gladys Maclean on March 11, 1911. As a military family, they spent two years in Scotland, two years in India, and eight years in Italy. Having been raised in a wealthy family and thereby given access to an excellent education, Gladys personally instructed Fitzroy in French, German, Italian, and English.

After having attended Heatherdown School, Fitzroy studied at Eton from 1924-29. Permitted to leave Eton before the normal graduation date, he studied Classics and History at King's College in Cambridge and Latin and Greek at Marburg University in Germany.

Afraid that Fitzroy might get injured as a soldier, his parents advised him to become a diplomat. Therefore, by the time Hitler was rising to power in 1933, Fitzroy had left academia and entered the Diplomatic Service. His entrance exam scores of 97% in French and German were the highest grades ever recorded which resulted with his first appointment in Paris from 1934-37, where he drafted handwritten telegrams and dispatches for the British government.

During this time, he met another Bond inspiration Commander Wilfred "Biffy" Dunderdale, who introduced him to the glamor of the city. The Dunderdales lived an extravagant life. Fitzroy first met them at their flat across from the Eiffel Tower where he and twenty-four other guests dined on French cuisine and champagne. After the party, Biffy took the group to Paris nightclubs where they drank more champagne until dawn, only to follow the festivities with a cruise down the Seine River in a private yacht with, of course, more champagne. During his stay in Paris Fitzroy met a young, playful Georgian princess named Madame Sert, or Roussi as she preferred to be called, and after a short romance with Fitzroy, Roussi influenced him to visit Russia as a diplomat.

In 1937 at the age of twenty-six, the playboy Fitzroy shocked the Diplomatic Service by applying for a transfer to Russia. When he arrived, he discovered that the glamorous life Roussi had painted was now gone. Under Stalin's iron fist, "Children were denouncing their parents to the NKVD (People's Commissariat for Internal

Affairs) and parents their children. Everyone lived in terror of the knock on their door at 3 a.m."[2] From a newly built government block of flats for the community, Fitzroy learned that scores of people were being arrested. "There were thousands living there then, and they were picking them up, twenty or thirty every night."[3]

Diplomats always assumed that their rooms were bugged and telephone conversations tapped. And with government communication limited they had been restricted to only meeting with other diplomats, as "anything one said to a Russian was immediately reported back to the NKVD."[4]

And following Fitzroy's new lifestyle, in Ian Fleming's twelfth and final novel *The Man with the Golden Gun* (1965), Bond inspects his hotel for bugging devices and signs that his room has been searched.

Bond is now working undercover for the professional assassin Scaramanga, who is known to have killed other MI6 spies. After traveling by car to the Thunderbird Hotel in Jamaica to meet a group of gangsters who may invest in a local hotel, Bond retires to his room. When he inspects the surroundings, he sees a large painting of a Jamaican market scene on the wall that he gently lifts off the nail. Nothing is attached to the wall or picture. "He then [takes] out a pocket knife, [lays] the telephone carefully, so as not to shift the receiver, upside down on a bed, and very quietly and carefully unscrew[s] the bottom plate."[5] Looking behind the plate he finds a small microphone that is connected to a main cable inside the cradle. "He screw[s] back the plate with the same care and put[s] the telephone quietly back on the night table."[6] Audio systems of this sort are capable of recording normal conversations anywhere in the room. To test the system he thinks he should, "say very devout prayers out loud before he went to bed. That would be a fitting prologue for the central recording device!"[7]

After inspecting the room, Bond pulls out his Walther PPK from under a pillow, pumps a single round onto the counterpane, tests the magazine spring, and practices shooting at targets. Off an inch due to the lighter weight of the unloaded gun, he places a round in the breech, sets the safety, and replaces the gun under the pillow. He decides that tomorrow he will whittle a wooden wedge to jam the door for added protection. "For tonight, he upended his suitcase just inside the door and balanced... three glasses on top of it. It was a simple booby trap but it would give him all the warning he needed."[8]

The next day, "Bond verified that his room had been searched sometime during the morning – and by an expert."[9] His safety razor of choice is the Hoffritz, which is similar to the Gillette that his CIA friend Felix Leiter had once bought him in New York. "The handle of a safety razor is a reasonably sophisticated hideout for the minor tools of espionage – codes, microdot developers, cyanide and other pills."[10] The nick placed on the handle screw next to the letter "Z" had been moved slightly to the right while he had been gone. "None of the other little traps, handkerchiefs with indelible dots in particular places arranged in a certain order, the angle of his suitcase with the wall of the wardrobe, the semi-extracted lining of the breast pocket of his spare suit, the particular symmetry of certain dents in his tube of Maclean's toothpaste, had been bungled or disturbed."[11]

ROOM INSPECTIONS WERE A COMMON PRACTICE TAUGHT IN ESPI-onage schools. Ian Fleming had been introduced to them during his training at Camp X in Ontario, Canada during the war. Therefore, Bond's inspection techniques were likely an extension of both Fitzroy Maclean's and Ian Fleming's similar training. Also, Fleming was well known to use the names of his friends as characters in his novels and short stories. Although Macleans toothpaste is an actual British product, by writing "Maclean's" in the singular possessive form of the name, Fleming may have made this subtle typographical error to establish an intentional correlation with his Bond inspiration.

On February 19, 1937, Fitzroy arrived in Moscow where for the next two years he would improve his Russian communication skills for meetings with Stalin that would never occur. Stalin had no time to meet diplomats, as he was too busy ruling the country.

During this time, Stalin methodically eliminated 75% of the military officers in the Army. He had many executed, while he had others simply disappear. And to gain control of the people, Stalin made fear and the mindless following of orders the only way to ensure a safe life. Heartless greed grew among the people who turned in family and friends with false accusations of disloyalty to the government, in return for which they received jobs, wives, or homes. As a result, the politically loyal citizens purged the country of the political dissidents.

In 1938, Fitzroy witnessed the trial and acquittal of a British oil engineer named Montague Grover,[12] who had fallen in love with a local girl named Yelena Golius during a business trip to Russia. Grover returned to England and divorced his wife, only to then be denied permission from Russian officials to retrieve his sweetheart. On November 13, 1938, he crashed a small plane near the village of Glukhovo, where he told his captors that he was looking for his fiancée. After being arrested, he was tried as a spy in Moscow.

At the same time, the Tory Under-Secretary to the Department of Overseas Trade, Rob Hudson, was in Moscow to renegotiate an Anglo-Soviet trade agreement. Among the British journalists covering the story for *The Times* was a young writer named Ian Fleming. One evening, while Fitzroy dined with Hudson and his wife, Mrs. Hudson said, "I do wish I could meet the nice Mr. Fleming. As he's staying in this hotel, couldn't you see whether he wouldn't like to join us for dinner?"[13] When Fitzroy went upstairs to retrieve him, he found him in bed with a girl. Upon returning, to the couple,

Fitzroy could only say, "he's very, very busy."[14] It is also said that Fleming gave the girl the bottoms of the silk pajamas he wore as a parting gift—unlike Bond, who wore pajama coats in *Diamonds are Forever* (1956) and *From Russia with Love* (1957).

After Fitzroy's encounter with Fleming, Grover received a commuted sentence, married Yelena, and was allowed to take her back to England. The Anglo-Soviet Trade agreement was also resolved, leaving Fleming and Fitzroy with excellent stories to report to *The Times* and the British government.

During his stay, Fitzroy took two trips through Russia that are of particular interest to the Bond stories. Always under close surveillance by the NKVD, he took one trip to Samarkand via the Trans-Siberian Railway (similar to one made by Ian Fleming), and a second to Soviet Central Asia (like Peter Fleming).

Fitzroy, now nicknamed "Fitzwiskers" for his Cossack mustache, became an authority on Russian culture and politics. When he returned to London on September 2, 1939, the day before Britain declared war on Germany, Fitzroy attempted to resign from the Foreign Office (FO) to enlist in the Army. However, as an expert on international political-military affairs, his request was denied.

Hitler invaded the USSR on June 22, 1941, under the codename OPERATION BARBAROSSA. Nineteen days before that attack, Fitzroy took advantage of a regulation stating that anyone wishing to enter politics must leave the FO. He immediately began a campaign to run for a Lancaster District Member of Parliament (MP) position while concurrently fulfilling his real desire of enlisting in his father's former regiment the Cameron Highlanders. After nine months of commando training, taught by Bill Stirling and Lord "Shimi" Lovat, he was commissioned a major in the Cameron Highlanders. Meanwhile, on October 16, 1941, Fitzroy was elected MP for Lancaster.

Fitzroy's time with the Cameron Highlanders made him an expert in the art of hand-to-hand combat, field sabotage, and destruction. In *Goldfinger* (1959) Fleming includes multiple references of hand-to-hand combat techniques, while in "Property of a Lady (1963) he introduces the use of gadget weaponry in field assignments.

M informs Bond that since there are no current field assignments, he will work the night shift at the office. It gives "him time to get on with a project he had been toying with for more than a year – a handbook of all secret methods of unarmed combat. It [is] to be called Stay Alive!"[15]

In order to make it the best Service manual, Bond decides that he will draw from techniques found in other secret service manuals. These include tricks and techniques "presented to M from sister Services such as OSS, CIA and the Deuxieme."[16] It will also draw from other techniques in manuals captured from enemy agents.

One particular prize is "a translation of a manual, entitled simply Defence, issued to operatives of SMERSH, the Soviet organization of vengeance and death."[17] In chapter two, "Come-along and Restraint Holds,"[18] Bond reads about conventional holds like the arm lock, forearm lock, and use of pressure points. When he reaches come-along locks, "Bond read[s] again the passage that had revolted him: 'A drunken woman can also be handled by using the thumb and forefinger to grab the lower lip. By pinching hard and twisting, as the pull is made, the woman will come along."[19] It's obvious to Bond that SMERSH and MI6 agents have very different perceptions of the need or desire to use such revolting violence against women.

During another slow period at the office, Bond has a chance to investigate information relating to field operation gadgets and their uses. He discovers "a jaw-breaking dissertation by the Scientific Research Section on the Russian use of cyanide gas, propelled by the cheapest bulb-handled children's water pistol, for assassination."[20] When the spray is directed at the face, it results in a near instant death that will later probably produce an autopsy outcome of heart failure, making it ideal for use on stairways or inclines that could be blamed for causing stress on the heart.

THE USE OF THE HAND-TO-HAND COMBAT TECHNIQUES HAVE become commonplace in numerous Bond stories, while the field use of the cyanide gun was employed by a SMERSH agent against Bond in Fleming's first novel *Casino Royale*, and by Bond against M in Fleming's final novel *The Man with the Golden Gun.*

Fitzroy also learned assorted field techniques to destroy the enemy. As a Cameron Highlanders officer, Fitzroy joined Captain David Stirling's Special Air Service (SAS) commando unit in Cairo, which was on a mission to disrupt German campaigns in North Africa through hit-and-run operations. There the men would slip under barbed wire defenses in the dark of night and set explosives on planes to go off after fifteen minutes, leaving them time to retreat safely. By using these tactics on lightly defended airfields, the SAS unit destroyed numerous supplies, petrol tanks, and ninety planes.

Next, armed with his new skills, Fitzroy traveled to Baghdad to meet with General Maitland "Jumbo" Wilson, Command-er-and-Chief for Persia and Iraq, with a request to raise his own SAS unit to work in Persia. And after securing permission, Fitzroy raised a mostly Scottish volunteer group of approximately 150 Non-Commissioned Officers (NCOs).

On November 1, 1942, Fitzroy received his first mission. General Zahidi, Governor-General of Isfahan, was believed to be working secretly with Nazi Germany. With orders to find evidence of the crime and remove Zahidi from the country, Fitzroy mastered a plan called OPERATION PONGO to kidnap the general without creating lethal or military conflict within the region. This was a difficult task, as security personnel usually surrounded the general when he traveled outside of his compound.

On December 7th, Fitzroy made an appointment to see the general. He took with him one officer in the front of the car and another fully armed under a tarp in the luggage compartment. Two trucks full of armed personnel remained just outside the security gate as a backup. Upon entering the home, Fitzroy drew his Colt automatic on the general, only to have Zahidi's thirteen-year-old son appear. Realizing the sensitivity of the circumstances, the general calmed his son, walked outside the house, and got into the awaiting car. He saluted the soldiers at the gate, was whisked into the desert, and put on a plane flight to Palestine, where he was interned for the remainder of the war.

Still unsatisfied, Fitzroy returned to Isfahan under the pretext that the general needed a change of clothing. There the group searched the premises, found further incriminating evidence of the general's collusion with the Germans, and sent the incriminating evidence to his superiors, ensuring Zahidi's conviction. The mission was an absolute success.

Within fifteen months, the SAS destroyed more than 250 aircraft and dozens of supply dumps, railways, and telecommunication systems in Northern Africa. Fitzroy was promoted to head "M Detachment" in Persia, where he worked until ordered by the Prime Minister to travel to Yugoslavia.

With the encroachment of World War II, King Alexander of Yugoslavia was assassinated leaving the eighteen-year-old King Peter to rule the country. Hitler's invasion army occupied Yugoslavia in eleven days, and the seven formerly freed countries of Serbia, Montenegro, Croatia, Dalmatia, Slovenia, Bosnia, and Herzegovina were divided among Germany, Hungary, Bulgaria, and Italy—creating the Independent State of Croatia.

With the establishment of the new state of Croatia, the Ustase (Rise up) Croatian Revolutionary Movement was created using a mix of Nazism and Croatian nationalism with the goal to create a racially "pure" Croatia. Initiating a genocide that paralleled the Nazi Holocaust, the Ustase killed 300,000 Serbs, Jews, and Romani (Gypsy) men, women, and children.

Two guerrilla resistance groups arose to fight the Ustase. The Serb nationalist Chetniks were organized under General Draza Mihailovic, and the second was the Partisans under the Croat Josip Broz (A.K.A. Tito). With Hitler threatening to kill one hundred Serb civilians for every German soldier killed, Mihailovic appeased the Germans by killing or turning over all Partisans to the Nazis. This resulted in a three-way war between the Ustase, Chetniks, and Partisans.

Working as an Inter-Services Liaison Department (ISLD) agent of MI6, Fitzroy was ordered to establish a cooperative relationship with Josip Tito and his Partisan resistance organization, oversee their espionage activities, and support the return of King Peter's royal government. However, Tito was a staunch communist who wanted to create a united nation-state comprised of the seven formerly free countries.

In 1943, Fitzroy parachuted into Croatia where he oversaw a distribution of British supplies to Tito and his 120,000 Partisans. "Fitzroy was a good delegator. He didn't interfere."[21] However, Russia was also giving assistance in an effort to spread communism. But, an ethical dilemma began to develop, as the resistance fighters were developing a reputation of being merciless murderers.

After a difficult battle, Fitzroy came upon the terribly shattered corpse of an Ustasa. "Seeing that capture was inevitable, [the Ustasa] had taken the pin from a hand-grenade and holding it against him, blown himself to bits."[22] A crucifix and Iron Cross still hung from his neck. Rather than be captured, "he had destroyed himself rather than fall into the hands of men of the same race as himself."[23]

Stories had spread throughout the land to strike fear into those who thought of supporting anyone other than the Partisans. One local traitor who was found selling information to the Germans for food was killed and his body fed to the pigs. When the Germans returned, the villagers made sure to feed the soldiers the pigs they deserved. Later, a German captain and a visiting actress went ashore on an island to have sex, only to look back and find a Partisan flag flying over his ship. All his men were dead. He shot the girl before killing himself in order to avoid facing the Partisans.

Soon Fitzroy's ability to support the return of King Peter to his former position fell apart as the king's preference for driving fast motor-cars, carousing with his aides, and occasional attention to government affairs was found disgraceful. On March 26, 1944, Tito officially declared that King Peter was not allowed to return to his country, and he further deferred any future decision about the king until the end of the war.

As the mission progressed, Fitzroy found Soviet soldiers wounded Tito's son, Zharko, in a night club and were involved in over 2,000 robberies and rapes. With growing uncertainty about future cooperation with the Soviet Union, Tito built a Democratic Federal Yugoslavia in 1943, the Federal People's Republic of Yugoslavia in 1945 and the Socialist Federal Republic of Yugoslavia in 1946.

At the end of the war, Fitzroy received the Croix de Guerre from France and the Order of the Partisan Star from Yugoslavia. In March 1945, Fitzroy returned to England where he received the standard award for a Brigadier—the Commander of the Most Excellence Award of the British Empire (CBE). He further returned to his position as MP for Lancaster and was re-elected to the House of Commons, a position he would hold until 1974.

Although Fitzroy possessed many Bond characteristics, his sex appeal was not one of them. Annette Street, an acquaintance of Fitzroy, said, "None of the girls I shared a flat with in Bari – there were six of us – wanted to sit next to him at dinner, he was that awkward."[24] With the girls living among hundreds of men, Fitzroy was totally undesirable. He was always very polite and could drink anyone under the table, but he had a custom of always calling the girls "dolls" and never seemed to show interest in any of them. "[He]] preferred more to be seen in his kilt, showing himself off as an approved Scot, rather than be seen gallivanting around town with a special woman."[25]

In 1945 Fitzroy met the Honorable Mrs. Veronica Nell Fraser-Phipps, who had lost her husband during the war. Now a 26-year-old widow with two children, she met Fitzroy at a dance. After a two-week whirlwind romance, Veronica said, "My initial feeling was that I wouldn't have minded an affair with Fritz, but he insisted on marriage."[26] They married on January 12, 1946.

Although Fitzroy had lingering war memories that caused him to wake during the night and roll on the floor, in 1946 he was chosen as one of five MPs to visit the Far East and Hiroshima with General Douglas MacArthur. In 1947, Fitzroy received his final promotion to Major-General with the mission of interrogating 70,000 displaced Yugoslavs in Italy and Austria to separate the war criminals from the general military. Afterward, Fitzroy returned to England and spent the remainder of his political career specializing in bills and programs relating to military matters, defense, and international affairs.

In 1949, he published his memoirs in the book *Eastern Approaches*, and in the 1960s he worked as an international affairs documentary filmmaker. He lived his remaining days at the family home in Argyll County, Scotland. On June 15, 1996, Fitzroy Maclean died at the age of 85[27] from a heart attack.

As a diplomat spy, Fitzroy's most important contribution to the field of espionage was gathering intelligence for political and military decisions by his superiors. From his extensive travels throughout Russia, the Middle East, and Yugoslavia, the reports and meetings that he shared with Ian Fleming were ideal sources for a better understanding of the political systems of those countries, as well as the espionage and political practices of their leaders. Fitzroy's SAS and MI6 fieldwork clearly evidences him as an excellent source of knowledge about specific cultures, people, and spy missions he experienced before, during, and after World War II. His stories were seeds for the young journalist and novelist to use in developing the Bond character, as well as the plots and settings of his novels.

CHAPTER 6

Sailor marries the girl he left behind in Oslo, Norway (28 June 1945)
Courtesy of the Imperial War Museum

PATRICK DALZEL-JOB

Field Agent

n his professional life Patrick Dalzel-Job[1], like Bond, believed that it should be the responsibility of the onsite agent to supervise all field activities, as they were more capable of responding to unexpected events than their superiors at the War Office in London. In his personal life Patrick, unlike Bond, fell in love with and married a girl to whom he remained devoted for the remainder of his life.

Patrick Dalzel-Job was born in London on June 1, 1913. At the outset of World War I, his father, Lieutenant Ernest Dalzel-Job, volunteered for overseas service in the Army where he quickly rose to command the 115th Machine Gun Company Corps. This exhausting and dangerous work required soldiers to use teams of mules or horses to transport heavy guns to combat locations.

On July 11, 1916, Patrick's mother rose from her prayers with the realization that something had happened to her husband. Ernest was killed that instant at Mametz Wood during the Battle of Somme—one of the largest battles in World War I. Patrick was three years old.

After the war, Patrick attended Berkhamsted School in Hertfordshire, where repeated fevers kept him at home more than school. By age fourteen, he was so weak and thin that to improve his health his French-speaking mother chose to move them to Switzerland. While there, Patrick became fluent in French and advanced his interest in navigation through correspondence courses. And as a result, Patrick developed an independent defiance of the traditional British school system.

During his time in Switzerland, Patrick discovered that skiing was a sport that he could perform without complications from his prior illnesses. As he grew in strength, he ultimately became an expert skier who could ski backward—a skill that Ian Fleming could also perform.

In 1931, at age eighteen, Patrick moved back to England with his mother, where he purchased an unreliable National lifeboat with two older motors. He honed his navigation skills by sailing around the Isle of Wight. From there he and his mother moved to the West Highlands, where he built a sixteen-ton schooner named *Mary Fortune*. The small boat was designed for one person to sail, and over the next few years Patrick became an expert sailor as he traveled around the British coast with his mother.

In July 1937, Patrick and his mother crossed the North Sea to explore the coast of Norway with the goal of spending two years navigating the deep fjords. In preparation, Patrick, who was now studying Norwegian, went in search of a deckhand to assist in the galley and communicate with the local people. "Her name was Bjorg (Bangsund). She was just thirteen, a slim child with enormous blue eyes and short, light brown hair. She was very musical... and had a sweet singing voice. She had an enchanting laugh and charmed everybody she met... She was enthusiastically interested in everything she saw and in every person she met. Patrick and his mother could not have made a better choice."[2]

Fleming had a way of describing his female characters in a sexual manner. Patrick, on the other hand, perceived Bjorg as an innocent child on the verge of becoming a woman. As one of ten children from a timber merchant family, her parents were pleased for her to work as the deckhand on Patrick's brigantine. At that time, Patrick was twenty-six years old. They sailed together for approximately seven months, during which time he became infatuated with her.

Like Patrick, Bond also becomes infatuated with a woman near the sea. In Fleming's eleventh novel *You Only Live Twice* (1964), Bond is sent on a mission to a Japanese island, where he meets, falls in love, and has an unusual outcome with a Japanese shell diver.

After the murder of his wife, Bond is given one month's leave that he spends in Jamaica. After returning to his job, he loses his ability to function over the course of seven months. During a conversation with Sir James Molony, the greatest neurologist in England, M prepares to dismiss Bond. M states, "He's a bachelor and a confirmed womanizer. He then suddenly falls in love... marries her and within a few hours she's shot dead by this super-gangster chap... 'Ernst Stavro Blofeld.'"[3] After Molony convinces him that Bond's erratic behavior is "just shock"[4] from the experience, M calls Bond into his office and gives him an assignment in Japan.

Upon his arrival, Bond finds that Blofeld, who has renamed himself Dr. Guntram Shatterhand, oversees the methodical, voluntary suicides of over five hundred Japanese citizens at the "Castle of Death,"[5] which he built. James is enlisted by the Japanese secret service "to enter this Castle of Death and slay the Dragon within."[6]

Disguised as a "deaf and dumb [Japanese] miner,"[7] Bond is sent to Kuro Island where he is to launch his assault. There he stays with the Suzuki family and their twenty-three-year-old daughter Kissy, also known as "The Japanese Garbo"[8]—a result of her trip to Hollywood, where she made a film that highlighted her as a Japanese diver.

Over the next few days, Bond assists Kissy in her awabi shell diving, learning the fundamentals and improving his strength to swim and dive. Their feelings for each other develop to the point where one day he takes her face in both hands and kisses her on the lips. He tells her that, "You are very beautiful and kind."[9] He then remarks, "tonight I have to swim to the castle and climb the wall and get inside."[10] She helps him get through the currents that night and promises to return every night at midnight for one hour to help him return home.

In late August 1939, the war between Germany and the United Kingdom became imminent. After the official declaration of war, on September 12th Patrick moored the *Mary Fortune* in Bjorg's hometown of Troms, said farewell, promised to return, and set off for London to inform the War Office of the importance of defending the coast of Norway.

On December 8, 1939, Patrick was commissioned into the Royal Navy Volunteer Reserve (RNVR). His first mission in January 1940 was to work as a navigating officer on a target-towing tug in Orkney. When the German invasion of Norway began on April 9, 1940, Patrick was sent to the cruiser *HMS Southampton* to work as an interpreter. His knowledge of the language, area, and culture was invaluable.

Norway was important for its natural resources and shipping routes needed to feed the German war machine. Norway was also a logical second military front north of France. From April 10-13, 1940, British warships surprised and fought the German Navy in Narvik harbor. As a result, the Germans had fourteen destroyers, one ammunition ship, six cargo ships, and one U-boat sunk or scuttled, while the British had two smaller, more maneuverable destroyers sunk and four damaged.

After the naval battles, Patrick supervised the British landing of an estimated ten thousand troops in the town of Harstad. With his knowledge of the language and people, he organized local fishing boats (called puffers) to transfer the troops to land. On April 15th, the troops disembarked at a rate of five hundred per hour. Patrick estimated that from April 4–June 7, approximately fifteen thousand troops and four thousand refugees were moved. For the next six weeks, the troops awaited the Narvik invasion.

Prior to the invasion, it was necessary to move the Narvik civilians to safety. On May 29th, Patrick informed Mayor Theodor Broch of a need to move approximately seven thousand civilians as soon as possible, before the German bomb attack. Within fifteen hours more than 1,500 women and children were moved to safety by the puffers. On May 31st, the Allied Forces Headquarters ordered a stoppage of the evacuation as the watercraft were needed in other locations. Believing that they knew better, Patrick and the mayor chose to disregard the order, and for the next two days they relocated another estimated 2,300 women, children, and older citizens.

On June 2nd, approximately thirty German bombers began to destroy the town center. Evacuations continued until June 7th, when it was estimated that the town contained approximately one hundred remaining people. On June 8th, the mayor was moved and Patrick returned to the *HMS Southampton*, likely facing a court-martial. Fortunately, the King of Norway sent a message of personal thanks to Patrick through the British Admiralty.

In the end, Patrick dodged a military trial and criticism from his government. Instead, while in London, he met with King Haakon of Norway, where he received the *Ridderkors* (Knight's Cross) of St. Olav. Throughout the rest of his career, Patrick would continue to believe that he was better equipped to manage field operations than his superiors.

From 1941-47, Lord Louis Mountbatten from the British War Office) was given the mission to harass the Germans in Europe through raids carried out by naval, air, and army forces. In 1942,

Patrick joined the "D" Class "Mobs" (motor torpedo boats—similar to the U.S. Navy "PT" patrol torpedo boats) to sink German ships in Norwegian waters. Because the Germans had little radar, they failed to monitor wireless transmissions between the Mobs and secret agents on shore. As a result, the Mobs sunk twenty-five ships, while only losing eighteen sailors.

This led to his transfer to the 12 Submarine Flotilla Special Forces Section, where he received further training in to operate one-man "Wolmans," two-man "Chariots," and the "X" Craft submarines that carried two-ton charges for detonation under a ship. During 1943, Patrick was further trained at the No. 1 Parachute Training School at Chesterfield, in Derbyshire, where British, Canadian, French, Polish, and Norwegian troops were required to perform eight successful descents.

Other collaborative operations by the British Navy and Norwegian Special Operations Executive (SOE) brought a halt to the Germans nuclear energy project that attempted to produce heavy water for the creation of a nuclear weapon. Much of this intelligence was shared with Ian Fleming while he worked for the Department of Naval Intelligence (DNI).

After completing the training, he became a field operative in the 30 Assault Unit Commando (30AU) that worked out of the DNI. It was there that he met the operation designer and chief, Commander Ian Fleming (RNVR). Throughout their relationship Patrick had minimal respect for Fleming and his fellow administrators, believing that agents should be left alone in the field and should only be reviewed and reprimanded when inevitable mistakes are made.

Commenting about Fleming, Patrick stated, "Our boss in Admiralty was Ian Fleming, better known as the later creator of James Bond. He was at that time PA to the Director of Naval Intelligence with the rank of Commander. He was quite kind to me, but somewhat cold and austere."[11] Patrick saw him as egotistical and in search of personal opportunities. He added, "My accelerated promotion to Lieutenant Commander, following the recommendation from Admiral Wells in Orkney and Shetland, was promulgated a few days after I started work in Admiralty. Commander Fleming was obviously delighted, but I soon understood the real reason for this was that it added to his own prestige to have a Lieutenant Commander in 'his' Unit."[12] He was also quick to point out that Fleming never took part in any operations; he appeared in the field only once and didn't stay long.

Patrick apparently did not understand that Fleming was too important to chance being caught in the field, as he was privy to classified information that would be a treasure trove to German interrogators. He also later stated, "someone said that I gave him the germ of the idea of James Bond, but I should think it unlikely."[13]

Due to his high-quality performance, Patrick was given command of his own 30 AU Commando Assault unit with orders to obtain as much German war intelligence as possible. Working from a master list of targets given to him by Fleming, Patrick was sent to work in the European Theatre.

In support of 30 AU units, before D-Day General Eisenhower gave all 30 AU commandos a card that read: "THE BEARER OF THIS CARD WILL NOT BE INTERFERED WITH IN THE PERFORMANCE OF HIS DUTY BY THE MILITARY POLICE OR BY OTHER MILITARY ORGANIZATION."[14] This autonomy in their missions to find German Naval Intelligence sites, intelligence, and equipment enabled them to bring back numerous treasures to the British War Office. The 30 AU commanders were so respected that they were given privileged D-Day landing plans before the operation. The classified information was one level beyond "Top Secret" called "Bigot."

Equipped with Q gadgets like those found in the Bond books, Patrick wore a flight jacket with a compass hidden in one of the buttons. He also smoked a pipe fitted with a hidden chamber for a map. On his command jeep, he mounted a field machine gun to look dangerous. And, like other 30AU commandos, he wore a green beret.

Patrick and his unit landed on Utah beach on June 10th. With his recce (reconnaissance) group, Patrick found a German Biber

(German for "beaver") midget submarine, in France, that was needed for a study to enhance the British "Wolman" midget submarine. He then found a new type of German mine in Cologne, Germany and, at the docks of Bremen, he found sixteen of the latest German submarines and two destroyers, with technical papers, equipment, and company directors. And, in his final operation on May 7, 1945, Patrick oversaw the German *Destroyer Z.29* surrender at the Bremerhaven Docks.

As a commando leader, Patrick was well known and respected for his commitment, leadership, and bravery. He also was proud to note that none of the soldiers under his command were ever killed or wounded.

After the war, Patrick returned to Norway in 1945 to find Bjorg. Not having seen each other in almost six years, Biorg immediately came to see Patrick upon hearing of his arrival. Describing her at the railroad station, Patrick said, "At nineteen she was taller, of course, than the child I had left, and her hair was longer and lighter; but she had the same enormous blue eyes under finely arched eyebrows, and the same white, even teeth, with a space between the two top ones in front. She was still a slim figure of a girl, with long straight legs; and she still threw her head back when she laughed, just as she used to do so long ago on my schooner, *Mary Fortune*. She took my arm as we walked slowly from the Vestbane station, up Ronald Amundersen's gate. We said very little; what is there to say after five and a half years?"[15]

On Saturday, June 23, 1945, Patrick went to the British Naval chaplain to ask about the procedure for getting married. Three days later, Patrick and Bjorg were married in a simple ceremony with her friend Dorothy as the bridesmaid and Patrick's friend Sven as the best man. On July 2nd, Patrick and Borg flew on an RAF Transport Command to Edinburgh, Scotland.

Returning to *You Only Live Twice*, Bond's unusual circumstances that lead to his falling in love with Kissy Suzuki began to unfold:

Before battling Blofeld, Bond thinks about Kissy. "She had brought a sweetness back into his life that he thought had gone forever."[16] During a sword fight between the two enemies, Bond manages to strangle Blofeld with his bare hands, blow up the castle, and escape using a helium balloon that is punctured by a bullet, sending him crashing into the sea.

When Kissy reaches him, she says, "It's Kissy... Kissy Suzuki! Don't you remember?' He didn't."[17] Fighting the currents for half a mile, she manages to "put her arms under his armpits and, with his head cradled between her breasts, she set[s] off with the traditional backwards leg-stroke."[18] Upon their return to the island, Bond fails to remember his name or anything about his past. As Bond falls asleep, Kissy thinks "she [[has] got her man back [and] she [is] desperately determined to keep him."[19]

While managing to hide Bond from the repeated visits of Japanese and Australian Secret Service agents, Kissy and James consummate their love for one another.

HOWEVER, UNLIKE BJORG AND PATRICK WHO WOULD HAVE A traditional and loving marriage, Kissy tries to take advantage of Bond's amnesia.

After their marriage, Patrick accepted a post in the Canadian Navy. Bjorg and Patrick had a son, Ian Dalzel-Job, who later served as a major during the Falklands War. In 1960, they moved to the West Highlands of Scotland where Bjorg sang in the Gaelic choir, learned to play the Highland bagpipes, and worked in her garden every day until her death in 1986. Patrick Dalzel-Job passed away on October 12, 2003, at age ninety. In his obituary, Dan van der Vat cited him as a "Real-life model for James Bond without the martinis."[20]

Both Patrick and Bond were daring, courageous, and passionate about ensuring the successful completion of any given mission. Their espionage training and need to have autonomy in the field were also very similar.

However, the personal lives of the two men were vastly different. Patrick was a devoted husband who respected, protected, and loved his wife for the rest of their lives. On the other hand, Blofeld crushed Bond's short relationship with his wife, and his relationship with Kissy was ruined by her withholding knowledge from him about his past.

Although Patrick is often cited as an inspiration for James Bond, he stated, "I have never read a Bond book or seen a Bond movie. They are not my style." He further emphasized that he personally "only ever loved one woman and was not a drinking man."[21]

*British MI5 photograph of Eddie Chapman aka
Agent ZigZag – double agent (1942)*

EDDIE CHAPMAN
Codename: (British) Agent Zigzag
(German) Fritz, and V-6523

E ddie Chapman[1] was a thief, safecracker, convicted criminal, womanizer, spy, and double agent who, like Bond, remained faithful to his Crown and Country.

On November 16, 1914, Edward Chapman was born in the Durham village of Burnopfield. As a student, he skipped school so much that on his sixteenth birthday he chose to run away from home. Although underage, at seventeen he enlisted in the Second Battalion of the Coldstream Guards, where he served sentry duty at the Tower of London. Nine months later he went to Soho, found his first female conquest, and lost his virginity, turning a six-day leave into two months. After returning to duty he was sent to a military prison for eighty-four days, released with a dishonorable discharge, and given his first prison record.

When he returned to Soho in the early 1930s, Eddie made money by seducing women. His Eroll Flynn-like appearance, complete with pencil-thin mustache, made him irresistible. During this time, he met James Well Hunt, who taught him to break into safes using gelignite. They joined forces with two accomplices and created the "Jelly Gang" in 1934.

In 1935 Eddie married Vera Freidberg, who taught him to speak German. Later he met Freda Stevenson, a stage dancer who he unknowingly left pregnant.

Eddie lived a high rolling, criminal life until 1939 when the gang was caught breaking into the Edinburgh Cooperative Society safe. The four burglars were placed in Edinburgh prison where, for an inexplicable reason, Eddie was released after fourteen days on a £150 bond. Soon afterward, he met an eighteen-year-old Shropshire farm girl named Betty Farmer.

Breaking his bond, Eddie took Betty to the La Page Hotel on the Jersey Channel Islands, where the police spotted him during lunch. He rose, kissed Betty, and said, "I shall leave, but I will always come back." He then jumped through a closed window and ran down the beach, evading capture from two men in hot pursuit. He was caught that same night.

On March 11th before entering the courtroom, Eddie received a letter from Betty professing her love for him. He received a two-year maximum "hard labor" sentence to be served on the island. On July 7th Eddie broke out of jail, only to be taken back to serve an additional year of harder time. Still facing an additional eleven-year charge for the Edinburgh robbery, Eddie expected to spend the next fourteen years in jail. Complicating his life further, a letter from Freda in London arrived informing him that they had a daughter named Diane Shayne.

As the only British territory to be captured during World War II, the Channel Islands were bombed by the Germans on June 29,

1940 and occupied three days later. On October 15, 1941, Eddie's and other non-violent prisoners' cells were unlocked and the inmates were allowed to walk freely around the inescapable island. He and his cellmate Anthony Charles Faramus wanted to dupe the Germans into believing that they would work for them in England, with a plan of later escaping into the general population.

In December the two were taken from their beds, arrested, handcuffed, and taken to Fort de Romainville in the eastern suburbs of Paris. Instead of being freed to help the Germans, for some unknown reason they were labeled enemies of the Third Reich. Romainville was essentially a hostage camp for Jews, political prisoners, and Nazi dissidents waiting to be killed. The day after their arrival, they learned that sixteen prisoners were killed for the assassination of a German officer in Nantes.

Despite hardships in the camp, Chapman and Faramus initiated and maintained regular sexual affairs with the female inmates. Chapman's partner was Paulette, a prisoner approximately ten years older than him, and Faramus partnered with Lucy, an inmate whom he believed to be his true love. In reality, female prisoners engaged in numerous sexual encounters with hopes of becoming pregnant to take advantage of the rule that any incarcerated pregnant inmate would be released into the general population.

While serving two weeks in solitary confinement for fighting with another inmate, Eddie was brought to the commandant's office and introduced to a German officer named Walter Thomas. Speaking perfect English, Thomas was familiar with Eddie's criminal record and incarceration in Jersey. After an hour of general conversation, Eddie was released from solitary confinement and allowed to return to the prison population. He was later sent back to the office and met Doktor Stephan Graumann, who offered him a chance to train as a spy if he was willing to send intelligence from Great Britain to their German command center. Eddie agreed and after a four-month incarceration, he left Faramus behind as a hostage.

Prior to OPERATION SEA LION (the German plan to invade Great Britain), twenty-one Abwehr agents were sent to England from September to November 1940. As amateur spies, most were quickly caught. Needing a new approach, in March 1942 Abwehr opened an elite espionage-training center at a French mansion in Nantes under the direction of the English-speaking officer Walter Praetorius (a.k.a. Walter Thomas) where Eddie would become their star student.

During a three-month training program, he studied German, French, Morse code, bomb construction, wireless communication, sabotage, espionage techniques, and parachute jumping. Having no experience with handguns, Eddie was taught to shoot a franc coin from a distance of fifty feet. He also learned how to blow-up bridges, trains, and military sites. He could booby-trap packages with a string containing two wires that would set off an explosive charge when cut and, arm an attaché case with an explosive set to an alarm clock muffled in a pair of pajamas. He also learned how to place an explosive charge in what appeared to be a large lump of Welch coal to sabotage locomotive and ship furnaces.

During his time training with the Abwehr, Eddie was instructed in the art of secret writing using matchsticks with special white heads. The process began by wiping a piece of white paper on both sides with a wad of cotton in a circular motion for ten minutes. Afterward, the paper was placed on a sheet of glass where a message was written in block letters using the matchsticks leaving no visible marks. In order to conceal the message, a normal-looking letter was written using a pencil on both sides of the paper. After being immersed in a chemical solution, green colored letters could be seen under the pencil marks.

In Fleming's tenth Bond novel *On Her Majesty's Secret Service* (1963), James uses a more unusual form of secret writing.

After Bond is informed of the location of Ernest Blofeld (head of the criminal organization SPECTRE), he travels to the dangerous man's Alpine base. While working undercover, Bond finds that Blofeld is brainwashing beautiful women into performing biological warfare practices that are intended to destroy Britain's agricultural economy. After finding the women's names and addresses, he must write the information in a safe place using secret ink.

"There are hundreds of secret inks, but there [is] only one available to Bond, the oldest one in the world, his own urine."[2] He enters the bathroom, cleans his pen, attaches a clean nib, fills the reservoir with freshly collected "secret ink," and begins to write. He transcribes the names and county locations of the girls from his list on a blank page of his passport. As he writes, the paper remains blank. However, when "Held in front of a flame, the writing would come up brown."[3]

After Bond escapes from Blofeld's training camp, he gets the passport information to M, who alerts all needed personnel to gather the brainwashed women when they return home and deprogram their conditioned behaviors.

During Eddie's Abwehr training, an errant wind caught his chute while he was making his first parachute jump, causing him to smash his face into the ground and lose consciousness. The mishap required the replacement of a front tooth, a canine tooth, and several molars with new gold teeth, leaving Eddie with easily identifiable facial markings and a 9,500-franc smile.

Upon graduating from the program, Eddie was given the codename "Fritz" and the spy number V-6523. Anxious to use an Englishman to spy in Britain, Abwehr had believed that Eddie would be the ideal candidate because he was a wanted criminal in his own country and an unscrupulous, money-driven thief. A few months later, British Radio Security Service code-breakers began deciphering German communications on Fritz, who was also referred to as "F" or "C."

As Eddie concluded his training, he was given his first operation, which was code-named "Walter" after Thomas/Praetorius, with the mission of destroying the De Havilland Aircraft Company factory near London. The British manufactured the De Havilland Mosquito airplane, nicknamed "the Wooden Wonder" because it was primarily made of wood. It carried a two-man crew, four thousand pounds of bombs, and no defense guns. With its two Rolls-Royce engines, the plane flew at four hundred miles per hour and could travel to Berlin and back without refueling. While the inexpensive aircraft was used primarily for target bombing, it was also utilized for night flights, photoreconnaissance, U-boat attacks, and general transport. The plane was a persistent threat to the Germans, and the De Havilland factory was considered an ideal target for destruction. If Eddie was successful, he was promised a £15,000 reward, the return of his friend Faramus, significant recognition, and the chance to see Hitler in a military parade.

In opposition to the German effort, Eddie began stockpiling written formulas for the various bombs he produced, assorted intelligence from obtained reports, and notes of eavesdropped conversations he heard through a secret hole in his room.

Shortly before Eddie was dropped into England, he was outfitted with a wireless transmitter to communicate with Abwehr, a handgun with a spare magazine, matches for secret writing, a compass, an area map, twelve detonators, a wallet with two ID cards, and Betty's love note. He was also given a brown potassium cyanide pill with which to kill himself if captured, and a canvas bag with £900 of used money with bands stamped "Reichsbank Berlin" and "England" written in pencil. Eddie realized that the money had been an oversight that would mark him as a German spy if he were to be found before the bands were discarded.

Disregarding the money band problem, Eddie parachuted into Britain on December 16, 1942. Initially, he got stuck in the opening of the airplane door and dangled for about ten seconds before being pushed into the open air. The jump was not without problems. He landed in a celery field near Cambridge around 2:30 in the morning. Around 3:30 a.m., Eddie arrived at an old farmhouse and surrendered to George and Martha Convine. They let the bloody-faced Eddie into their house, called the constables, and gave him three cups of tea and four slices of toast. When the constables arrived an hour later, Eddie surrendered his gun and asked to be taken to representatives of the British Intelligence Service.

MI5 created OPERATION NIGHTCAP to capture Fritz on his arrival. Although they called him Agent X, the British believed all along that Fritz was actually Chapman. After his capture, he was sent to the "Camp 020" British secret interrogation center, which was headed by Lieutenant Colonel Robin "Tin Eye" (so nicknamed because of his monocle) Stephens. Tin Eye interrogated Eddie, who unexpectedly shared everything he could remember about his Abwehr experiences.

Despite the fact that he still believed that he was going to serve fourteen years in prison, Eddie willingly volunteered to become a Double Agent (XX) and was given the codename "Agent Zigzag." For all future radio communication, the codename of ZINC was given to keep recognition of the letter Z in the agent's name. On New Year's Eve, Eddie sent a message to Abwehr stating that "Walter" can be successfully completed.

Like all double agents, Eddie had been given a case operator, wireless operator, a housekeeper, two guards to protect him, and a safe house. The team's greatest challenge was keeping the known criminal out of the public eye.

The seclusion made Eddie depressed. To address the problem, he was taken to a pub where he was allowed to spend time with a local a prostitute. Unfortunately, Eddie then sank into a deeper depression and requested to see his wife Freda and daughter Diane. Unbeknownst to Eddie, in August 1941 Freda had married an older man named Keith Butchart who managed a balloon works. The marriage dissolved after Freda left Keith one night while he was out drinking.

The following day, Freda and Diane moved into the safe house where Eddie told Freda that he had escaped from Jersey, had his other charges dropped, and he would soon join the army overseas. It had been almost four years since their last meeting. Since Eddie had divorced Vera Friedberg while he was in prison, he was free to propose to Freda with the two agreeing to marry after his return from duty.

To gain the confidence of the Abwehr officers, Eddie needed to make them believe that he succeeded in blowing up the De Havilland Aircraft Company factory.[4] Needing a master illusionist to complete the charade, the magician Jasper Maskelyne, under the supervision of Sir John "Conky Bill" Turner (head of the Air Ministry Camouflage Section), was called to create a visual appearance of a destroyed aircraft factory that would be photographed aerially by German aircraft from 2,000 feet. By camouflaging buildings to appear destroyed with debris spread over the surrounding one-hundred-foot radius, Maskelyne succeeded in creating the illusion.

To further convince the enemy, the *Daily Express* agreed to print a supporting article. The operation was planned to take place on the night of January 29th. On that evening the camouflage was set, debris was strewn about, and an explosion was heard by the local people. On Monday, February 1, 1943, the first edition of the *Daily Express* read:

"FACTORY EXPLOSION"
Investigations are being made into the cause of an explosion at a factory on the outskirts of London. It is understood that the damage was slight and there was no loss of life.

The operation was called Maskelyne's masterpiece. The Germans bought the deception hook, line, and sinker. As a reward, Eddie was promised the honor of attending one of the Führer's parades. He volunteered to use the honor to assassinate Adolph Hitler as an XX mission, but the proposal was rejected by the MI5 administration.

In his twelfth and final Bond novel *The Man with the Golden Gun* (1965), Fleming presents an alternative use of the XX assassination when James is sent on a mission to kill M.

⸻

Bond picks up his hotel phone at the Ritz, calls MI6, and asks for "Admiral Sir Miles Messervy. He is head of a department in your Ministry."[5] Bond has been missing for a year, so the individuals he contacts first are shocked to hear his voice. After passing through security at MI6, he finally gets to see M. With a distant smile and glazed look, Bond seems out of sorts. Upon entering M's office, he explains how he was hit on the head during a mission in Japan, lost his memory, traveled to Vladivostok, was sent to the local branch of the KGB, and ended in Leningrad where he was interrogated for weeks. Over time his memory has returned as minute details of his past have been revealed to him.

Still speaking in a distant manner, Bond says, "They gave me VIP treatment. Top brain-specialists and everything"[6] after which he states the "need for East and West to work together for world peace."[7] Then looking "across the table Bond says, "for most of my life you've used me as a tool. Fortunately that's all over now."[8]

Clearly brainwashed by his captors, Bond pulls a bulb-butted pistol out of his pocket and releases a poisonous liquid out of the barrel at M just as a "great sheet of Armourplate glass hurtle[s] down from the baffled slit in the ceiling and with the last sigh of hydraulics, brake[s] on the floor."[9] The brown fluid splashes harmlessly against the glass, distorting M's face. The Chiefs of Staff and Security burst into the room and pounce on Bond. Realizing that the fluid was cyanide, they kick away the gun and rush everyone out of the office.

⸻

THE CYANIDE GUN USED IN *THE MAN WITH THE GOLDEN GUN* WAS a later, more sophisticated version than the earlier one used by a SMERSH agent in *Casino Royale* (1953). Fleming loved to present numerous gadgets he studied or saw used during his time at the DNI. His further understanding of the XX system and use of brainwashing practices gave him additional information to enhance his novels and short stories.

In the case of Eddie, he used his newfound knowledge and skills to teach MI5 personnel how to use electrical bulb filaments and watches as bomb fuses and detonators. Having completed his mission to "destroy" the De Havilland factory, Eddie said farewell to the most recent prostitute he had befriended and made passage to Lisbon on the three-thousand-ton merchant marine ship *City of Lancaster*. There he sent a message to the Germans that he wanted to blow up his ship. After having two coal bombs made by local German saboteurs, he gave them to the ship's commander for later MI5 inspection and returned to Paris. Afterward, a staged attempted sabotage on the *City of Lancaster* was reported through sailor gossip with Eddie identified as the saboteur.

With Abwehr administrators believing that he had blown up the Havilland Aircraft Company factory and attempted to sabotage the *City of Lancaster,* Eddie was praised and sent to Norway. There he was given 100,000 reichsmarks for his work in England and 10,000 reichsmarks for his attempted sabotage of the *City of Lancaster* that he could draw upon as needed.

The only British subject ever to receive such an honor, Eddie was awarded the Iron Cross (das Eiserne Kreuz)—the highest award given by the Third Reich for outstanding bravery and accomplishment.

Shortly thereafter, Eddie met Dagmar Lahlum, the daughter of a Norwegian shoemaker and recently divorced wife of an older man named Johanssen. In addition to her work as a model and dressmaker, she also worked for the Norwegian Resistance. With his new abundance of money, Eddie showered her with every luxury available at the time, and eventually, she moved into his residence.

The new love affair resulted in an unwanted pregnancy. Worried about what others might think, Eddie found her a German doctor willing to perform an abortion. Believing that he would someday return to marry her, Eddie made sure to set her up with a very comfortable life. In a further attempt to keep Dagmar's affection, Eddie confessed his position with the British Secret Service. This confession enabled Dagmar to share her similar relationship with the Resistance.

After residing in Norway for eleven months, Eddie left for Paris on March 8, 1944. Dagmar was left behind to monitor German activities with a promise that her lover would return as soon as possible. The D-Day invasion in France on June 6th constrained Eddie's movement, but on June 27th he left from Holland for England with a new XX mission of improving accuracy for the V-1 bombing missions in London.

On June 29th, Eddie parachuted into Cambridgeshire and surrendered to a farmer's wife. Within two hours, Eddie was reunited with Tin Eye Stephens at Camp 020 and pledged his allegiance to England and Dagmar, whom he now planned to marry instead of Freda at the end of the war.

With MI5 assistance, over the next two months, Eddie sent inaccurate information to the Germans in regard to their V-1 rocket blitzes. Unfortunately, 6,184 people were killed by the bombs before the U.S. developed new technology that neutralized the rockets.

One last major deception for Eddie was OPERATION SQUID. For this mission, he presented inaccurate information about a new exploding device called the "hedgehog" in which a fuse would trigger numerous depth charges guaranteeing U-boat destruction. This exaggerated report struck terror into the minds of the enemy who saw altered photographs to evidence the claim. And with this deception having a direct impact on Naval Intelligence, it was Ian Fleming who was well informed of Eddie's efforts.

On November 2, 1944, Eddie signed a copy of the *Official Secrets Act*, preventing disclosure of his clandestine activities during the war. And, on November 28, 1944, the Eddie Chapman file was officially closed, bringing his secret agent life to an end.

Having saved thousands of lives through his wartime activities, Eddie was given an "unofficial" pardon for his earlier alleged crimes, awarded £6,000 by MI5, and allowed to keep £1,000 given to him by the Germans. Ironically, he also still had the Iron Cross for his services to Germany.

Finally, Eddie resolved his female relationships. He avoided making contact with Dagmar in Oslo, Freda and his daughter, his ex-wife Vera, and the numerous prostitutes with whom he kept company during his periods of loneliness and depression. Instead, he set out to find Betty Farmer. During a chance meeting at the Berkeley Hotel, Eddie sat down next to her and reiterated, "I shall leave, but I will always come back." Betty and Eddie married on October 9, 1947, and their daughter Suzanne was born in October 1954. Eddie continued to have periodic minor criminal problems with the police and judicial system during the remainder of his life. He was also had problems being faithful to Betty, engaging in affairs with at least six mistresses during the remainder of his life.

Eddie Chapman died of heart failure on December 11, 1997, at the age of eighty-three. Although he never drew a pension from his three-year war service, approximately one month after his death Betty received a check for £2,500 from a representative of the Ministry of Defense. The film *Triple Cross*, directed by Terrence Young, was loosely based on Eddie's life.

Included in the MI5 files released in 2001 is a January 7, 1942 report written by Robin Stephens that reads, "The story of Chapman is different. In fiction it would be rejected as improbable… The man essentially vain, has grown in stature and in his own estimation, is something of a prince in the underworld. He has no scruples and will stop at nothing. He makes no bargains with society and money is a means to an end… In a word adventure to Chapman is the breath of life. Given adventure, he has the courage to achieve the unbelievable. His very recklessness is his standby… Without adventure, he would rebel … For Chapman, only one thing is certain, the greater the adventure, the greater the chance of success."[10]

Eddie Chapman's life is the story of a spy who manufactured a perfect cover for espionage activities that contributed to saving Britain from Nazi domination while simultaneously maintaining a compulsively satisfying sex life. Ian Fleming's personal familiarity with Eddie's spy career must have been a great source of Double-X field behaviors and gadget designs for the Bond novels and short stories.

CHAPTER 8

Escaping from France by sea (November 1940)
Courtesy of Thwm100

MERLIN MINSHALL

Self-Proclaimed Codename:
One-Man-Minshall-Army
(Intelligence) or OMMA(I)

M erlin Minshall[1] was a master sailor, winning motorcar racer, inventor, professional photographer, adventurer, and spy. As a self-trained spy, he worked for himself gathering intelligence for Britain until he was allowed to work for MI6 under the supervision of Ian Fleming where he fed the young author with detailed spy stories that could be copied verbatim for the Bond novels and short stories. An army of one, Merlin exhibited persistence, dedication, and serendipity.

A spy similar to the One–Man-Minshall-Army (Intelligence) is introduced in Ian Fleming's eighth novel *Thunderball* (1961).

Giuseppe Petacchi was an ideal recruit for SPECTRE. "At the age of eighteen he had been a co-pilot of a Frocke 200 [and] one of the few hand-picked Italian airmen who had been allowed to handle these German planes."[2] While on a mission, he decided to go into business for himself by shooting a pilot and navigator in the back of the head. After landing the plane safely in the harbor of Bari, he surrendered to the RAF. "He had told a highly coloured story to the Intelligence people of having been a one-man resistance ever since he had been old enough to join the Italian Air Force, and he emerged at the end of the war as one of Italy's most gallant resistance heroes."[3] Maintaining his cover as one of six Italians chosen for the NATO Advance Striking Force, he hijacked a plane with an atomic bomb. "He didn't mind in the least who wanted the plane so long as he was paid."[4]

ALTHOUGH PETACCHI IS A VILLAIN, FLEMING USED MERLIN'S concept of a one-man resistance figure to portray a rogue agent who works for himself.

Merlin Theodore Minshall was born on December 21, 1906, in Chobham, England. His father Thomas was a successful newspaperman who owned the London evening *Globe*. His grandfather started the Swan-Hunter shipyards, which made Merlin seem destined to take to the sea.

Merlin first experienced the world of espionage at the age of ten. Accompanying his mother on a London bus, he spotted two nuns with a pair of men's boots under one of their habits. Surprised, he informed his mother of the odd circumstance. She said, "Stay on the bus. I'm getting off. Whatever happens don't lose sight of the nuns."[5] After leaving the bus at the end of the line, Merlin followed them only to see his mother waiting with two uniformed police, who arrested the "nuns." Unbeknown to anyone in the family, his mother worked for the Foreign Office (FO) as a spy during World War I. His mother later committed suicide due to the pressure of her job, leaving Merlin to become a self-trained spy.

Merlin was educated at Charterhouse School and Oxford University, where he received an honors degree in Modern History. Shortly before graduation, he vacationed in Bavaria where he met an attractive German girl named Marlene Dörnberg. When they later traveled to Venice, Marlene said, "You do realize, *mein Liebe*, that my body and my virginity are both wholly dedicated to the Führer."[6] Then disregarding her German fanaticism, they both lost their virginity that same day.

In the fifth Bond novel *From Russia with Love* (1957), Ian Fleming uses this story to introduce how sex is used to gather intelligence by a similar young Russian secret agent.

Corporal Tatiana Romanova meets with the Head of the SMERSH Otdyel II (Department of Torture and Death) Rosa Klebb (Russian word for bread) who "would let no torturing take place without her."[7] Terror-stricken as she sits in front of Klebb, Tatiana hears that her record is considered excellent, and "The State is pleased with you."[8] Now chosen for a special operation, she will seduce an English spy who is possibly the most famous of them all. As an instrument of the State, she will be taught certain foreign customs and trained in the arts of allurement in order to fulfill her mission. Klebb strictly states, "Your body belongs to the State. Since your birth, the State has nourished it. Now your body must work for the State."[9]

BELIEVING THAT HIS LIBERAL ARTS EDUCATION FAILED TO PREPARE him to succeed in life, Merlin studied architecture in London.

While working as an architect's apprentice, he fell head-over-heels for a charming, sexy blonde appropriately named Elizabeth Loveday. Foreshadowing Ian Fleming's trademark use of sexually suggestive names for women in his Bond novels, in 1931 Merlin married "Liz Loveday" with a commitment to live on love and travel the seas.

Having little savings, Merlin dropped out of school and traded his £200 secondhand Wolsey Hornet sports car for a sixty-year-old yacht called *Sperwer*. With little to no knowledge of sailing, he and Liz set out to be the first British subjects to sail across Europe to the Black Sea. However, the stress of traveling put a strain on the relationship, and eventually Liz left to find a more traditional suitor and lifestyle.

As Merlin continued to follow his fantasy, Germany was preparing for war. Since the Germans had never seen an Englishman sail across Europe, they kept a close eye on Merlin, who was stopped on numerous occasions and accused of being a British spy.

Traveling down the Danube River, he observed that Germany was actively transporting oil and wheat to the Motherland. Seeking a location to destroy the supply route, he found a narrow passage in the river that could be blocked.

When he went ashore in Vienna, he met an undercover female German agent named Lisa Kaltenbrunner who seduced him. Believing that she was the daughter of a history professor (whom he had met earlier in his travels), Merlin allowed her to travel with him as his lover and mistress. Soon a Gestapo officer repeatedly appeared in other ports of the river. The officer who turned out to be Hermann Goering, the President of the Reichstag, presented a cover that Lisa's father was a German dissident. Merlin naively thought the meetings were coincidental and his newfound love for Lisa Kaltenbrunner was kismet—until Lisa stole Merlin's film and photos of the Danube River shipping route, as well as his notes describing the ongoing transport of oil and grain supplies to Germany.

After abandoned by Liz and made to look like a fool by Lisa, Merlin decided to continue his travels when he met Count Mihaili Fock, a man posing as a potential buyer of his yacht. During their initial discussion, Frock invited Merlin to drive his speedboat in the Danube Gold Cup Boat Race. With absolutely no experience in high-speed motorboat racing and given only one day to practice, Merlin won the race and the prize money of one thousand guineas.

Feeling insulted, a Hungarian member of the Royal Budapest Motor Yacht Club slapped Merlin's face and challenged him to a duel. In traditional fashion, the challengers were supplied with fine quality pistols and the gentlemanly conditions in which to kill one another. After the challenger's discharged bullet missed his target, Merlin pointed his weapon and deliberately shot the pistol out of his opponent's hand. Like a scene right out of a Bond novel, the Hungarian was shamed, Merlin won a victory without having to kill his opponent, and the self-proclaimed spy continued his mission with the conclusion that Germany was preparing for another world war.

Returning to *Sperwer*, Merlin found Lisa Kaltenbrunner naked sunning herself on the deck of his ship. "Did you miss me very much, *mein Liebling*?"[10] she cooed as she threw her arms around him. He responded, "What do you think?"[11] as he picked her up and carried her down into *Sperwer's* great cabin. After explaining that she had accidentally packed his photos with her belongings because she needed to get home to see her ill brother, Merlin didn't seem to care. She whispered in his ear, "But now I think we are wasting time. You must make love to me."[12] And, beginning to better understand the life of a spy, Merlin took her back.

In a bizarre turn of events in 1933, Merlin managed to steal one of the very few maps of the Danube in existence. He then sailed to the very narrow Gorge of Kazan, which he believed was an ideal location to create a river blockage. Taking advantage of her vanity, Merlin photographed Lisa in less-than-appropriate bathing attire in front of the narrowest section of the river. Then he mailed the photographs and map to England for safekeeping.

Shortly thereafter, realizing that her spy mission was compromised, Lisa poisoned Merlin. Fortunately—or unfortunately, as Lisa would have it—Merlin didn't die and Lisa was not able to steal any sensitive documents before leaving for the second time. Apparently, she misjudged the amount of poison it would take to kill him. The day after she left, Merlin was found lying on the floor of *Sperwer* and rushed to the hospital.

After four weeks in intensive care, Merlin was released from the Bucharest General Hospital. The doctors assumed that he had tried to commit suicide. Merlin felt it best not to explain the reality of the situation. Feeling embarrassed that he had let a female spy make a fool of him twice, he returned to *Sperwer* only to find the ship stripped of all usable parts. Unable to continue his trip, Merlin loaded *Sperwer* on a ship bound for England, where he sold the boat for his same original purchase price.

By the end of this chapter of his life, Merlin had spent eighteen months on the Danube River, lost two loves, won a major motorboat race, survived a pistol duel, stole a valuable map, and avoided being poisoned to death. With all of his adventures, Merlin became possibly the only credible British expert on the Danube River.

Unsure of his future as a spy, Merlin used a substantial amount of inherited family money to enter the 1935 Monte Carlo car rally. To cover a distance of three thousand miles, from Lapland near the Arctic Circle to Monte Carlo, in approximately ninety-six hours of near non-stop driving, he acquired a new 1½-litre Singer Special that had recently nearly won at Le Mans. Like his motorboat racing experience, Merlin believed that an amateur could beat the professionals.

Redesigning his headlights to turn with the steering changes, he improved the illumination of the road. He also learned to keep food and drink warm using his exhaust manifold and how to monitor his route with a large-scale map of the course. He was soon ready to compete against the other hundred cars in the race. Traveling with his new English mistress Yvette, Merlin secured the position of first place at the end of the third day, in part because his car had been performing exceptionally well. Unfortunately, his overall advantage soon slipped to second and then fifth place, while he still maintained first place in the under 1500cc class. Although he didn't win his first rally, he developed a reputation as a quality driver and car modifications inventor.

In 1936, Merlin entered the grueling four-thousand-mile, three-day Mussolini Gold Cup. Averaging speeds above 90 mph at times, Merlin performed well. Beating many Italian entrants, at the end of the race more than half of the cars had dropped out and four drivers were dead. Mussolini himself presented the Foreign Challenge Trophy to Merlin. As he awarded the cup he stated, "Now that you have seen, *Seniore Inglese*, how we Italians can vanquish everybody, go back and tell your compatriots, your League of Nations, your mister Baldwin, that they had better stop annoying me. Yes, you *Inglesi* are great hypocrites. Throughout your history you have been murdering untold millions of innocent natives to gain your British Empire. Now you have the effrontery to try and stop Italy rebuilding her glorious African Empire in Abyssinia by entirely peaceful methods."[13] Like his meeting with Goering, Mussolini's arrogance for seeking world dominance further prompted Merlin's desire to work for British Intelligence.

When Merlin returned to England, he discovered that Yvette had married another eligible bachelor. After losing yet another love, Merlin chose to forget his heartache by taking an eight-week cruise around Africa.

Merlin next teamed up with a Dutch journalist named Alfred Mazure with the goal to cross the Sahara Desert on a motorcycle. Instead of the water-cooled four-wheel vehicles commonly used in the area, Merlin purchased a new three-wheel air-cooled motorcycle for £105. The duo set off on February 28, 1937. Aside from his desire to be the first to cross the Sahara on a motorcycle, Merlin wanted to study Germany's interest in the area. The Nazis were in need of rubber, tin, copper, and uranium raw materials to support their growing war effort, and by crossing the desert Merlin and Alfred believed that they could gather intelligence on how Equatorial Africa could effectively be used as a trans-Saharan supply route.

Beginning their adventure in Algiers, the duo traveled to Beni Isguin where they were believed by French authorities to be spies and asked to leave the country. Ignoring the instructions, Merlin and Alfred left undetected to cross the desert. Traveling at a maximum speed of 33 mph, they occasionally met individuals believed to be members of the German Afrika Korps or other spy organizations. Near the end of the trip, a French Secret Service military vehicle stopped them. After inspecting their passports and other papers, they were taken to the edge of the French territory where their visas were canceled.

Returning to England, their Sahara adventures became big news. Although Merlin made history as the first person to cross the Sahara on a motorcycle, the manufacturer's three-wheel vehicles ended production. Believing that he had revolutionized desert military operations, Merlin went to the War Office to offer his expertise but was turned away.

Next, Merlin gave his Sahara trip photographs to a London agent to sell. Not knowing that the agent was a German spy, he later learned that the images were sent to Berlin where it is believed that they contributed to the development of prototype air-cooled vehicles used in the Nazi African desert campaign and the production of Doctor Porsche's air-cooled Volkswagen Beetle. This new technology gave Germany state-of-the-art tanks and jeeps, which resulted in a military transportation advantage.

Remaining in England, Merlin was invited to a party where he met Isolde Llewellyn, whom he married twenty-one days later. Because Isolde's mother had been a Lady in Waiting to the Queen, their wedding became a major social event. After a honeymoon in Paris and Africa, where Merlin found more evidence of German war preparations, in 1939 he reported his findings to the Director of British Military Topographical Intelligence. He was insulted and asked to leave.

Undaunted, he went to the Department of Naval Intelligence where he met Lieutenant Ian Fleming, who upon hearing his knowledge of the Danube River immediately allowed him to read a 'Top Secret" document labeled "Lower Danube Intelligence Report." The document, which contained intentionally inaccurate information, was used as a way of testing Merlin's knowledge of the topic. Believing that the Danube could play a role in the defeat of Germany, Merlin was allowed to meet an individual believed to be Admiral John Godfrey DNI (Director of Naval Intelligence), who unfortunately didn't agree that the Danube was a priority, leaving Merlin feeling insulted, frustrated, and deflated.

Upset by the experience and still wanting to help, Fleming sent Merlin to an individual known as "M." Speaking from another room and never seeing M's face, Merlin divulged all of his knowledge about blocking ship movements to Germany. Not only was his interviewer significantly more knowledgeable about the Danube, but he also knew about Fräulein Kaltenbrunner. At the end of the conversation, Merlin was given command of a mission that needed to be completed within the next one hundred days: to block the largest river in Europe.

First Merlin was instructed on how to act as the new British Vice-Consul to Romania. He was further instructed in various types of explosive devices as well as unarmed and armed combat techniques. He received instruction in camouflage, disguise, cover stories, and codes. Near the end of his training, Merlin received a commission to the rank of Lieutenant in His Majesty's Royal Navy Volunteer Reserve (RNVR). Before leaving, he was given final instructions on how to kill himself instantly with a potassium cyanide pill that was drilled into his upper left wisdom tooth.

On January 1, 1940, twenty-six days into his assignment and one hundred nineteen days into Britain's declaration of war, Merlin set off across the continent on the Simplon Orient Express, carrying a briefcase containing five pounds of plastic explosives disguised as bars of Mackintosh De Luxe Toffee and what looked like ordinary electric cartridge fuses.

Upon arriving in Bucharest, he checked into one of the finest hotels. Arming himself with a shoulder-holstered Walther PPK pistol and a Beretta .25 that was hidden in a fob pocket set near his groin, Merlin set out to find all of the fifty British ships used in the Danube River. After learning that the ships were British only in name and sailed by professional sailors, he regained control of the ships yet was unable to remove the riverboat pilots who had extensive knowledge of the Danube and its idiosyncrasies. On the eighty-third day, he developed a new plan.

The goal was to take five to six ships to the Gorge of Kazan just above the Iron Gates and sink them, thereby creating an impassable blockage. While scouting the area, Merlin met a man claiming to be a botanist on holiday. Staying at the same hotel, he was found rifling through Merlin's luggage. When Merlin was returning to Bucharest on the Orient Express, the stranger appeared again. After noticing his German passport, Merlin fed him poison while dining together. Not feeling well, the man went to the toilet, where he died. Merlin found his stall, stole the passport proving that he was a Gestapo agent, took his clothes for a later disguise, and threw the body out the window.

A similar scene can be found in the Richard Maibaum screenplay *From Russia with Love* (1963), adapted by Johanna Harwood and based on the Ian Fleming novel.

Following Klebb's orders, Tatiana Romanova seduces Bond, falls in love with him, and assists him in stealing a Lektor (aka 4-rotor Enigma) cipher machine. Traveling back to London on a European train, Bond meets SPECTRE assassin Donald "Red" Grant who is impersonating an MI6 agent. After gaining Bond's confidence, Grant tranquilizes Tati-

ana by pouring chloral-hydrate in her wine. Then on returning to the compartment he "pulls a pistol from a holster under his pant leg"[14] and hits Bond on the base of his skull. After Bond recovers, Grant explains that SPECTRE was "keeping you alive till you could get us the Lektor... Now that we've got it, you and the girl are expendable."[15]

Trying to bribe Grant with 50 gold sovereigns from his "Q gadget" briefcase, Bond follows the secret procedure for opening the case. After receiving the coins, Grant tries to open the second similar case only to have "a gale of smoke shooting from the case. Bond lunges through the smoke at Grant... They struggle over the gun. The gun fires... Bond grabs the gun and throws it... Bond lunges forward... Grant reaches for his watch. He pulls the garrote from his watch"[16] and wraps it around Bond's neck. Bond pulls a knife from his briefcase and plunges it into Grant's shoulder. As he falls backward, Bond wraps the garrote around Grant's neck and keeps pulling tighter until "Grant's head slumps back and he lands on the couch dead."[17]

AFTER MURDERING THE GESTAPO AGENT, UPON HIS RETURN TO Bucharest Merlin teamed with a group of British demolition experts to crew his ships. However, with the Gestapo controlling all river transportation, the foreign ships were refused fresh drinking water, thereby preventing them from leaving the port.

Time was running out and Merlin had to remove the Nazi Naval Attaché in order to carry out his plan. Having befriended the Madame of the best bordello in Bucharest, he talked her into supplying the Attaché with a favored companion to take to his room in an elegant hotel that prohibited such behavior. Prior to their arrival, Merlin cut a sliver off a Gillette safety razor blade and placed it in the slit of the Attaché's door lock. Sneaking back into the hotel and ripping off half of her clothes in the lift, the Attaché found himself standing next to a half-naked girl unable to open the door to his room. Because his behavior had been witnessed by another hotel patron, the next day he was removed from his office and forced to return to Berlin. Fortunately, on this day, another twenty-five pounds of Mackintosh toffee plastic explosives arrived in a diplomat's bag, marking the ninety-second day of the mission.

Moving quickly, Merlin drove the explosives through snowy areas from Bucharest to Braila. He arrived at 3 a.m. and bribed the guard at the locked Braila harbor gates to gain entrance. Shots rang out immediately and Merlin sped away under a barrage of bullets. Minutes later he reached the gangplank of the *Oxford*. He carried the twenty-five pounds of explosives on board but forgot the cigar box of detonators. He ran back, retrieved the box, and was stopped by the Rumanian harbor police who were actually German Gestapo. They searched his car only to find the unidentified clothes of the dead Orient Express agent. Upon learning that Merlin was the British Consul General, they allowed him to return to the boat. This marked day ninety-seven of the operation.

The following day Merlin was called to the British Legation. Believing the letter that summoned him to be authentic, Merlin followed its instructions, which led him into a trap. Always prepared for danger, Merlin took his Walther PPK and Beretta .25 with him. As soon as he entered the house, he was hit on the back of the head and bound from head to foot with ropes. Awakening in a chair, Merlin was unable to raise his head beyond the waist as his neck and wrists were tied with rope close to his feet. Looking up slightly he saw a Gestapo with a Luger who knew his real identity, remembered his travels down the Danube with Lisa Kaltenbrunner, and even knew his rank in the British Navy. Realizing that his cover was destroyed and his future in dire straits, the Gestapo gave Merlin a complete written confession to sign, acknowledging him to be British spy on a mission to sabotage the Danube transportation system.

After finally agreeing to sign the confession, Merlin's hands were untied and, when given a moment to stretch, he reached down to rub his groin and pulled out the Beretta. He shot the German in the left temple. Retrieving his Walter PPK and the Luger from the German, he raced out of the house and down to the harbor.

Merlin had missed the ships, but he had a backup twin-engine high-speed Air Sea Rescue Launch (ASRL) that Ian Fleming had sent to Braila in case of an emergency. Exiting the harbor and cruising the boat to deceive the Iron Gates supervisors, he managed to clandestinely catch up to his ships only to find that they had run out of fuel. Apparently, the Germans had won again.

To Merlin's surprise, the same Gestapo who had stopped and inspected his car reappeared on the ship. With his plan to block the river now totally collapsed, Merlin boarded the ship, was accused of being a lieutenant in the British RNVR, and was immediately arrested.

Needing to escape, Merlin requested permission to return to the ASRL to change into his Naval uniform. Respecting his military formality, emerging in full uniform, Merlin moved to the cockpit, started the engines, and took off just ahead of a bullet that broke his windshield and another that hit the deck inches away from his foot. With two Rumanian vessels in hot pursuit, the superior ASRL easily sped away.

A scene similar to Merlin's escape from the Gestapo appears in Maibaum's screenplay and film *From Russia with Love* (1963):

———————◆———————

Having survived an assassin and a helicopter attack, Tatiana Romanova, now known as Tania, and a SPECTRE senior agent named Rhoda run down the jetty to an awaiting boat. "Bond follows carrying the Lektor, rifle and Rhoda's coat. He unties the front rope and the three of them climb aboard. Bond starts the engine and they move off."[18] Since they are within swimming distance of the shore, Bond pushes Rhoda into the water. Moments later a motorboat appears with the captain, Morzeny, yelling into a megaphone: "Heave to! Heave to! ... You're trapped, Mister Bond! You're trapped! You cannot escape!"[19] One more boat appears and then another. All begin firing machine guns and rifle grenades.

Then "Bond glances back at the fuel drums. Bullets puncture each of them and fuel pours out. Bond keeps looking. More fuel.... Bond unties the drums and pushes three of them off the boat... PAN BACK to show the drums floating between Bond's boat and the others... The three boats pass one of the fuel drums... Bond rolls the last fuel drum off the boat... Bond raises his hands as Tania looks back."[20]

Tania says, "Why are you giving up? Without those drums the boat must be lighter. We can go faster."[21] Bond aims and fires a Very (aka flare) gun. The water is set on fire and the boats become engulfed by the flames. They begin to collide and screams to abandon the boats are heard as their gas tanks, explosives, and ammunition blow up. Bond cleverly quips, "There's a saying in England: where there's smoke there's fire."[22]

NOW WELL BEYOND THE POSSIBILITY OF CAPTURE, MERLIN WENT into the cabin and removed the last twenty-five pounds of Mackintosh's De Luxe toffee blocks, to which he attached thirty-second mercury detonators. The night began to set. Turning about, a Rumanian boat approached the ASRL at a high rate of speed. Merlin started the engine and headed toward the boat in a game of chicken. Not wishing to die, the Rumanian barely missed a collision only to have his searchlight shot out by Merlin.

In a final attempt to complete his mission and delay shipping for up to a few weeks, Merlin charged the ASRL toward a collection of railway lines used to move ships through the Iron Gates. At 23:59 of the hundredth day of his mission, the twenty-five pounds of plastic toffee exploded, destroying the train and tracks in its path.

Emerging from the Danube wearing a soaking wet uniform, Merlin found the passport from the deceased Orient Express spy and lots of Rumanian lei, dollars, and British pound notes in his pockets, which he used to buy new clothes. He then impersonated the German doctor, whose passport was now in his possession, and traveled back to London. Two days later, he reported to Ian Fleming about his adventure wreaking havoc with the Germans in the international waters of the Danube.

In the summer of 1940, Merlin was recruited by the Special Operation Executive (SOE) and in November of the same year supervised a small party of Frenchman in OPERATION SHAM-ROCK whose mission was to study German U-boat movements about the Gironde Estuary. Next, he spent time in New Zealand organizing special Naval intelligence. And in autumn of 1943, Merlin was promoted to commander and placed in charge of the Allied Naval Mission to establish relations with Tito's Yugoslavia.

After the war, Merlin made a brief and unsuccessful attempt to enter politics. He spent the remainder of his life in Norfolk with his fourth wife, Christina Majorie Zambra[23], and their four sons. Merlin Minshall died[24] on September 3, 1987, at the age of eighty-one.

Touted as a major James Bond inspiration, Merlin loved women. He was also a master at driving boats and cars as well as infiltrating enemy territories and bombing military sites. It is clear to see how Fleming used many of Merlin's adventures in his stories. Lastly, his One-Man-Minshall-Army (OmmA) antics and adventures certainly contributed to the subtle British humor of the fictional spy.

CHAPTER 9

Conrad Fulke Thomond O'Brien-ffrench, Marquis de Castelthomond
(1919 est.) Courtesy of John ffrench

CONRAD O'BRIEN-FFRENCH

Title: Marquis de Castelthomond
Codename: S.T. 36 & Agent Z3

Conrad O'Brien-ffrench[1] knew Ian Fleming and his brother Peter. Like many other Bond inspirations, Conrad was an avid skier, mountaineer, car enthusiast, and author. In addition to his work as a Canadian Royal Northwest Mounted Policeman, he also worked as one of Claude Dansey's War Office "Z" Network undercover business agents in foreign countries. Today such individuals are termed "corporate spies." In Conrad's day, the "business spy" sought specific company military-related intelligence that contributed to the war effort. This included investigating and reporting German World War I military operations as well as World War II war preparations. Many of Conrad's field agent adventures paralleled Fleming's fictional character.

Conrad Fulke Thomond O'Brien-ffrench[2] was the second son born to Henry and Winifred on November 19, 1893, in London. His father was the Marquis de Castelthomond. Shortly after Conrad was born, the family moved to Rome, where he and his brother Rollo studied English, Italian, and French with private tutors. Growing up in the Catholic faith, the boys moved to Florence and studied art at the Uffizi and other local galleries. Desiring to give the children an English education, Harry moved the family to Brighton, where it is believed that he permanently left them due to the baptism of their new daughter Yvonne into the Protestant rather than Catholic faith.

Unlike Rollo who was an accomplished student, Conrad fell below acceptable academic standards. Instead, he learned to train hounds and became an accomplished horseman. Accepted at the Bradley Court Agricultural School, Conrad took courses in farming, poultry management, horsemanship, carpentry, game-keeping, and estate management. Once he became a "keeper" he was allowed to carry a gun and hunt with his own ferret and dog.

In November 1909, when Conrad was sixteen years old, Rollo died in a football accident at Wellington College. Having lost his best friend, Conrad moved to Evesham Valley to study farming. There, he heard stories about Canada and the Royal Northwest Mounted Police. He became so enamored with the country that in April 1910 Conrad booked passage on the *Empress of Britain* to Quebec with hopes of joining the Mounties.

Upon his arrival in Canada, he took a train to the Tuxford Buffalo Lake Regina Royal Northwest Mounted Police barracks where he passed a physical examination, pledged allegiance to the Crown, and completed five rigorous months of training. At graduation Conrad received a revolver, scarlet jacket, and Stetson hat, and in return he vowed to adhere to the Mountie philosophy that he was to resolve problems through resourcefulness and not violence.

His first and only felony case of the year dealt with a man who stole wooden railings from a rancher to use for firewood. Conrad found the man, arrested him, and followed the court guidelines sentencing him to pay a fine of $250 or spend six months in prison. Believing that the felon was a good man and didn't deserve jail time, Conrad talked the judge and rancher into hiring the convict to work for the owner until the cost of the stolen goods was paid. The proposed outcome was satisfactory to all parties and justice prevailed, without the unproductive incarceration of a citizen.

Canadian citizens were a respectful society and truly violent crimes were minimal. During his two years of active duty, Conrad only encountered two violent incidents: one man who murdered his wife before committing suicide, and two other men who were killed by accident in a freight yard. Such was the typical life of a Canadian Mountie. And it was these experiences that began to mold Conrad's future investigative abilities to seek out German intelligence while disguised as a respectable and impartial businessman.

In the summer of 1912, Conrad received word that his mother was dying of cancer. When he returned home to be near her, he developed an obsession with fast cars—an obsession that Bond and Ian Fleming shared. Trying to improve his driving abilities, he purchased a 1909 chain-driven, two-seater Mercedes-Simplex that he modified to reach a speed of 60 mph and used to compete at the Brooklands racetrack. During this time, he also met the artist Augustus John who later became Evelyn Fleming's lover and father of their illegitimate daughter, Amaryllis.

After his mother's death, Conrad went to Ireland and joined the Royal Irish Tipperary Militia. Given the rank of captain, he traveled to France in August 1914 to fight the Germans at the Battle of Mons. On the first day of battle, he led his men in a certain death charge where they were riddled with machine gun bullets. He was the only officer to survive. Stricken with wounds, he was sent first to an asylum and then to a prisoner-of-war camp, where he met a Siberian named Docia Logwinoff who taught him Russian in return for learning English. While incarcerated, the two prisoners drank tea and read Shakespeare, Milton, Trotsky, and Pushkin in their original languages. After numerous escape attempts, in the spring of 1916, Conrad was sent to an inescapable camp, *Garrizone Arrestanstalt* in Augustabad, where the prisoners were locked in individual cells and let out once a day to exercise in a guarded prison yard.

While incarcerated, Conrad met captured RAF pilots who shared information about their sorties and observed enemy troop movements. Needing to share this intelligence with London, Conrad developed a process of sending covert messages to Cathleen Mann, an old acquaintance who was working for the War Office. He obtained potassium iodide (which was used to treat wounds) from the prison hospital that he used to write secret invisible letters between the regular lines of a letter on glossy paper. He sent the messages to his fictitious aunt, *Mrs. Washit of Innk Road, Bath, England*—a code which meant to "wash it in ink bath."

After successfully sending a covert communication to Stewart Menzies at the War Office, Conrad's new work was considered more important than fighting in the trenches. Using the secret ink, he asked Cathleen to send five one-hundred-mark notes in a false bottom biscuit tin. Conrad gave one of the notes (which equaled more than a year's wages) to a gate guard, who in turn agreed to look away at a predetermined time, enabling Conrad and an accomplice to escape and find two second-hand bicycles outside the camp. Prepared with civilian clothes, maps, and food, they awaited instructions from the War Office.

However, the escape plan never reached fruition. The camp was divided into two sections, allowing inmates to travel between them as long as they promised not to attempt escape while visiting prisoners in the other area. As fate would have it, the Senior British Officer (SBO) residing at the other camp, Captain Barry Bingham, sent a message to see Conrad. Apparently, he and sixteen other men had dug a tunnel from their barracks cupboard to a shore outside the camp. Exercising the right of passage, Conrad traveled to the neighboring camp, where Captain Bingham showed him a piece of paper slightly smaller than a postage stamp. Using a magnifying glass, Conrad found that the message listed potential escapees desired by the War Office and that he was prominent on the list.

Realizing that his breaking of the honor system of travel would result in dire repercussions for the remaining men, he chose not to accept the escape offer and returned to his camp section. All the prisoners that escaped that night were captured and the consequences were great. All mail was more closely censored, preventing the use of invisible ink. Conrad and other prisoners who had been incarcerated in the camp for three or more years were transported to Holland until the end of the war. After his 1918 release, Conrad went back to England, where he found it difficult to adjust to the post-war culture. As a result, he had to find a new direction in life.

Fortunately, it didn't take long before he was called to report to the London War Office. There he ran into Cathleen Mann, who was now the secretary to Colonel Stewart Menzies in the Secret Intelligence Service (SIS). Menzies had a job for Conrad as an Assistant Military Attaché in Stockholm. Explaining that the job was a cover for secret agent missions in Russia, he took Conrad to meet Chief Captain Mansfield Smith-Cumming from MI6. Already fluent in Russian from his incarceration, Conrad began learning as much as possible about the country. He soon created a communication network in Russia with secret agent Paul Dukes, codename S.T.25. Conrad was given the codename S.T. 36. Their mission was to make sense of Vladimir Lenin's application of Karl Marx's socialist theories during the Russian Revolution.

While in Stockholm, Conrad first learned to ski and fly an airplane. He also met his cousin Kathleen ffrench, whose estate on the Volga was seized, looted, and returned to the people. Fortunately, she escaped death and reached Finland in March 1920—a broken and impoverished woman.

By autumn of 1920, the operation was moved to Helsingfors,

Finland in order to be closer to the action. During this time, Conrad escorted the Leonid Krasin Russian trade delegation to meet with Prime Minister Lloyd George in London, where they negotiated an Anglo-Soviet Trade Agreement in March 1921.

From 1921-22, Conrad was sent to work as an Aide-de-camp for one of the British governors in India. During his stay, he observed how Mohandas Gandhi and later the first Prime Minister Jawaharlal Nehru used passive demonstrations and violent riots to achieve Indian independence from Britain. He witnessed the Mundera Bazar shooting of three freedom demonstrators. The crowd's response was to burn the Thana City Hall, killing twenty-two police officers trapped inside. The unrest ultimately led to Gandhi's arrest and incarceration on March 10, 1922. Although Conrad left well before the independence of India, he became sensitized to their plight.

He also developed a passion for mountaineering in the Himalayas during his time in India. This led to skiing and climbing adventures that ultimately supported his 1933 nomination to the Alpine Club in London. As a member, he became associated with other notables like Sirs Edmund Hillary, John Hunt, and Frank Smythe.

Conrad writes in his autobiography, *Delicate Mission: Autobiography of a Secret Agent*, that after his service in India he underwent numerous operations at the Grover Crescent nursing that failed to result in any cure for his developing case of phlebitis. Then entering a sanitarium, he found that massage therapy, diet, and the drinking of saline waters for their curative effects returned him to an acceptable level of physical health, served as a natural cure for his phlebitis, and improved ocular and aural acuity. He also states, "I met a nineteen-year-old American named Jane, the like of whom for sheer physical beauty I had not known… More than physical appeal she was to me an open declaration of oneness—no hidden fantasies, romanticism or cheap sentiment. She was the embodiment of sexual union."[3]

These health concerns and curative outcomes mirror a similar storyline in Fleming's eighth Bond novel *Thunderball* (1961), as well as those found in the fourth Bond film *Thunderball* (1965) with Bond encountering a new spy, violence, and sex.

M orders Bond to his office. After Bond exits the lift at the eighth floor, greets Moneypenny, and enters the room, M addresses him as James instead of his number, implying that this is going to be a personal rather than business conversation. M reads from a report, "Despite many previous warnings, he admits to smoking sixty cigarettes a day. These are of the Balkan mixture with higher nicotine content than the cheaper varieties. When not engaged upon strenuous duty, the officer's daily consumption of alcohol is in the region of half a bottle of spirits of between sixty and seventy proof... The tongue is furred. The blood pressure a little raised at 160/90. The liver is not palpable... the officer admits to frequent occipital headaches."[4] M concludes that Bond is in need of a two to three-week visit to a sanitarium to rehabilitate his body into his previously high level of physical fitness.

Beginning with an interior shot of the massage room at Shrublands sanitarium, "JAMES BOND, face down on a table with only a towel round his middle, is being vigorously massaged by PATRICIA FEARING, an athletic-looking beauty in a thin short-sleeved smock with very little underneath it. Her expert manipulations evoke a series of involuntary grunts from him as she works on his spine."[5] She then picks up a pair of large mink gloves and gently runs her hand over a heavily bruised welt on his back. She says, "Funny looking bruise... a fall?"[6] Bond responds, "A poker... in the hands of a widow."[7]

Noticing a small, red, lightning bolt tattoo on another guest's arm, Bond later calls Moneypenny to verify its origin with a crime syndicate. When he returns to Patricia, she places him on a Motor-

ized Traction Table—for stretching the spine. She pulls a lever control beside a big dial that begins the whine of the motor, which alternates tightening and relaxing the straps.

After Patricia leaves, the distinctive hand of the tattooed guest enters the frame and adjusts the machine control to maximum. "Whine of the motor builds, the straps tightening and loosening more rapidly and with increasing violence. BOND struggles desperately as his back is racked by powerful wrenches. He tries to shout, but can only manage choked, intermittent gasps... His features contort agonizedly as the couch seems to go berserk. The face is coming and going in great jerks and then suddenly the sound ceases."[8]

Fading into a new shot of Patricia's hand moving from the switch to her mouth, she remarks that her quick return to retrieve her watch was fortunate. Having saved him from certain death, Patricia takes Bond to the steam room where he proposes a price for keeping silent and not complaining to her superiors. "Steam billows around the camera as it moves forward, and it is with difficulty that we can just make out a woman's bare feet as she stands on her tiptoes stretching upward. A few inches away are the man's feet and legs. CAMERA PANS UPWARD, past a thicker bank of steam which conveniently covers everything until from out of the mists emerge bare arms and shoulders and then faces as PATRICIA'S mouth comes away from his... The steam rises higher making it even more difficult to see anything at all."[9]

In both the novel and film versions of THUNDERBALL, Fleming establishes a parallel between Conrad and Bond in their use of curative massage, diet, and sex to assist in improving their failing health and rebuilding their strength.

Due to his early love of art, in between his espionage assignments, Conrad studied at the Slade School of Fine Art in London from 1926-29 and the Andre Lhote's Academy in Paris from 1930-32. In 1930 he decided to forgive his father, and the pair traveled to Jamaica where Conrad gave lectures on modern art, drew portraits, and sold a few of his paintings. He later exhibited his work at the Claridge Gallery in London and became modestly well known for his drawings and paintings of Jamaica and portraits of the British social elite.

In 1931, the thirty-seven-year-old Conrad found a woman whom he believed to be the love of his life. While visiting his father in Rome, he met Maud Astrid, the sweet, sensitive daughter of Colonel Bo Tarrass-Walhberg of Stockholm, Sweden. They were married on June 31, 1931, in the Paris Registry Office, and honeymooned in Vienna before moving to Kitzbühel, where Conrad opened a tourist business called Tyrolese Tours.

Conrad's new business was actually a cover for spy missions to investigate an increased German military presence in Austria and the manufacturing of their war supplies. Having difficulty staying away from the spy work that he enjoyed, he worked for the "Z" Network headed by Lieutenant Colonel Claude Dansey with the new codename of "Z3." Intentionally keeping Maud in the dark about his real business, Conrad built a network of spies to gather the necessary intelligence.

Tyrolese Tours received approval from the National Tourist Board to bring English tourists to the area. The cover of his business allowed Conrad to inspect potential hotels and tourist sites in Germany. It further opened these areas to British spies who could travel undercover. His Kitzbühel spy operations required Conrad to speak fluent English, French, Russian, Italian, and German.

For the next six-and-a-half-years, Kitzbühel was Conrad and Maud's home, and they often ran into the Fleming brothers. At this time Peter was married to the British actress Celia Johnson, and Ian was often on the prowl for female companionship. At this point in his career, Ian was a foreign correspondent for Reuters. The friends frequently met at the local bars, restaurants, mutual friends' houses, and ski areas.

Ian later referred to the location by including an homage to his old teacher (and his love of skiing) in the short story "Octopussy," which appears in his last short story collection *Octopussy and The Living Daylights* (1966).

While working for the Miscellaneous Objectives Bureau (MOB) from the Secret Service and Combined Operations, Lieutenant-Colonel Dexter Smythe is given the mission to clean up the Gestapo and Abwehr hideouts at the end of the war. Sent to Tyrol, he travels about a mile east of Kitzbühel where he knew some Nazi gold was buried. He informs local resident Hannes Oberhauser that he will be cleared as a Nazi sympathizer if he cooperates in leading Smythe to the gold bars hidden in the mountains. In good faith Smythe says, "We will spend the day climbing on the Kaiser and I will then drive you back to Kitzbühel and report to my commanding officer that you have been cleared at Munich."[10] After finding the two gold bars, Smythe shoots Oberhauser with two bullets in the skull and covers the body in a crevasse of the glacier.

After bringing the gold back to England, Major Smythe retires with his wife in Jamaica. Years later James Bond finds Smythe, gets him to confess to his crime, and informs him of an impending court-martial. "It was a small glacier. Oberhauser's body came out at the bottom earlier this year... Some climbers found it. All his papers and everything were intact. The family identified him. Then it was just a question of working back. The bullets clinched it."[11]

Bond further adds the personal statement, "Oberhauser was a friend of mine. He taught me how to ski before the war, when I was in my teens. He was a wonderful man. He was something of a father to me at a time when I happened to need one."[12]

IN 1927 IAN FLEMING WAS SENT TO A SMALL PRIVATE SCHOOL IN

Kitzbühel to study for the Foreign Office (FO) exams under the tutelage of former British spy Ernan Forbes Dennis and author Phyllis Bottome. Although Ian improved his language and writing skills (yet later failed the FO examinations), he never forgot his past friends and felt a need to honor them in his novels and short stories.

A rather strange competition between Conrad and Ian occurred at a popular swimming lake at Schwartz Zee. Ian, surrounded by the social elite, performed an exhibition dive off a diving board. Believing that he could outperform his competitor, Conrad approached the board and performed his best swallow dive. As he hit the water in perfect style, he immediately found himself completely naked. His new pair of swimming trunks was missing a belt, and the hard impact into the water had caused them to fly off his body. Embarrassed and naked until they eventually floated to the top, he tried to cover his exposed body parts, proving that not every 007 inspiration is as smooth as Bond.

Conrad found Ian accepting of his own limitations, yet intolerant of the failure of others. Desiring to help Conrad, in 1934 Ian told him to beware of a local German whom he believed to be a Gestapo. When Conrad was away in London, the man took Maud out to dinner and gave her a lot of wine. During the evening, he openly asked if her husband was a secret agent. The naïve wife responded, "Conrad a secret agent? Oh, no, he's much too stupid."

Her comment verified the need for spies to share intelligence only on a need-to-know basis. Not even Ian was aware of Conrad's business. As a Section Z agent, he was paid less than a window washer and frustrated with Dansey who took all the credit for the information he supplied.

During the same year, two other personal disappointments occurred. First, on October 28th, Conrad and Maud chose to separate, not realizing that their daughter Christina had already been conceived. Secondly, three days later Conrad was called to his father, who passed away shortly after he reached his bedside.

Now truly alone, Conrad dived into his work. His new cover was that of a playboy who very openly traveled for work and pleasure. Through his tourist bureau, Conrad freely crossed the Austro-German border. Finding that Germany was buying as much iron ore as possible to rearm their war effort, Conrad verified that many mines were supplying between 300 to 500 tons a day to Germany. As the intelligence was found, he sent reports with photographs to London. He further became aware of Hitler and the Nazi party's interest in occultism. These reports were of significant interest as they later affected German military strategy.

Like Ian Fleming, Conrad had an opportunity to take the Trans-Siberian Express to Harbin, Manchuria. His mission was to gather intelligence throughout the trip that might be of use to Britain's war effort. Undercover, he visited his cousin Kathleen who had lost her land and wealth to the Russians. Before World War II, Harbin was a horribly corrupt town that had grown to a population of 200,000 Asians and 65,000 Europeans, many of whom had fled from Chinese, Russian, or German oppression. Within the squalor of the city, Russian heroin addicts lived next to Chinese beggars in the streets. In this chaotic, depraved environment, military police regularly victimized the local population.

While living under Japanese rule, Conrad observed a Japanese officer decapitate a bandit whose remains were pushed into a river. He further learned of a type of Japanese torture that used a tube to push water into the stomach of a victim through their nose only then to have someone jump on their stomach. This pressure on the intestines continued until the individual confessed to their crime or died in the process. As the danger of his work increased, Conrad began carrying a small automatic pistol for protection.

Kathleen lived in a secluded home where she continued to entertain in lavish style with the little money she had left. While in the town, Conrad obtained detailed descriptions of Japanese military operations in Manchukuo through a Russian officer who worked for the Japanese military headquarters. The information was worth the entire trip to the British War Office because they needed it to deal with expected future Japanese military confrontation. Soon after Conrad traveled back to England with his report, Kathleen died.

After he returned to Kitzbühel and began living with his three-year-old daughter Christina, Conrad received word that the German military was going to invade Austria. Realizing that London needed the information immediately, Conrad used the Austrian telephone lines to send a report. After taking an hour to send the message, he realized that the wires were tapped and his cover had been blown. The attack came at 9 a.m. on March 12th. His news was the first received by the War Office and was credited with saving numerous lives by allowing time for Jews and other residents in danger to leave the country. Conrad immediately sent Christina and her nurse to Switzerland. He remained to help others.

Conrad stayed in the home of a fellow agent, which was visited by the Gestapo. He left unnoticed through the back door where his Ford V8 engine sports car was parked. He speedily made his way to the Austro-Swiss border where he was stopped. With a pistol in hand and car prepared to run the border, after an excruciatingly tense wait, the guard returned with permission to cross. Then suddenly he heard the words, "Halt, Halt!" Failing to heed the commands, Conrad sped across the border with a trail of bullets behind him. Almost failing to stop at the Swiss guardhouse, he reached safety and decided that his life as a secret agent was over.

Conrad returned to London, delivered his final report to Claude Dansey, and resigned from Military Intelligence. By 1940 it was reported that he was in the "Black Book" of war criminals to be executed if ever captured by the Gestapo. Unable to further contribute as an agent, Conrad returned to Canada where he purchased a home with property. Now seeking seclusion, his only contact with the world was through a car radio.

However, Conrad felt a need to contribute after Britain declared war against Germany in 1939. Unable to physically serve as a fighting soldier, he returned to England and was assigned to inspecting export goods going to politically sensitive foreign countries. Working in Scotland, Conrad used his observation and investigation skills to unearth illegal activities that might compromise the British war effort. The job became so intense that he worked seven days a week for six months before having a day off.

In April 1941, Conrad was called back to London and given instructions to report to the Imperial Censorship in Trinidad after a short furlough in Canada. While returning home on a whaling ship, he found himself in the middle of a battle where the *HMS Hood* was destroyed shortly before the German battleship *Bismarck* was finally sunk to the bottom of the sea.

Conrad reached the Trinidad Imperial Censorship office in the midsummer. He later defined his new job as follows: "To the average individual, censorship consists of merely opening up letters to see if they contain any information of a military nature."[13] He elaborated that, "Censorship makes a minute study of the endless means of sending or collecting information and exploits them [sic] in the interests of its country to the full."[14] In essence, similar to Ian Fleming's work at the Naval Intelligence Department, Conrad spent his time in search of minute and accurate political, military, or economic intelligence that could be used against Britain.

Using his foreign language background, he was able to read correspondence from passengers arriving at the Piarco airport or interview captains with cargo arriving at the Port of Spain. Through this work, Conrad oversaw investigations for the Security and Contraband Control offices of the Imperial Censorship. Unfortunately, he had an attack of malaria with reoccurring symptoms of phlebitis, and in October 1942 he was flown to Bermuda and then Canada. After what he felt was a satisfactory recuperation, he was told that he was now too old and unfit for wartime activities.

Able to make it back to England, the fifty-year-old Conrad settled in Oxford where he met Rosalie (Rosie) Isabelle Baker at a party. They immediately became daily companions and soon were hardly out of each other's sight. As the war began to wind down in early 1945, Conrad became severely ill. Unable to visit a hospital (due to the overwhelming need to treat the returning soldiers), Rosie nursed him back to health. Realizing that they could no longer live without one another, the ex-spy married Rosalie on May 1, 1945. They lived in London until the end of the war and then moved to Canada.

The damp weather in Vancouver was incompatible with Rosie's health, forcing the couple to move to Banff, where they purchased a home in Canada's largest national park, 4,735 ft. above sea level. The sunshine and drier air quickly improved her health. They purchased a plot of land, built a cottage with stables, and added a fourteen-room lodge they called *Fairholme Ranch*, where their two sons Rollo and John were born and raised.

In 1948, Conrad joined the faculty of the Banff School for the Fine Arts as a watercolor professor. Conrad also reunited with Lloyd Arthur (Uranda) Meeker, whom he met near the end of the war. Uranda founded a new spiritual movement called Emissaries of Divine Light. Indoctrinated into the following, Conrad described his new life as follows: "I had been a secret agent working for a cause I believed in, a human cause, now I would serve a universal cause, neither human nor limited in scope, the cause of all causes."[15] And accepting this mission, he left political life for a new life of cosmic power and spiritual harmony.

In 1954, Conrad studied the teachings of Uranda for six months, ended his marriage to Rosie, and sold *Fairholme Ranch* back to the Parks Department. When Conrad retired from teaching, he took up permanent residence at the international headquarters of the Emissaries of Divine Light in Loveland, Colorado, where he spent the remainder of his life painting and lecturing on art, philosophy, and theology. Conrad Fulke Thomond O'Brien-ffrench died at the age of ninety-two, on October 23, 1986.

Conrad spent six-and-a-half years working in Kitzbühel and was a friend of Ian Fleming. The handsome agent loved to race automobiles, ski, climb mountains and fly airplanes. However, unlike many other inspirations, Conrad was a business spy, which meant that he never used a weapon to kill or keep the enemy at bay. Instead, his job involved the art of observation and investigation. It was also quite likely that Ian was aware of Conrad's trips to Jamaica, Norway, Austria, Germany, Italy, India, and Manchuria either during or after the war. Espionage is a profession that necessitates a very subtle character that results in even subtler behaviors. Conrad O'Brien-ffrench was a master of this subtle art of espionage.

CHAPTER 10

Duško Popov - Serbian double agent
National Archives and Record Administration

DUŠKO POPOV

Codename: (British) Scoot & Tricycle (German) Ivan

Dedicated to the Allied war effort, Duško Popov[1] was one of the greatest British double agents of all time. While living the cover of a playboy spy, he acquired information that ultimately helped the Germans to defeat themselves. Duško shared early intelligence with the FBI of an impending Japanese attack on Pearl Harbor, and he advised the Germans to send troops to a false Allied Forces landing beach on D-Day. Due to Duško's ability to live his cover, tenacious spirit to succeed, control of his emotions, love for gambling and women, intelligence, and aptitude for gaining the confidence of others, Ian Fleming used him as an inspiration for James Bond.

In 1912, Dušan "Duško" Popov was born to a wealthy family in Titel, Serbia. His father was a successful industrialist who moved to Dubrovnik, Croatia where he became president of a powerful and influential provincial political group. After attending schools in England and France, Duško graduated with a law degree. In 1936 he enrolled at Freiburg University in Breisgau, Germany with the intent of completing a doctoral degree. At this time most of the Jewish professors had been fired and the remaining Jewish students were being methodically flunked out. As a student, Duško met Johann "Johnny" Jebsen, the orphan son of a rich Hamburg ship owner. While pursuing their degrees, the two friends openly mocked the German Nazis who were just coming into power.

After completing his degree, Duško was arrested by four Gestapo soldiers on the morning he was to leave Germany for a graduation celebration in Paris. For the next eight days the Gestapo interrogated him around the clock, trying to get him to admit to a Communist allegiance. After they failed to get a confession, he was transferred to Freiburg prison. In an attempt to find Duško guilty of treason, the interrogators questioned approximately two hundred individuals about his political affiliations.

Learning that Duško had been placed in solitary confinement, Johnny managed to cross the Swiss border, telephone Duško's father in Dubrovnik, and inform him of his son's incarceration. After soliciting Prime Minister Dr. Stojadinovic of Yugoslavia to intercede on his son's behalf, Duško's father arranged for his son's release from the Gestapo, who gave him twenty-four hours to leave the country. Duško was fortunate because typically in such situations with no official charges, the prisoner disappeared into a concentration camp never to be heard from again.

After Johnny saved his life, Duško began practicing business law in Dubrovnik. Three years later, Johnny and Duško met in Belgrade, where Johnny wanted to sell his family ship to the British through a camouflage scheme.

His ship was moored with four others, also for sale, in the British and French occupied Mediterranean port of Trieste. During this pre-wartime period, ship owners were allowed to sell their boats to neutral countries. If Duško could negotiate a sale of the five boats to Yugoslavia, then they could be resold to England to help the war effort. Unaware of their intended future use, the German government permitted the contractual sale of the ships within two weeks.

Although German, Johnny couldn't support the Third Reich ideology. Required to work for the cause, he joined the Brandenburg (Sabotage) Division of the Abwehr (Nazi Intelligence Agency), where he felt safe from openly fighting what he believed to be an unjust war. With Germany soon to overrun France, Johnny asked Duško to use his family position to infiltrate and produce a list of influential French citizens who may sympathize with the German occupation. Excited with the idea, Duško agreed. He also gave the report to the First Secretary of the British Embassy, an act that created the opportunity for Duško to become a double agent.

Also interested in Duško's list was a German Abwehr officer who, at a party, asked him to spy on the British, offering payment in the form of a high position in Yugoslavia after Germany won the war. Believed to be a Nazi sympathizer, Duško asked for time to think about the request. He then spoke to Johnny, who said, "If you want to destroy a team, the best way is to become part of it."[2] Since both men shared the same political ideology, they decided to covertly collaborate for the destruction of Nazi Germany. And as a result, Duško became an official German spy.

The following day, Duško met with Mr. Dew at the British Embassy to offer his allegiance but instead was sent to see an agent (codename Spiradis) in charge of the MI6 Balkans Section British (espionage) Passport Control Office (PCO). There, Duško agreed to act as a double agent for Britain. To assist him, Spiradis gave Duško "Navy Certs" that permitted him to travel and conduct business freely between Great Britain and Yugoslavia. The only condition of the agreement was that Johnny, who was also made a double agent (codename Artist), was not to have access to any intelligence that would potentially jeopardize British interests.

Duško's first mission, OPERATION SEA LION, was to find evidence of England's ability to withstand an invasion. However, before leaving Belgrade, he had to have six double cross meetings with Spiradis at the PCO. Duško was not aware that his father's chauffer Bozidar was spying for the Germans, and consequently the numerous meetings at the PCO came under suspicion. After realizing the situation, the only solution was to eliminate the spy. Duško met with two criminal offenders he had helped pardon for an earlier crime and hired them to murder Bozidar and make it look like a robbery gone afoul. It was a success, and Duško experienced his first lesson in how to maintain a cover.

Now safe, he traveled to England with information that OPERATION SEA LION had been canceled due to the inability of the German Army, Navy, and Air Force to cooperate in the attack. British Intelligence used the information in restructuring their plans for offensive action in case of a future invasion.

Around this time Duško began to meet alluring female spies who were searching for information behind bedroom doors. On a mission, he met an amorous woman who went to his hotel room where she used sexual advances to obtain information. Finding him in possession of what she felt to be worthless intelligence, she turned off her affections and was thrown out of the room by Duško. After reflecting on his first encounter with sexual persuasion by a female agent, he learned to use similar and more improved techniques to obtain information needed for Britain.

As a new double agent, Duško was assigned a case officer named Bill Mathews, who followed him in the field. Duško was also required to have a female case officer who could play a "social mistress" and solicit future German recruits. In London, Duško met with individuals from MI5, MI6, Naval Intelligence, and Air Intelligence. Considered a high-quality recruit, he was desired by numerous departments. After meeting with J. C. Masterson, the head of the Double-Cross (XX) Committee, whose purpose it was to coordinate British interest activities among spies working for two or more opposing secret service agencies, Duško was sent to Major-General Stewart Graham Menzies, the head of the British Secret Service (MI6), who welcomed him into the agency.

While attending a London soiree, Duško met Gerda Sullivan, with whom he quickly found himself in lust. Gerda was a divorced Austrian socialite who now supported the British. She began escorting Duško to many high society functions where he could gather intelligence. After a short period of time, they broke the unwritten espionage code of never moving beyond social friendship. The result was their belief that they had become the ideal spy couple.

After having received numerous reports and observation about each of his new agents, Menzies took a personal interest in the case. During a meeting with Duško, the head of MI6 felt a need to share an assessment of his new spy's personality and warn him about a flaw in his character. He told Duško, "You are honest without scruples. Your instincts and intuitions are stronger than your intelligence, which is far more above average. Your conscience never bothers you, and you are mentally shortsighted and long-sighted at the same time. You are ambitious and ruthless and you can even be cruel. But when you are cruel, it is an animal cruelty, not a sick cruelty. You like to hit back but you are not in a hurry to do so. When you are frightened, you don't panic. Danger is a stimulant for you. You think more clearly and make better and quicker decisions when pushed by the instinct of self-preservation, than by contemplation... You have the makings of a good spy except you don't like to obey orders. You had better learn or you will be a very dead spy."[3]

And so, it is with James Bond in Fleming's ninth novel *The Spy Who Loved Me* (1962). Bond shows himself to be a cold and ruthless killer when placed against gangsters who are equally prepared to kill him and a young woman who innocently finds herself in a life-or-death situation. By presenting a realistic view of a spy's life, Fleming compares Bond to Menzies' analysis of Popov's lifestyle as hard, cruel, and dangerous.

After Bond kills the two thugs who burned down the Dreamy Pines Motor Court and tried to kill Vivienne Michel, the New York State Troopers arrive to speak with Viv. Captain Stonor concludes that the girl, who knew the spy for less than six hours, had sex with Bond after their horrible ordeal.

Stonor speaks to Viv as if he is a concerned father, "The top gangsters, the top FBI operatives, the top spies and the top counter-spies are cold-hearted, cold-blooded, ruthless, tough, killers, Miss Michel. Yes, even the 'friends' as opposed to the 'enemies.' They have to be. They wouldn't survive if they weren't.... Keep away from all these men. They're not for you, whether they're called James Bond or Sluggsy Morant... So don't go and get sweet dreams about one or nightmares from the other. They're just different people from the likes of you... Like hawks and doves, if you'll pardon the comparison."[4]

Leaving the troopers, Viv kick-starts her Vespa and speeds away with a cheeky hand in farewell and a short glance back. Considering what the captain said, Viv thinks, "The scars of my terror had been healed, wiped away, by this stranger who slept with a gun under his pillow, this secret agent who was only known by a number... I knew exactly who he was and what he was. And everything, every smallest detail, would be written on my heart forever."[5]

WHILE STONOR PRESENTS A REALISTIC COMPARISON OF SPY AND criminal lives, Viv's image of the spy lovingly remembers Bond's gallantry and sexual prowess in the same way they are depicted in the Bond films. *The Spy Who Loved Me* was published in 1962, which happened to coincide with the release year of the first Bond film, *Dr. No*. Could it be that during this year Fleming discovered that his stories about murder and sex in espionage work well in both print and film? Could he also have realized that Duško is a major contributor to his fictional spy's life?

As Duško became more involved in covert operations, he learned tricks of the trade from his fellow agents. He was taught to place a pretty girl in any photograph he took that contained visual information important to a mission. He also learned how to communicate with another agent through roulette. He did so by placing three chips on the numbers for the date, time, and minute of the meeting. The signal was sent three times while the other agent would play 0 for one rendezvous location or 36 for another. Additionally, he learned such practices as looking into the reflections of windows to see if he was being followed and exiting trains immediately before the doors closed to evade a tail. Lastly, he learned how to send and receive messages through a microscope and "mikropunkt" (photographic microdot) the size of a typed dot above a letter "i."

To enhance the double cross, Duško recruited Gerda Sullivan and Dickie Metcalfe as new German agents. Gerda now claimed allegiance to her homeland in support of her father's membership in the Nazi Party, and Dickie played the role of an irresponsible army officer whose rich desires for fast cars, faster women, drink, and horse racing placed him in the position of endlessly needing money. This growth required Duško to change his codename from "Scoot" to "Tricycle" because he now had his own double-cross team of three agents. Gerda was given the codename "Gelatine" and Dickie was named "Balloon." However, "There was only one appropriate codename for a playboy double agent who had a penchant for ménage à trois,"[6] and Duško's codename of Tricycle also represented his desire for excessive sexual relationships while living within his cover.

With Yugoslavia overrun by Germans, Duško's family was in jeopardy. Fortunately, Johnny interceded and helped the family to receive Abwehr's protection. It was appropriate, as the organization needed to placate their top German spy. This also offered Duško's older brother Yvo (codename Dreadnought) an opportunity to become involved in resistance operations. Like the Flemings, the Popovs became a family of spies.

During one of Duško's fourteen trips to Portugal to meet with his German handlers, Fleming, who happened to be spending time with a friend in Estoril, observed him at the casino. There, a Lithuanian named Bloch was boisterously yelling "banque ouverte," implying that he would match any bet on the baccarat table. Frustrated by the obnoxious behavior of the player, Duško accepted the challenge and placed $30,000 on the table. The man, although wealthy, was unable to match the amount and left the table in disgrace.

Duško's excessive gambling became part of James Bond's personality. Years later Duško was informed that Ian Fleming used the baccarat gambling incident as a major topic in his first novel *Casino Royale* (1953). Since many readers had difficulty understanding the game, Bond explains the rules for the most popular French variation of baccarat *Chemin de Fer* to the American CIA agent Felix Leiter.

Bond says, "It's much the same as any other gambling game. The odds against the banker and the player are more or less even… there will be ten players, I expect, and we sit around the banker at a kidney-shaped table… In front of him he has a shoe containing six packs of cards, well shuffled… by the croupier and cut by one of the players."[7] Bond continues to explain how the banker announces a bank that may be covered entirely by each player in a counter-clockwise direction. If no single individual can gamble against the full amount, it is then parceled to the players in the same order of play with the possibility of using spectators until the bank is covered.

After describing the basic operation, Bond feels it's "time to explain the mechanics of the game… 'I get two cards and the banker gets two and unless anyone wins outright, either or one of us can get one more card. *The object of the game is to hold two or three cards which together count nine points, or as nearly nine as possible. Court cards and tens count nothing; aces one each; any other card its face value. It is only the last figure of your count that signifies. So nine plus seven equals six – not sixteen. The winner is the one whose count is nearest to nine. Draws are played over again."*[8]

Presenting the strategy of play, Bond explains that if two dealt cards equal eight or nine they are known as a "natural" and should be turned over, allowing the player an immediate win unless the bank has a better natural. "If I haven't got a natural, I can stand on seven or a six, perhaps ask for a card or perhaps not, on a five, and certainly ask for a card if my count is lower than five... According to the odds, the chances of bettering or worsening your hand if you hold a five are exactly even."[9]

Acknowledging that some players always stand on five while others draw, Bond reveals that his strategy is to always follow his intuition. After losing all of his money to Le Chiffre, Bond is anonymously delivered thirty–two million francs from Felix Leiter, which he uses to beat his opponent.

BACCARAT IS SIMILAR TO TWENTY-ONE, WHICH IS COMMONLY played in the U.S. Fleming loved the game, as did Duško and, consequently, Bond. In the 2006 film version of *Casino Royale*, a decision was made to play the card game Texas hold 'em instead of baccarat while maintaining the same intensity, style of play, and outcomes as found in the original novel.

In 1941 Abwehr requested that Duško travel to the United States to develop a new spy ring. Their current German spies were being arrested at an astoundingly high rate due to their inability to operate as a unit. The answer was to have Duško recruit new agents who would work independently of one another under his authority. Believing Duško's three-agent team system was successful, Abwehr officers agreed that a similarly structured team could also work in America. This meant that the British XX Committee also believed that Duško could use his double-cross team to give Britain and the U.S. information about German espionage that would give them an advantage. However, nobody envisioned the havoc that the FBI director J. Edgar Hoover would create.

After Duško traveled to New York on August 10, 1941, he began to build his cover as a rich playboy. Arriving with $68,000 in his pocket, he purchased a new Buick coupe with a sliding sunroof and rented a penthouse on Park Avenue and Sixty-First Street that would serve as his center of operations. His first job was to report new intelligence to William Stephenson's Canadian/British spy headquarters on the thirty-fifth floor of Rockefeller Center.

On August 12th, he showed an FBI representative a new German mikropunkt that contained information for a covert Abwehr operation in the U.S. and that he had been sent by Abwher to develop a double agent spy system. The microdot contained a copy of an intelligence questionnaire that explained how the Japanese were planning to attack Pearl Harbor. It contained requests for detailed descriptions and sketches of ammunition dumps and mine depots, railway lines, airfields with hanger and communication stations, seaplane stations, petrol installations, submarine stations, wharf and pier installations, anchored ships, and assorted land and underground installations. He lastly elaborated that he was to receive a microdot system in Canada with orders to carry and use it in the U.S.

After FBI representatives told him that Hoover would meet him in two weeks, Duško decided to travel to Florida for a vacation with his friend, the delicate, rich English model Terry Brown, who he knew was working in New York City. They took his Buick to Miami, where, while lying in the sun, two FBI agents approached Duško and informed him that he would be arrested if he didn't send the woman home immediately and drive back to New York by himself. Apparently, Duško was breaking the Mann Act, which made it a federal offense to cross a state line with a woman for immoral purposes. Such was Hoover's welcome that laid the foundation for their future relationship.

Astounded by this reception, Duško returned to New York and met with Hoover, who read him the riot act for his immoral and unprofessional behavior. Duško explained that he had given the FBI the latest form of German microdot communication. He divulged his plan to develop a double agent system for the U.S similar to the one he had made successful in London. And he explained in detail how the Japanese planned to attack Pearl Harbor. Unaware of Duško's double agent playboy cover, Hoover accused him of selling information to the highest bidder and threw him out of the office, screaming "good riddance" as he left.

In a move that almost destroyed his cover, the FBI bugged Duško's apartment and demanded that he give them the incoming transmission communication system from Abwehr. They then failed to receive the microdot system by interfering with Duško's pre-specified shipping arrangements with Abwehr. The most damaging outcome of his trip was the information about Pearl Harbor. Even though Duško shared his intelligence with the FBI four months before the attack on December 7, 1941, it never reached the appropriate authorities, resulting in the loss of 4 battleships, 65 army aircraft, 196 navy and marine aircraft, over 3,000 navy sailors and marines, and 226 army soldiers.

Adding insult to injury, Hoover took credit for finding the microdot communication system in an April 1946 edition of *Reader's Digest* magazine. In essence, the mission and follow-up communication with the FBI was a disaster.

Undeterred, Duško left the U.S. and returned to his Lisbon/London covert operation. In 1943, he supported OPERATION MINCEMEAT by reporting false information to the Germans for the invasion of Sicily that helped the Allied armies to quickly overrun and control the island. He also helped obtain information on the V-1 (Doodlebug missiles) used to bomb England. In 1944, he became involved in OPERATION FORTITUDE, where he and other highly reliable agents reported that the landing for the D-Day invasion was to be in the northeastern site of Pas-de-Calais in France, which resulted in Hitler sending over 100,000 soldiers to protect an area that he believed would be attacked in the first or second wave of the invasion. Because this attack never occurred, OPERATION FORTITUDE saved countless Allied lives and turned the war to their advantage. This mission may be considered Duško's most significant contribution to the war. For these and other successful missions, he was awarded the Most Excellent Order of the British Empire (OBE) as the Battle of Normandy continued.

Three weeks before the June 6th D-Day invasion, Johnny Jebsen, who was sending false intelligence to the Germans, was arrested by the Gestapo for illegal money manipulations. With the Gestapo increasing its power, Johnny was the among the first Abwehr agents to be removed from their positions of authority. Thinking that he was arrested for being a double agent, the British believed if he cracked under torture, then the D-Day deception would be ruined. Five weeks later Ivo Popov, who was working under Johnny in the deception, was also arrested for the same charge. Fortunately, Johnny never divulged any sensitive information and D-Day gave the Allies the foothold necessary to change the course of the war.

Ivo managed to escape from his incarceration and was escorted back to London to be with his brother. Unfortunately, Johnny was murdered in a false escape attempt fabricated by the Gestapo. Furious over the death of his friend, Duško wanted revenge. At the end of the war in August 1945 and after a long search in Germany, Duško found the man who had ordered Johnny's murder. He captured him, took him into the countryside, and prepared to shoot him. Unable to pull the trigger, he beat him senseless and threw away his gun. Duško the spy had finally learned that assassination for revenge is simply murder.

At the end of the war, Duško ended his career as an agent and psychologically worked to clear his mind of the deception, debilitation, and death he experienced. Realizing that the Allied victory was a moral victory that saved the lives of countless innocent people, he felt somewhat vindicated.

Duško Popov died in Opio, France on August 21, 1981, at the age of sixty-nine, leaving a widow and three sons. Numerous documentaries on his life portray Duško's career as a superspy who may have made the greatest espionage contributions to the Allied forces during World War II. After reviewing new millennium released documents from London's Public Records Office, Claire Hills from BBC News writes, "But although Agent Tricycle may have come across as a James Bond-type, he was vital to Britain's intelligence gathering and, some say, the country's most important agent."[10]

Courtesy of Bajoman1
Firefly statue & house

Firefly bedroom

Firefly bedroom 2

Firefly bar & living area

Firefly statue

Firefly grave

Blue Harbour House

Blue Harbour swimming pool & ocean view

Goldeneye house

Goldeneye pool

Goldeneye master bedroom

Goldeneye guest bedroom

Goldeneye living & dining room

Goldeneye party room

Goldeneye outdoor tub

Goldeneye outdoor vanity

Goldeneye ocean view 1

Goldeneye ocean view 2

Goldeneye beach view 1

Goldeneye beach view 2

CHAPTER 11

Canadian passport photograph of William Stephenson (1942)
Courtesy of Intrepid Society

SIR WILLIAM STEPHENSON

Codename: Intrepid,
Quiet Canadian & Little Bill

William Stephenson[1] was a man of courage, cunning, and mystery. In a meeting with Winston Churchill, Bill was appointed to head the British Security Coordination (BSC) with the mission of persuading the United States government and its people to support the British war effort against Nazi Germany. During the course of their conversation, Churchill said that he must be a leader who is dauntless, fearless, and "intrepid." The latter description was adopted as his codename for the remainder of his spy career. Stephenson was a visionary well-organized spy who Ian Fleming knew well and who may have inspired the incorporation of cryptographic communication techniques in the Bond stories.

Also known as the "Quiet Canadian," Bill never drew attention to himself as an agent. He received the name "Little Bill" while working with William "Big Bill" Donovan, who was head of the U. S. Office of Strategic Services (OSS), which later became the Central Intelligence Agency (CIA). In this capacity, their relationship was very similar to Ian Fleming working as the Personal Assistant (PA) to Rear Admiral John Godfrey.

Bill's life is full of contradictions. Good spies live anonymously in the public eye, and Bill was among the best. He performed and/or supervised so many missions it was believed that he lived in constant fear of retaliation. This fear became evident in his later years when he retired to a highly guarded private island in Bermuda.

On January 23, 1897, William Samuel Clouston Stanger was born to William and Sarah Stanger in Winnipeg, Manitoba. In 1901 his father died from advanced muscular atrophy. Unable to care for her three children, Sarah allowed William to be adopted by foster parents named Stephenson, giving him his new last name.

As a young man, he preferred to be alone during which time he quietly developed a passion for reading and experimenting with electricity, steam engines, and crude airplanes.

Due to an early interest in Morse code, Bill worked delivering telegrams for the Great North West Telegraph Company. On December 3, 1913, a local bank manager named H. M. Arnold was killed during a robbery by a disguised shooter. Winnipeg pawnshop records traced an expensive watch found in the getaway car to John Krafchenko. From his work delivering telegrams across town, Bill recognized the man and contacted police, who then arrested Krafchenko. As a result, Bill was labeled a "stool pigeon" for a fugitive whose charismatic image had charmed many local women. While awaiting trial for murder and robbery, Krafchenko escaped from prison. He had a revolver, skeleton key, and rope smuggled into his cell. He used the key to get out and the rope to shimmy thirty feet down to the ground. He was captured nine days later to the chagrin of many women and delight of Bill, who lived in fear of retribution. With Krafchenko's fellow criminals still at large, Bill withdrew from society.

In July 1916, he enlisted in World War I and was immediately sent to the trenches with the Royal Canadian Engineers. Within a week of his arrival, he survived a gas attack and was sent to England to convalesce for about a year where he studied communications, navigation, flight theory, and combustion engine operation at a school of aeronautics near Oxford.

Not wanting to leave the fight, in April 1917 Bill transferred into the Royal Flying Corps, whose pilots were known to have very short lives. While flying a Shopwith Camel biplane for the No. 73 Squadron, he shot down twelve planes and won further recognition for shooting down Lothar von Richthofen—brother of "The Red Baron" Manfred von Richthofen.

Known as "Captain Machine Gun" due to his lightning-fast fists, Bill won the lightweight world boxing championship. At the same time, the great Gene Tunny won the heavyweight title for the U. S. Marines. The two eventually became friends and business partners. Bill managed to keep his undefeated title until 1928 when he decided to retire.

While flying a solo sortie on July 28, 1918, he was shot in the leg by a bullet that penetrated his plane, forcing him to crash behind enemy lines. While fleeing the site he was shot a second time in the same leg, captured by the Germans, and sent to a prisoner of war camp. After several attempts, he managed to escape in October 1918. Making the guards believe that his leg injury was still severe, he escaped using a crude knife, wire cutters, and compass while serving kitchen duty. Wearing a German overcoat, he cut through the fence before daylight and reached the Allied lines three days later. Bill was awarded the Military Cross and Distinguished Flying Cross for having shot down twenty-six airplanes during the war.

After the war, he returned to Winnipeg where he started the Franco-British Supply Company, which patented and manufactured can openers called the Kleen Kut. Based on a twin-handled opener still used today, the unit left a clean cut around the can, replacing the jagged cut created by former single-handle models. Due to the bad economy, he and his partner Charles Winfred Russell lost $30,000 of company stock. Bill hastily left for England, leaving a bad taste in the mouths of his investors who faced bankruptcy a year later.

In early 1920, Admiral William "Blinker" (so named for a chronic facial twitch) Hall asked Bill to work on electronic communications and cryptanalysis, which he believed had a future in espionage. In mid-1922, Bill reopened Stephenson-Russell Ltd. in London and purchased interest in General Radio and Cox-Cavendish, which ultimately sold thousands of home radios. By August 1923, at the age of twenty-six, he was the managing director of both companies, making him a millionaire.

He also published research papers on a new invention called "Tele-vision" or a method of transmitting moving pictures through radio waves. In December 1922, Bill transmitted his first radio wave photograph, which was claimed to be a revolutionary breakthrough in the field of electronics. In 1924, he went to the U. S. where he studied the new talking picture industry. By the early 30s, Bill controlled the largest film recording studios outside of Hollywood. He also owned coal mines and steel factories in the Balkans and Scandinavia.

On a voyage back to England, he met a pretty, young American tobacco heiress from Tennessee named Mary French Simmons. Infatuated with her beauty and company, Bill proposed at the end of the trip and they were married on July 22, 1924, at the South Kensington Presbyterian Church. An August 23, 1924 headline in the *New York Times* read, "American Girl Weds Canadian Scientist." On the recorded General Register Office wedding certificate, Bill's age, his father's name and occupation, and the couple's address were all incorrect.

Contradictions like these were to follow him throughout the remainder of his life, with his Winnipeg family only finding information about him through public media. Although he lived in the public eye, Bill continued to misrepresent facts about his life to conceal his covert espionage operations.

In 1924, the Germans introduced a commercial version of their new rotor cipher machine. Acquiring a unit to study, Bill believed that it could be remodeled into an electric portable format. Little did he know that the prototype would become the Nazi secret cipher communication system "Enigma" used during World War II. He also had no idea that his analysis of this machine would be the catalyst for Blinker Hall to recommend him to head a new British secret service agency designed in part to decipher German and Japanese cryptic military messages.

As Ian Fleming reached the midpoint of his Bond novel series, he decided to introduce clandestine communication systems into his stories. Having experienced the German Enigma and Japanese PURPLE secret communications systems during the war, he introduced the use and practice of covert communication in espionage in his fifth novel *From Russia with Love* (1957).

In his meeting with M to discuss his new mission, Bond learns that a female Russian agent is prepared to bring a new cipher machine to Britain. M says, "If she could come over to us, she would bring her cipher machine with her. It's a brand new Spektor machine. The thing we'd give our eyes to have."[2] Possessing this machine would enable them to decipher the "Top Secret traffic of all ... Russian embassies and spy centres all over the world."[3] Understanding the importance of the mission, Bond readily accepts it. Even after walking into a trap, Bond manages to turn Tatiana Romanova to his side, kills the SMERSH agent sent to kill him, and delivers the girl and cipher machine to his superiors.

THEN IN HIS SIXTH NOVEL *DR. NO* (1958), FLEMING PRESENTED
information that describes how the cipher system is used.

In his next mission, that would ultimately lead him to Dr. No, Bond
travels to Jamaica to investigate a communication problem with the
Jamaican Regional Control (SIS) Officer for the Caribbean–Commander John Strangways, RN (Ret.). "Every day, at eighteen-thirty
local time, unless [Strangeways] gave warning the day before that he
would not be on the air – when he had business on one of the other
islands... or was seriously ill – he would transmit his daily report
[to London] and receive his orders."[4] If he failed, a second "Blue" call
would be made exactly thirty minutes later, and if no contact is made
a third and final "Red" call would be made at exactly nineteen-thirty.
If silence continued, emergency methods would urgently begin to
identify the problem.

On the way to send his daily radio message, three men who appear
to be blind shoot Strangways using sausage-shaped firearms with
silencers and place him in a hearse.

Strangways' secretary Mary Trueblood and former Chief Officer
Women's Royal Naval Service (WRNS) waits at the bungalow where
his radio is hidden. As his No. 2, she was instructed in "fist" communication that ensures secured Secret Service transmission measured
through "the weight of each pulse, the speed of each cipher group, the
stumble over a particular letter."[5] She knew if any slight variation
occurred, contact would automatically be broken due to the fist's signature being compromised. "And, if an agent had been captured and
was being forced to contact London under torture, he had only to add
a few hair-breath peculiarities to his usual 'fist' and they would tell
the story of his capture as clearly as if he had announced it en clair."[6]

While waiting for Strangways, Mary hears the lock blown out of the door and is then shot three times in the left breast, lifted into a bag, carried to the hearse, and thrown on top of her controller. As the hearse drives away, the secret communication station burns out-of-control.

IN 1933, THE GERMAN NAZI PARTY WAS FOUND USING CODIFIED communication. By 1937, in order to break their codes, Britain began intercepting German Enigma messages while the U.S. was doing the same with the Japanese, who were using a modified version of the same machine. In 1938, the new Heydrich-Enigma machines were being mass-produced. Unable to break the German codes, the Polish Cipher Bureau worked from 1932-39 to decipher the system. On July 25, 1939, they presented their basic decryption techniques and equipment to the French and British.

With this significant contribution to the Allied forces, a new cipher headquarters called Bletchley was established in Buckinghamshire with the mission to decipher the intercepted messages. The codes, although basically understood, did not reach a point of reasonable decryption until April 1940.

Eight days after the official declaration of war between Great Britain and Germany on September 3, 1939, President Roosevelt (codename - POTUS) and Winston Churchill (codename - Naval Person) were in confidential communication. The United States was in a period of isolationism, with no intention of entering the war in Europe. This clandestine relationship between the two leaders could have easily been perceived as illegal and thus precipitated impeachment proceedings against Roosevelt. A new covert communication system needed to be created and monitored by secret operatives. As a result, Bill Donovan and Bill Stephenson became the administrators and operators of the TeleX system that allowed for secured communication between the U.S. and Britain.

In the first eight months of the war, the Nazis used secure landlines to send messages. Then as resistance operations began to cut the lines, the enemy needed to use more radio communication that could be picked out of the air by Allied cipher operators. The covert communication system most widely used by the Germans was the Enigma machine. However, in 1942 the Lorenz SZ42 also came into use by the German High Command, while the PURPLE machine was used by the Japanese. As the messages were deciphered, under the codename ULTRA, they were sent to need-to-know parties only. These included very few British leaders with one additional report sent to POTUS. With TeleX and ULTRA, the Allies ultimately achieved dominance in covert communication.

Early in the war German blitzkriegs caused countries to fall like bowling pins. Poland was overrun in twenty-six days, Norway in twenty-eight days, Denmark in twenty-four hours, Holland in five days, and Luxembourg in twelve hours. The Battle of Dunkirk in France from May 26-June 4, 1940 was a catastrophic defeat despite the OPERATION DYNAMO evacuation of 338,226 soldiers.

With MI5, MI6, SOE, and British Security Coordination (BSC) fully operational, on May 10, 1940, Churchill told Bill, "You know what you must do at once … You are to be my personal representative in the United States. I will insure that you have my full support of all the resources at my command. I know that you will have success, and the good Lord will guide your efforts as He will ours."[7]

However, nobody knew where the Head of BSC's authority started or ended. Time was of the essence and results were expected yesterday. Bill and Mary Stephenson reached New York City on June 21, 1940. Once there, Bill opened his headquarters and made connections with J. Edgar Hoover, Director of the FBI, and William Donovan.

Although relations with the FBI were minimal, "Big Bill" Donovan from the U.S. Office of Strategic Services (OSS) and "Little Bill" became a successful team working synchronously for the remainder of the war. A telegram sent by Little Bill to King George VI with the label

"For Your Eyes Only" reads: "THE AMERICAN GOVERNMENT IS DEBATING TWO ALTERNATIVE COURSES OF ACTION. ONE WOULD KEEP BRITAIN IN THE WAR WITH SUPPLIES NOW DESPERATELY NEEDED. OTHER IS TO GIVE BRITAIN UP FOR LOST. DONOVAN IS THE PRESIDENT'S MOST TRUSTED PERSONAL ADVISOR DESPITE POLITICAL DIFFERENCES AND I URGE YOU TO BARE YOUR BREAST TO HIM."[8]

On a trip to England, the King gave Donovan a July 16th ULTRA message from Hitler stating his decision to invade England. Needing to work fast, the two Bills successfully proposed to transfer fifty older U.S. destroyers to Britain to protect the country from a potential invasion. Although the U.S. still maintained a policy of isolationism, an agreement was announced in September 1940 to release the destroyers for rights to create U.S. air and naval bases in Bermuda, Newfoundland, the Caribbean, and British Guiana for ninety-nine years. Both countries also shared other developments in radar, nuclear warfare, radio communications, aviation systems, and military strategies. The improved diplomatic relations led to the creation of an alliance that ultimately won the wars against Germany and Japan.

Realizing that Britain and America may soon fight together in another world war, Little Bill gave a prayer to Eleanor Roosevelt that she kept in her purse. It summarized his mission as follows:

Dear Lord
Lest I continue
My complacent way
Help me to remember
Somewhere out there
A man died for me today
-As long as there be war
I then must
Ask and answer
Am I worth dying for?[9]

Bill's early operations used Noël Coward and Roald Dahl to rally support for Britain and the war. Coward epitomized the celebrity agent who used his fame as an entertainer to lure support for England. Dahl, on the other hand, used his fame as a war hero to attract British support. Early in his work, Dahl also learned to write effective propaganda stories that gained the support of American hearts in addition to preparing him for his future career as an author.

As Anglo/American relations improved, in October 1941 Donovan established a London OSS office and began cooperative relations with the British BSC, SOE, MI5, and MI6. One significant OSS contribution was the creation of Camp X in Canada, which was used to train U.S. and British espionage agents (one of whom was Ian Fleming).

Like the SOE that was primarily attacked by other related British agencies, the U.S. Department of State and the FBI attacked the BSC. The Assistant Secretary of State Adolph Berle believed that the BSC was running a secret operation for British ships to illegally receive war supplies from the U.S. He found three hundred agents employed at ten BSC satellite offices located in major U.S. cities, raising a concern whether it was legal for the State Department to work in collusion with the BSC. Biddle further uncovered the clandestine relations between Churchill and Roosevelt that could be interpreted as an illegal alliance. As a result, Berle requested all foreign agents to register with the government in order to maintain close surveillance of their activities. However, with the December 7, 1941 attack on Pearl Harbor and the February 9, 1942, U.S. declaration of war, there was little to be done except allow Bill Stephenson to continue his work.

Bill tried to maintain positive relations with the FBI but since their first meeting, J. Edgar Hoover's obstreperous behavior had interfered in numerous BSC agent missions. Hoover wanted a more specific definition of legal operations, and Bill, using a get-it-done-anyway-you-can approach, was quick to give all the credit for publicly perceived successes to the FBI.

With expanding cooperation between the U.S. and Britain, Donovan recognized a need to monitor Nazi influence in South America. As a result, Little Bill met with the American Ambassador to Colombia to develop South American operations that supported Allied interests. Throughout the war, Bill's influence became ubiquitous, while the Quiet Canadian remained an enigma to many trusted friends and colleagues.

After the war, Bill received Knighthood in the New Year's Honours List. He was also the first non-American to receive the U.S. Medal of Merit, the nation's highest civilian decoration. The award acknowledged his unpaid service for supervising American wartime intelligence and special operations.

In his last few Bond novels, Fleming addresses the public recognition of his fictional characters through British distinguished honors. In Fleming's tenth novel *On Her Majesty's Secret Service* (1963), M irritably refuses to acknowledge congratulations from friends and colleagues for his KCMG (Knight Commander Order of St. Michael and St. George) award. And in the same novel, Bond has a nightmare that he publicly wears his CMG (Companion Order of St Michel and St. George) medal when he marries Tracy.

Having saved the world from nuclear destruction in "Operation Thunderball," M is awarded the KCMG. He states, "Well, I think it's all a pack of nonsense"[10] and in response refuses to reply to a single note of congratulations. He tells "Miss Moneypenny not to show him any more but to throw them in the wastepaper basket."[11]

While working on his mission to find and destroy Blofeld's Swiss biological warfare center, Bond dreams that he marries Contessa Teressa "Tracy" di Vicenzo in a ceremony in which he "dressed in tails... and the white collar [that] stuck into his neck below his chin. He was wearing his medals, and his order as CMG, on its blue and scarlet ribbon, [that] hung below his white tie."[12] On entering a gilt and white drawing room they are announced as Commander and Mrs. James Bond to a hushed crowd. Tracy says to the hostess, "And this is James. Doesn't he look sweet with that beautiful medal around his neck? Just like the old De Reszke cigarette advertisements!"[13] at which time Bond awakens from his dream in a sweat. After completing his mission Bond really does marry Tracy, who is shot dead hours after the ceremony by Ernst Blofeld and Irma Bunt.

———————◆———————

THEN IN FLEMING'S 12TH (AND FINAL) NOVEL *THE MAN WITH THE Golden Gun* (1965), James is slated to receive the KCMG, only to later decline it.

———————◆———————

In his last major mission, Bond kills the assassin Scaramanga who unsuccessfully tried to poison him. Ready to leave the Jamaican hospital, his secretary Mary Goodnight enters his room with what appears to be a Triple-X deciphering machine and a message from M.

After adjusting the cylinder settings, she cranks the handle, receives the message, and reads, "M PERSONAL FOR 007 EYES ONLY STOP YOU HAVE DONE WELL AND EXECUTED AYE DIFFICULT AND HAZARDOUS OPERATION TO MY ENTIRE REPEAT ENTIRE SATISFACTION... THE PRIME MINISTER PROPOSES TO RECOMMEND TO HER MAJESTY QUEEN ELIZABETH THE IMMEDIATE GRANT OF KNIGHTHOOD STOP THIS IS TO TAKE THE FORM OF THE ADDITION OF KATIE AS PREFIX TO YOUR CHARLIE MICHAEL GEORGE."[14]

Acknowledging the KCMG as the same honor given to M, Bond declines the award saying, "I'd like all those things. The romantic streak of the SIS – and the Scot... I just refuse to call myself Sir James Bond... I know M'll understand. He thinks much the same way about these things as I do. Trouble is he had to more or less inherit his K with the job."[15]

FLEMING'S CHARACTERS BELIEVE THAT THEY DO NOT NEED A LEGACY presented through a medal or knighthood. Instead, their greatest honor is to serve their Crown and Country. Ian Fleming never received any of the British distinguished honors after the war, a circumstance that may have affected the crafting of his fictional characters' opinions on the topic. Bill, on the other hand, welcomed the honors.

From 1946-51, Bill semi-retired in Montego Bay, Jamaica where he socialized with local residents like Ian Fleming and Noël Coward. In his new social group, he continued his reputation of preparing the best martinis in large glasses, reading avidly, and collecting paintings. He also contributed funds for a new church on the island. After leaving Jamaica, he lived in New York City on an entire floor of a building under the Luce's, publishers of *Time* and *Life*, and above the recluse Greta Garbo. In the early 1960s, he suffered a stroke that deteriorated his speech.

Soon afterward he moved to a secluded island of Bermuda, where Mary was diagnosed with cancer. Nurse Elizabeth Baptiste faithfully attended to her every need until her death in 1977 when she continued to give the same attention to Bill, who over time began to appreciate her as the daughter he never had.

Bill was not awarded the Companion of the Order of Canada until 1980. Unable to travel to receive the honor, Governor General Edward Schreyer performed the ceremony in Bermuda. In 1983, Bill was awarded the William Donovan medal from the veterans of the OSS. Barely able to walk, he accepted the honor on the aircraft carrier *Intrepid*, permanently moored in New York City. In a September 12, 1983 letter, President Ronald Regan writes,

> *"I was delighted to hear through Bill Casey that you would be the recipient of the William J. Donovan Award. I can think of no person more deserving. What an extraordinary life you*

have led in the service of freedom. Your career through World War I, World War II, and the post-war years adds up to one of the great legends, one of the great stories of personal valour and sake of country and fellow men.

All those who love freedom owe you a debt of gratitude; but we, as Americans, are particularly grateful to you for all the warmth and friendship you have always shown to our nation. We want you to know that the friendship is reciprocated tenfold; and I want to assure you that as long as Americans value courage and freedom there will always be a special place in our hearts, our minds, and our history books for the 'Man Called Intrepid.'"[16]

In 1983, Bill adopted Elizabeth as his daughter. On January 31, 1989, William Stephenson died in Bermuda at the age of ninety-two. According to his wishes, notice was not released until he was buried. In attendance were his daughter Elizabeth, her son Rhys, Bill's doctor and physiotherapist, and a few local police who acted as pallbearers. His life ended with no communication with his Winnipeg family. Instead, the adopted William died with only his newly adopted family by his side.

The best way to summarize Bill Stephenson's contributions to the Bond legend is to quote respected notables in *The Intrepid Society,*[17] a website dedicated to his memories and achievements. Lesley Hughes from the *Winnipeg Free Press* writes, "After the Second World War, Fleming and Stephenson owned neighboring properties in Jamaica, where Fleming did most of his work. By the time Fleming sat down to write the first Bond novel, he'd known and admired Stephenson for about 10 years." Bill MacDonald in *The True Intrepid* adds, "Ian Fleming was one to serve under him, and there's not much doubt that elements in Bond's make-up were derived from Stephenson, not least his love for fancy gadgetry." And, in *The Life of Ian Fleming* John Pearson writes, "Ian Fleming came to regard the Canadian as 'one of the greatest secret agents' and a man who had 'the quality of making anyone ready to follow him to the ends of the earth.'"

In the video *The True Intrepid*,[18] Bill was shown to possess many characteristics similar to Bond's, and in the 1979 miniseries titled *A Man Called Intrepid*[19] (directed by Peter Carter and starring David Niven as William Stephenson), audiences viewed fictionalized portrayals of his career. With so much attention and so many accolades given to his life's work by the Canadian, U.S., and British governments, press, and media, Bill Stephenson proved to be a significant inspiration for the field of espionage as well as for Ian Fleming and James Bond.

CHAPTER 12

Noel Coward (31 December 1962)
Courtesy of Erling Mandelmann

NOËL COWARD

Celebrity Spy

N oël Coward[1] is a prime example of a celebrity spy who worked with Section D, the "Dirty Tricks Department" of MI5, to continually promote Britain throughout World War II. Noël initially gathered intelligence in France, Russia, and contiguous countries of significance to Great Britain. He was then used to carry intelligence between President Roosevelt and Prime Minister Churchill, and later traveled around the world gathering assorted intelligence to support the war effort.

Noël Coward influenced Ian Fleming in two ways. As a celebrity producer, playwright, director, actor, composer, singer, dancer, and comedian, he helped sway the opinions of world leaders to enter World War II while carrying out spy missions in the public eye. And for that work, Noël represented particular characteristics of the James Bond fictional character. Noël also had the second distinction of being Ian Fleming's personal friend and writer colleague who lived a short distance away in Jamaica. In this capacity, the two authors were in constant contact and able to discuss the creative development of their individual works.

Noël Pierce Coward was born to Arthur and Violet Veitch Coward on December 16, 1899, in the London suburb of Teddington. Since he was born close to Christmas, his parents named him Noël. He began his studies at the Royal Chapel Choir School in London where at twelve years old he first appeared in a children's stage play titled *The Goldfish,* which was followed one year later with his playing the part of "Slightly" in *Peter Pan.*

Receiving his first public acclaim, Noël decided to make a professional commitment to the theatre. In 1917 at the age of eighteen, he wrote his first play called *Rat Trap.* In 1929 Noël played the lead in the Broadway musical *Bitter Sweet.* Throughout the next ten years, he wrote and starred in a variety of British comedies that made him a popular public figure.

At age thirteen, Noël began homosexual relations with another child actor named Philip Tongue. This alternative sexual lifestyle followed him for the remainder of his life in a unique manner, where gender reversal roles became staples in his future plays. As it was customary in those days to maintain discretion in such matters, Noël lived a life of clandestine personal relationships.

In 1914 at the outset of World War I, fifteen-year-old Noël was too young to serve in the military. When finally called into military service in 1918, he secured a simple assignment in the Artists Rifle Corp., where he incurred a head injury that led to an honorable discharge.

Returning to civilian life, he experienced difficulty finding employment in the theatre. In 1924 he experienced his major breakthrough with the play *The Vortex,* which he wrote, directed, and starred in. As an emerging star, his songs and plays made him a household name. He maintained this successful career until the late 1930s when England once again found itself moving into an inevitable war with Germany.

Robert Vansittart, the undersecretary of the Foreign Office (FO), began to recruit citizens who could unofficially acquire intelligence for Britain. In early 1938, one year before the official declaration of war, Noël was recruited to travel to Paris and open the Bureau of Propaganda in close cooperation with the French Commissariat d'Information. There, he used his social contacts to follow the mood and actions of the country regarding the advancement of Hitler's army.

Noël felt his time in France was ill spent, with one exception. Understanding that Germany could use cross-bearing transmissions from a broadcast music station to aid their flight guidance systems, he recommended that Radio Fécamp, one of the most successful radio stations in Europe, be shut down. Despite all radio transmissions being shut down during an enemy alert, he argued that the German guidance signals were so strong they could lock into their tower before the alert signal was sounded. Winning the argument, he began to feel like he was contributing to the war effort.

In June 1939 he was sent by the FO to Vansittart, Warsaw, Danzig, Moscow, Leningrad, Helsinki, Stockholm, Oslo, and Copenhagen to continue the same mission. On an early assignment, he was given sensitive materials by the British Minister to carry from Stockholm to Oslo. Armed with a courier's passport, Noël boarded the train, spent a night dreaming of being caught as a spy, and ultimately delivered the items safely to a man in a bowler hat who met him at the train station.

Unaware of Noël's FO work, Winston Churchill approached him later that year to entertain the troops in an attempt to keep up morale. In a response to the Prime Minister Noël wrote, "During the last war to end all wars, I'm conscious that I made little or no contribution – and that is something that has stayed at the back of my mind ever since...This time I am determined to play as much of a part as the powers-that-be allow me... You may count on my doing whatever I am called upon to do and to do it to the best of my ability."[2]

On September 3, 1939, Noël was taken to the Secret Intelligence Service (SIS) Headquarters at Bletchley Park in Buckinghamshire where he officially enlisted in Section D of MI5. Afterward, on January 26, 1940, Noël moved back to Paris and wrote to his friend, actor, and American drama critic Alec Woolcott, "I can honestly assure that I have never worked so God damned hard in my life ... I can not unfortunately go into details about what I am doing because of the... spies who can't wait to read my letters, listen to my telephone conversations and follow me in and out of public lavatories. All I can tell you is that I am learning a whole lot of things about a whole lot of other things and I dread to think what I shall be like at the end of it."[3] Hearing that other actors were concerned with his absence from the theatre, he writes, "I am an Englishman and my country is at war! ... There really is a great deal to be done. This is a sinister and deadly war, in many ways more so than the last one."[4]

Faithful to his duties, Noël was sent to the United States at the end of April to rally support for the British war effort. During his crossing on the SS *Washington*, he met a man who, for no apparent reason, tried to befriend him. Suspicious of his actions, Noël returned to his cabin and found the man's name on a list of Soviet and German agents. Having been indoctrinated into the international world of espionage, he had learned to suspect everyone.

On his first day in Washington, Noël was invited by Eleanor Roosevelt to dine at the White House, where he heard about public demands for U.S. isolationism but also emerging political voices sympathetic to Britain. On June 3, 1940, the President invited him back to dinner where they discussed the need to support Britain in greater detail.

Despite a rule that prohibited hard liquor in the White House, Roosevelt kept an excellent bar stocked with assorted mixing equipment, glasses for different drinks, and mixers like bitters, brown sugar, and lemons that permitted him to make excellent whiskey sours and martinis. As a result, social drinking parties became an ideal way for Noël to obtain information necessary for the war effort.

In a letter sent to the President, Noël writes, "It was a great privilege to be with you and there will be many times when I am back in Europe that I shall long to be in the warm friendly atmosphere of your study enjoying your very special cocktails."[5]

Like Roosevelt and Noël, Fleming's Bond character had a fine taste for alcoholic drinks. In his first novel *Casino Royale* (1953), third novel *Moonraker* (1955), and fourth novel *Diamonds are Forever* (1956), Bond presents the perfect mixture for a martini.

———•———

While playing a successful series of bets on a roulette table, Bond finds what looks like an American CIA agent duplicating a number of his moves from across the table. After completing his game, Bond leaves with the man who introduces himself as Felix Leiter. Having a drink together to celebrate the successful run of luck, Leiter orders a Haig-and-Haig on the rocks. Bond orders "A dry Martini... One. In a deep champagne goblet. Three measures of Gordon's, one of vodka, half a measure of Kina Lillet. Shake it very well until it's ice-cold, then add a large thin slice of lemon peel."[6] He then explains that the drink is his own invention that he plans to patent after he finds an appropriate name. When the drink is served, Bond notices, "the deep glass became frosted with the pale golden drink, slightly aerated by the bruising of the shaker,"[7] and after taking a long sip he adds that it tastes even better when the vodka is made with grain rather than potatoes.

Later when meeting Vesper Lynd, he recommends she order a very cold glass of vodka, which is the foundation of the martini. On hearing her first name and describing his special martini Bond says, "I think it's a fine name, ... The Vesper, ... It sounds perfect and it's very appropriate to the violet hour when my cocktail will now be drunk all over the world."[8] Requesting her permission to use the name, she agrees as long as she can try one first.

———•———

And while preparing for another mission with M, who pours three fingers of vodka from a frosted carafe, Bond takes "a pinch of black pepper and drop[s] it on the surface of the vodka. The pepper slowly settle[s] to the bottom of the glass leaving a few grains on the surface which Bond dabbed up with the tip of a finger."[9] After knocking the drink down his throat he says, "It's a trick the Russians taught me... There's often quite a lot of fusel oil on the surface of this stuff... when it was badly distilled... It takes the fusel oil to the bottom. I got to like the taste and now it's a habit."[10]

Later while on a mission in New York City, Bond runs into Felix Leiter, who buys him a martini at Sardi's famous restaurant and bar, where he finds "a medium dry Martini with a piece of lemon waiting for him."[11] When he tastes the drink, Bond is unable to recognize the Vermouth. Leiter says, "Made with Cresta Blanca... New domestic brand from California. Like it?" Bond replies, "Best Vermouth I ever tasted."[12]

AND SO BOND BEGINS THE EVOLUTION OF THE MARTINI AND HIS years of drinking them while on his missions.

After moving on from the cocktail parties in Washington, Noël traveled to New York City where he was taken to the thirty-fifth floor of Rockefeller Center to meet William "Little Bill" Stephenson, head of the BSC. This British Security Coordination was commonly called the Baker Street (named for Sherlock Holmes' urchins who could pass unnoticed in a crowd) Irregulars (opposite of Regulars in the infantry). From there, Noël was taken to Camp X on the north shore of Lake Ontario, Canada, where he was taught the subtle art of espionage.

"I was to go as an entertainer with an accompanist and sing my songs and on the side do something rather hush-hush. I was to go all the way through the continent of South America because at that time the Nazis were running all over South America. I spoke Spanish so that was all right."[13] His cover was to be a flamboyant, somewhat idiotic playboy. "I was a perfect silly ass. Nobody... considered I had a sensible thought in my head and they would say all kinds of things that I would pass on to Bill [Stephenson]. All my reports were written for him alone-nobody else."[14] He learned to search for the smallest details in conversations with important political and high society individuals that may have proven to be significant to Britain. Noël said, "I ridiculed the whole business of intelligence, because that's the best way to get on with it... I never had to do any disguises. Except occasionally I had to look rather idiotic – but that wasn't all that difficult. I'm a *splendid* actor!"[15]

During the remaining war years, Noël visited Australia, New Zealand, South Africa, and the Far East. As an entertainer his celebrity status allowed him to freely travel the world. However, in late 1941, a problem developed when the British government accused him of two counts of tax evasion. Based on a recent wartime law, he had not appropriately claimed the amounts of money he took out of the country for personal trips to the United States. The fine was set at £11,000. He pled innocent and, being unable to disclose the official purpose of his travel, the situation required personal intervention from high officials in both countries to ensure an innocent verdict was rendered. Noël was fined £200 and £20 for court costs.

Since he was working as a spy, various government departments needed to remain unaware of Noël's clandestine activities. After the tax evasion incident, he was sent on a public mission throughout the United States working for the British War Relief. The effort paid his expenses while permitting him to continue his spy work.

Because Noël was a notable celebrity who was constantly in the public eye, his most significant contribution to the war was the propaganda he spread through his theatre, film, and music, as he found it was art that moved both politicians and individual citizens to rally for the war effort.

Although not a direct form of propaganda, the play *Blithe Spirit*[16] first opened in London in 1941 and set a new record of 1,997 performances for a non-musical play. Later that year, it ran on Broadway for 657 performances. The play, originally written in five days, was a great source of entertainment that managed to move the minds of audiences away from the horrors of war for a short period of time—and as such validated the importance of art in supporting war efforts.

In 1942, Noël was commissioned to produce the film *In Which We Serve*.[17] The story was based on the life of the king's cousin Lord Louis Mountbatten, who served in the Royal Navy. Written by Noël, the story is based on Mountbatten's command of the destroyer *HMS Kelly* that was sunk in 1941 during the Battle of Crete. Co-directing the film, producing the score, and playing the lead, Noël presented audiences with a very personal insight into the war. Using flashback memories of seamen in a lifeboat awaiting rescue, the film dealt with many of the political, professional, societal, and personal issues facing the British people during that difficult time.

The film premiered on September 17, 1942, and received two Academy Award nominations for Best Picture and Original Screenplay. One reason for the accolades was that it showed current war footage and used actual military personnel as extras to enhance the realism of the story. The film featured Celia Johnson, who also happened to be the wife of Peter Fleming. Noël had met Johnson at a party the previous year and later contacted her for a casting call, where he found her suitable for the role.

In an October 24, 1942 letter sent to Noël, Mountbatten writes, "The King and Queen kept their promise and ran *In Which We Serve* at the official dinner for Mrs. Roosevelt."[18] All the invited politicians and dignitaries found the work excellent.

In 1943, Noël created the song "Don't Let's Be Beastly to the Germans," which included the lyrics,

Don't let's be beastly to the Germans
When our victory is ultimately won
It was just those nasty Nazis who persuaded them to fight
And their Beethoven and Bach are really far worse than their bite
And be meek to them and turn the other cheek to them
And try to bring out their latent sense of fun
Let's give them full air parity
And treat the rats with charity
But don't let's be beastly to the Hun[19]

As a spy who understood how to effectively use propaganda, Noël maintained that the German people should be forgiven and the blame for the war should be placed solely on the Nazis, who very effectively used propaganda to persuade their people to fight.

As the war continued, Noël performed quality work for his country. In 1943, he committed to a Middle East and Southeast Asia tour to help raise soldier morale. Never saying no, he agreed to travel to Gibraltar, Malta, Algiers, Iraq, Syria, Iran, and Cairo. He further traveled to Ceylon and Burma where, after eight months of continuous performances to troops, he collapsed from exhaustion, after which he was sent home. Finally, Germany surrendered unconditionally on May 7, 1945, and Japan followed suit on September 2, 1945.

For his notable work, Noël was recommended for Knighthood before the end of the war. However, due to differences of opinion among the various sectors of the government that were unaware of his clandestine activities, on December 29, 1942, Churchill sent a letter to the King that read, "conferment of Knighthood upon Mr. Coward so soon… would give rise to unfavorable comment. With considerable personal reluctance I therefore come to the conclusion that I could not advise Your Majesty to proceed with this proposal on the present occasion."[20]

Noël became upset when his friend and writer Dame Rebecca West informed him that both their names were on the official Nazi blacklist of British agents to be killed after the country was occupied. By pulling a few strings he could have easily become a Welfare Officer Royal Navy Volunteer Reserve (RNVR), which would have allowed him to perform his duties openly in public. He wanted to tell the truth about his intelligence work but, due to the nature of his missions, he was unable to disclose any information. Fortunately, he finally received his well-deserved Knighthood in 1970.

After the war, following celebrities like Betty Davis, Claudette Colbert, and Clara Bow, all of whom had homes in Jamaica, Noël rented Ian Fleming's *Goldeneye* home in Jamaica for three months at £200 a month. Having experienced the Spartan décor, deplorable abundance of snake pictures, and lack of hot water, he decided to change the name to "Golden Eye, Ear, Nose, and Throat." However, he was smitten with the surrounding beauty of the island and decided to make his own home on a beach approximately five miles away from Fleming. In an attempt to avoid post-war taxes, Noël became an expatriate. He designed a house he called *Firefly* with guesthouses that he named *Blue Harbour* (See Photos).

During the years Noël lived in Jamaica, he often complained that Ian's taste in food and wine was awful. Typical meals at Ian's included stewed guavas and coconut cream, salted fish with ackee fruit, conch gumbo, goatfish, shrimp, and fried octopus tentacles in tartar sauce. A typical breakfast would be papaya, scrambled eggs, and coffee. The cuisine seemed absolutely contradictory to that of James Bond. In Noël's opinion, the food Fleming loved tasted like armpits. Unlike the fine wines that Bond loved, Fleming would make a concoction called "Poor Man's Thing" that included orange and lemon skins heated in a bottle of rum with lots of sugar.

While Noël and his friends considered Fleming's food distasteful, Bond always appreciated and ordered the finest food and wine. In his first novel *Casino Royale*, Fleming presents Bond and his dinner partner Vesper Lynd as connoisseurs of French cuisine, while in his fourth novel *Diamonds are Forever*, Felix Leiter and Bond share a mutual appreciation of American food while dining at Sardi's in New York City.

As they drink their vodka, Vesper chooses to order caviar to start her meal, followed by "rognon' de veau with pommes soufflés [and]... fraises du bois with lots of cream."²¹ Bond follows suit with caviar explaining, "The trouble always is... not to get enough caviar, but how to get enough toast with it..., but then I would like a very small tournedos, underdone, with sauce Béarnaise and a Coeur d'artichaut While Mademoiselle is enjoying the strawberries, I will have half an avocado pear with a little French dressing."²² When he orders a bottle of Taittinger 45 champagne, he decides to take a recommendation from the sommelier instead who says, "the 'Blanc de Blanc Brut 1943 of the same marquis is without equal."²³

And while on a mission in New York City, Bond appreciates the martini that Leiter orders at Sardi's. Leiter says, "I've taken the chance and ordered you smoked salmon and Brizzola... They've got some of the finest meat in America here, and Brizzola's the best cut of that. Beef, straight across the bone. Roast and then broiled."²⁴ Acknowledging that the two friends have shared enough meals together to know each other's tastes, Bond accepts the recommendations.

As neighbors, Noël observed that Ian and Lady Anne Rothermere were having an open affair in front of her husband Lord Rothermere. Shortly after they divorced, Ian and Anne married on March 24, 1952, with Noël and his secretary Cole Leslie witnessing the event in the magistrate's office. The ceremony was followed with black crab and green wedding cake at *Goldeneye*. The next day, Ian and his new wife went to New York with an early copy of *Casino Royale*. Later when the first Bond film *Dr. No* was produced, as a well-acclaimed actor and friend, Noël was offered the role of the villain—a part he refused.

In England, Ian and Anne purchased a house from Noël in St. Margaret's Bay. There, Anne became the hostess to such honored guests as Noël, Evelyn Waugh, and Somerset Maugham. In honor of their friendship, Noël became godfather to Ian and Anne's only son Casper.

On January 16, 1973, Noël traveled to Jamaica with friends. On the morning of Monday, March 23rd, he suffered a stroke and died peacefully, at the age of seventy-four, on the island he loved. On March 29th a simple funeral was held with all attendees wearing white. He remains buried near his house that now remains as a museum to his life (See Photos).

Noël's contributions to espionage can be appreciated through the art of his life. As much of today's espionage is conducted through Internet websites, social media, and general media, as well as social functions and presentations, Noël Coward served his country through his writing and acting skills as well as his ability to obtain information while disguised as a dim-witted, harmless actor. And it is in this capacity as a celebrity spy that made Noël so important to Ian's life as a writer and colleague as well as Bond's life as a fictional character.

CHAPTER 13

Roald Dahl (20 April 1954) Courtesy of Carl Van Vechten Collection at Library of Congress

ROALD DAHL

War Hero/Celebrity Spy

Roald Dahl[1] and Ian Fleming were friends, collegial writers, and espionage collaborators during World War II. Like Fleming, Roald wrote stories that blended facts, fiction, suspense, and fantasy. While Fleming placed his espionage facts into Bond novels, Cubby Broccoli, creator of the Bond films, hired Roald to write the fifth James Bond screenplay *You Only Live Twice* (1967). Both authors also wrote children's stories. Fleming's *Chitty Chitty Bang Bang* (1964) and Dahl's *James and the Giant Peach* (1961) and *Charlie and the Chocolate Factory* (1964) were examples of their obviously similar writing styles and sufficient rationale for Broccoli to hire Roald to write the *Chitty Chitty Bang Bang* (1968) screenplay.

Roald first published war propaganda stories in newspapers and magazines; later he wrote fantasy books and screenplays that were eventually turned into films or television shows. As a journalist, Fleming published in newspapers, magazines and later Bond fiction novels that would be turned into feature films. Working for MI6, both men were inspired to translate their World War II experiences into espionage stories. Roald's first wartime experience, published as "A Piece of Cake," was transformed into the more fictional propagandized version titled "Shot Down Over Libya,"[2] while Fleming's report of military life in Russia, "Russia's Strength, Some Cautionary Notes," which was published by *The Times* was later transformed into parts of *From Russia with Love* and other Bond stories.

Like Fleming, Roald's life experiences became his stories. His use of language in his writing was simple yet elegantly complex. He smoked, drank, and gambled too much and proclaimed himself an anti-intellectual, developing lasting relationships with similar-thinking contemporaries like Noël Coward and Ian Fleming. As a fighter pilot and war hero, Roald became a celebrity spy who gathered intelligence, created British propaganda, and gathered support for the U.S. to enter World War II.

On September 16, 1916, Roald Dahl was born to Harald and Sophie Dahl in Cardiff, where his father became a wealthy shipbroker. In 1920, Roald lost his fifty-seven-year-old father to pneumonia. At thirty-five years old, Sophie was left with six children to raise. The bulk of Harald's £150,00 estate, valued at £5 million or $7.5 million today, was left in trust to the children, leaving his wife in minimal control of the finances.

Roald was sent to the Llandaff Cathedral School when he was seven years old in 1923 and remained there until 1925. After he was caned for putting a dead mouse in a jar of gobstoppers at a local store, he was sent to St Peter's boarding school across the Bristol Channel, where he spent four very lonely years. When he came home for vacations, he became uncontrollable. To appease her children, Sophie repeatedly told Scandinavian folk stories that became an inspiration for Roald's future publications.

From 1930-34, he attended Repton School in Derbyshire, where he grew into a six foot five inches tall handsome young man with a love for photography, squash, and football. In this draconian environment, where the cane and strap were often used to punish students who committed minor offenses, Roald's fantasized view of the world evolved.

His teachers often criticized him for being "'Rather dazed,' 'curiously dense and slow,' exhibiting 'fits of childishness' and 'fits of the sulks …'" who was a "persistent muddler, writing and saying opposite of what he means."[3] They believed he had very little ability, was apathetic, stupid, lethargic, languid, obstinate, and too pleased with himself. Ignoring their opinions, by age fifteen Roald had developed a unique sense of self and imagination.

After graduation, he was hired by the Shell Petroleum Company in 1934, which sent him to Salaam, Tanzania from 1934-36 to help set up a new oil terminal. During those two years of luxurious living, he took up golf, along with excessive drinking and gambling on horses and greyhounds—habits that would plague him for the remainder of his life.

In the summer of 1939, Roald became a Special Constable responsible for arresting German nationals and sending them to internment camps. On one occasion a threatened German national pointed a Luger pistol at Roald's chest. Immediately, one of the guards fired his gun and blew the man's head into fragments that then fell on Roald's face and khaki shirt.

Next, Roald was informed about the assassination of a mean German national by one of his servants. The servant had crept up on the man and cut off his head with a sword he had received from Roald. Comparing the two deaths, the servant claimed both killers to be warriors of equal status, not realizing the difference killing in self-defense versus cold-blooded murder. The fictional version of this short story titled "The Sword" was published in *The Atlantic Monthly* in August 1943, and the factual story was published in the book *Going Solo* in 1986.

Since Fleming and Dahl were both writers and friends, it was likely that they read each other's work. Elements of Roald's "The Sword" resonate with the Double O rite of passage concept in *Casino Royale* (1953), which suggests that Fleming may have used Roald's story as a source of inspiration.

Upon hearing that she would be working with a Double O agent, Vesper Lynd says, "Of course you're our heroes,"[4] to which Bond frowns and replies, "It's not difficult to get a Double O number if you're prepared to kill people... That's all the meaning it has. It's nothing to be particularly proud of."[5] He explains that the people who get killed are decent people who happen to be caught in particular problems or circumstances. Bond admits, "It's a confusing business but if it's one's profession, one does what one's told,"[6] making him sound like a blunt instrument used by others who can't perform the work themselves.

After beating Le Chiffre at baccarat and later being tortured by him, Bond is fortunate to still be alive after a SMERSH assassin kills his torturer. Lying in a hospital bed and recuperating from his wounds, he decides to resign from the service. He tells his MI6 colleague Renè Mathis that he killed two targets in cold blood. "The first was in New York–a Japanese cipher expert cracking our codes on the thirty-sixth floor of the RCA building in Rockefeller centre."[7] After getting a couple of Remington .30-30s with silencers and telescopic sights, he and another MI6 agent from New York got a room across the street from the target. The agent shot a hole in the window, which allowed Bond to shoot the man through the hole and into his mouth.

The second target was a Norwegian double agent who had been responsible for the capture of two British agents. "'For various reasons it had to be an absolutely silent job. I chose the bedroom of his flat and a knife,' says Bond. 'The only problem is that he didn't die very quickly."[8] *And it was for those two jobs that Bond was awarded his Double O number.*

While still in his hospital bed, Bond begins to question whether any assassination is good. He concludes that good or evil sides are based on one's allegiance, and he questions if his is correct. It takes Mathis' help for Bond to regain an appropriate perspective. He tells Bond, "when you get back to London you will find there are other Le Chiffres seeking to destroy you and your friends and your country... And now that you have seen a really evil man, you will know how evil they can be and you will go after them to destroy them in order to protect yourself and the people you love."[9] He adds that Bond will always know the difference between good and evil individuals by their actions.

BOTH ROALD'S SHORT STORY "THE SWORD" AND FLEMING'S *CASINO Royale* contend with the complicated issue of killing. Roald justified the difference between killing in self-defense versus cold-blooded murder, while Fleming justified assassination by Double 0 agents to protect and defend a nation against evil. Psychologically rationalizing missions to murder people in cold blood would plague Bond for the remainder of his fictional career.

In November 1939, Roald joined the Royal Air Force (RAF) and trained at the Initial Training School in Nairobi with sixteen others, thirteen of whom would be dead within the next two years. He flew the De Havilland Tiger Moth biplane for eight weeks before being sent to Habbaniya, Iraq for six months of further training. And in September 1940, Roald headed for action with the 80th Squadron in the Western Desert of North Africa. While flying a new Gloster Gladiator biplane across the desert to an airfield in Northern Egypt, he became lost and crash-landed. He managed to crawl away from the burning plane and avoid one hundred rounds of ammunition whizzing around his body that had been set off by the fire. The next day he was found barely conscious, blind, and with numerous facial injuries. His sight was restored after a month and, after face reconstruction by a plastic surgeon, he suffered frequent, painful headaches.

As the headaches began to subside, in February 1941 he was placed on active duty and sent to Ismailia near the Suez Canal to train on the new Mark I Hurricane. By April 1941, he had been sent to the 80th Squadron in Greece.

On April 6th, the Nazis invaded Athens and air battles began with approximately 800 German and 300 Italian planes against 192 British and Greek aircraft. It was an absolutely hopeless suicide mission. Roald later described the Battle of Athens as "the most breathless and exhilarating time I have ever had in my life."[10] Totally out-gunned, he had no time to think. While shooting wildly at anything that looked like the enemy, he saw a fellow pilot "whose Hurricane was in flames, climb calmly onto a wing and jump off."[11] Fortunate to survive the day, he returned to the airfield with no ammunition left in his guns. Of the twelve British planes that entered the battle, five were shot down against a loss of twenty-two German planes. Due to the intensity of the aerial battle, nobody could tell who had downed any of the planes.

As the Germans moved farther into Greece, Roald moved to Egypt where he flew missions every day for four weeks until he started having blackouts, which led to his dismissal in September 1941, with a final promotion to Flying Officer.

When he returned to England, Roald refused a desk job or flying instructor position. In March 1942 he met Harold Balfour, who was responsible for the RAF interests in Churchill's War Cabinet. After their meeting, Balfour promoted Roald to Flight Lieutenant and made him an assistant air attaché on the staff of the British Embassy in Washington DC.

This British Secret Intelligence Service (SIS/MI6) position required Roald to supply intelligence gathered in America to William Stephenson of the British Security Coordination (BSC), who then sent it to the SIS. The goal of the mission was to get the United

States to abandon its isolationistic policies and declare war on Nazi Germany. As a wealthy, handsome, womanizing, garrulous, war hero, soon-to-be author, Roald Dahl was in the midst of a British propaganda force to lure the U.S. into the war in Europe. And in such a capacity he worked as a celebrity spy for MI6.

In his first week, Roald delivered four lectures on the war in Greece to audiences in New Jersey, New York, and Washington. After ten days, the British novelist C. S. Forester contacted him to write a story about his war experiences. Roald wrote his story titled "A Piece of Cake"[12] within five hours. After significant editing to increase the propaganda value, the story "Shot Down Over Libya" was published in the *Saturday Evening Post* on August 1, 1942. This was Roald's first attempt at changing fact into fiction. Roald used this same strategy of embellishment in many of his other stories, and this kind of fantastical storytelling became an integral aspect of his unique writing style.

From this point, all future stories were rewritten to maximize their propaganda value before being published in the U.S. and England. Roald even sold the rights for the film *The Gremlins* to Walt Disney, who helped the war effort by producing the propaganda feature film *Victory Through Air Power*, the satirical Donald Duck cartoon *Der Fuehrer's Face,* and assorted war-training films. Although *The Gremlins* film was not produced at that time, it was published as a children's book in April 1943.

Working for the BSC required Roald to ingratiate himself into U.S. high society, where he became friends with Noël Coward and Hoagy Carmichael. He also mingled with political society, where he became a favorite of Eleanor Roosevelt and, by virtue of his writing, was invited to the Hyde Park presidential retreat where he conversed with the President. Their conversations were polite and candid, with Roald making covert notes of the President's opinions that were later reported to British Intelligence.

Roald also befriended Roosevelt's Vice-President Henry Wallace. One evening when they were together, Wallace shared a report titled "Our Job in the Pacific" with a mutual friend of Roald's. The content of the report stated how the U.S. should endorse the emancipation of Asian countries from British rule and initiate a monopoly in the field of civil aviation. The latter part of this ambition was realized shortly after the U.S. entered the war in Europe and negotiated an agreement that Britain cease production of cargo planes until the end of the war, resulting in sufficient time for the American transport aircraft industry to become a global leader.

Given the report to edit, Roald told his friend that he would go downstairs, work on the document, and return with suggestions for revisions. He quickly phoned his contact at the BSC, met him outside the house, and told him to copy the document and return it in fifteen minutes. Roald later wrote, "The man buzzed off to the BSC Washington offices and duly returned the pamphlet to me on the dot,"[13] which allowed him to return to the house and the mutual friend who suspected no foul play.

This event epitomized the type of intelligence demanded by the BSC and MI6. Although the information was published a year later and received official condemnation from Britain, the early acquisition allowed time for analysis and counteraction.

As the work progressed, Roald was called back to London in October 1943 after having lost his position for assorted complaints from the RAF Washington officers. Refusing to lose his spy, William Stephenson hired him back with a promotion to Wing Commander, ensuring that the RAF officers would never interfere in his work again.

Trying to make contacts in the field of communications, Roald was invited to numerous parties, dinners, and gatherings with the Washington and New York elite. One of these individuals was Drew Pearson, whose *Washington Merry-Go-Round* gossip column was syndicated to 430 newspapers throughout the country. Others included women of influence who appreciated Roald's social and sensual charm, such as Beatrice Gould, co-editor of *Ladies Home Journal*, who published a number of his early propaganda stories. Others included Helen Rogers Reid, wife of Ogden

Mills Reid, who owned the *New York Tribune* and the *New York Herald Tribune*, as well as the author Claire Booth Luce, whose husband owned *Time* and *Life* magazines. As a result of these relationships, Roald was able to spread the message of Britain's need for support.

Moving from communication moguls to socialites, Roald continued to maintain his sensual appeal. He attracted the attention of prominent socialites such as Evelyn Walsh McLean (owner of the famous Hope Diamond), the Standard Oil millionairess Millicent Rogers, and the French film star Annabella, who toured the country after becoming a U.S. citizen to support Allied war efforts. Using his charms, he swayed these and other influential individuals to help promote British propaganda.

After V-E Day Stephenson asked Roald to travel to espionage spy training at Camp X near Lake Ontario, where he wrote some history of the BSC from records transported from their office at Rockefeller Center. The document was released in the 1999 text *British Security Coordination: The Secret History of British Intelligence in the Americas, 1940-1945* by William Samuel Stephenson and Nigel West.

After four years in America, Roald returned to England. In February 1946 he found that his work was no longer desired or popular; he finally sold two stories in 1948 and began to rebuild his reputation. When he returned to New York City, Roald met Patricia Neal, a twenty-six-year-old Tony Award-winning actress from Tennessee. After a three-year affair with Gary Cooper and much persuasion, Pat married Roald in a small ceremony at Trinity Church in downtown New York City on July 2, 1953.

Over the next thirty years, the couple had five children, Roald rebuilt his reputation as a writer, and Pat won a Best Actress Academy Award in 1963 for the film *Hud*. The couple divorced in 1983 and Roald married Felicity Crosland, the woman with whom he had an affair that caused the divorce, that same year.

In the 1960s, Roald was approached by Cubby Broccoli to write the screenplay for the fifth Bond film (1967) and twelfth Bond novel

You Only Live Twice (1964), which is considered by many reviewers to be among Fleming's weakest novels. As a result, Roald was given enormous latitude to alter the storyline as long as the stylistic formula for women, gadgets, and the Bond character remained the same. Collaborating with Harold Jack Bloom, who shared the credit for additional story material, Roald wrote the first draft in eight weeks.

You Only Live Twice was published in March 1964, five months before Ian Fleming's death, and the film was released in 1967, three years after the author's death. Since Cubby Broccoli did not follow the numerical order of Fleming's stories for his Bond films, the chronological order of events for Bond's career was altered.

In the *You Only Live Twice* novel, Fleming addresses the issues of killing for good vs. evil and, Bond's desire to kill for revenge.

Bond finally finds Ernst Blofeld—the man who murdered his wife on the day of their marriage. Blofeld is living with Irma Bunt in a "Castle of Death" on an island in Japan where he spends his time assisting Japanese citizens to commit suicide.

Sent by M to kill Blofeld, Bond begins a new amorous relationship with the local awabi shell diver, Kissy Suzuki. With her help, they swim to the island where he enters the castle and awaits his battle to the death with Blofeld. "But then he thought of Kissy, and he wasn't so sure about not fearing for himself. She had brought a sweetness back into his life that he thought had gone forever."[14] However, realizing that he is outnumbered, Bond is captured by two guards and brought to Blofeld, who pompously explains that his suicide assistance service "is a public service unique in the history of the world."[15]

Then finding an opportunity to grab a nearby stave, Bond engages Blofeld in a difficult sword fight. Finally getting the upper hand, Bond wraps his fingers around Blofeld's neck and "whisper[s] through his gritted teeth, 'Die, Blofeld! Die!' And suddenly the tongue was out and the eyes rolled upwards and the body slipped down to the ground. But

Bond followed it and knelt, his hands cramped around the powerful
neck, seeing nothing, hearing nothing, in the terrible grip of blood lust."[16]

While escaping Blofeld's castle, Bond plummets into the sea and hits
his head. He is retrieved by Kissy but left with a case of amnesia. Then,
after remembering only a little about his past, Bond leaves the island
without emotionally confronting his revengeful killing of Blofeld, and
without Kissy divulging the news that she is pregnant with his child.

WITH REVENGE ADDED TO THE PSYCHOLOGICAL MIX OF KILLING
for good vs. evil, Fleming portrays Bond as a revengeful assassin
who has no problem killing someone like Blofeld, an evil nemesis
who murdered other people, including Bond's wife. Yet, with Bond's
lingering amnesia, Fleming fails to assure his readers that James
will ever be able to return to his former Double O life. Concurrently,
in the second to last chapter of the novel, before James leaves Kissy
to search for his past, M pens a *London* Times obituary for his spy.

Unlike the *You Only Live Twice* novel, in the screenplay of the
same name Roald avoids scenes that show Bond as an assassin
seeking revenge for his wife's murder, and instead presents him as
a third-party agent defending the United States and Russia from
entering into nuclear war while being unknowingly provoked by
the head of SPECTRE Ernst Blofeld.

When a United States spaceship is captured in orbit by a rocket
believed to be of Soviet origin, M discovers that the captor has landed
on an island near Japan. When M discusses a mission for Bond to
find the rocket's owner, he says, "That's what you've got to find out
and fast, before the real shooting starts. This damn thing could blow
up into a full scale war."[17] Then Bond meets his MI6 contact in Tokyo,
who is stabbed in the back during their conversation. Bond pursues

and engages the assassin who draws a flick-knife during their struggle, at which time Bond strangles him.

Later as Bond sleeps with a Japanese geisha, an assassin enters the room through a window and moves across the rafters until he is over the sleeping couple. He unrolls a spool of thread and places drops of poison that run down the string toward Bond, only to reach the lips of the girl who suddenly moves into the unfortunate, receiving position. After licking her lips, she panics and dies next to Bond, who grabs his gun from under the pillow and shoots the murderer. Bond tells Tanaka when he enters the room, "She's dead…poisoned. Tiger, we must get to that island."[18]

Over the next few days, Bond is trained in ninja fighting, kills another assassin, is made to look like a poor Japanese villager, marries a girl named Kissy, fails to consummate the marriage, and departs on a boat for Blofeld's island with Tiger and Kissy.

Finally reaching the island, Bond enters a control center through a disguised crater lake, is captured by Blofeld, launches an all-out attack with Tanaka and his ninjas, and fights Blofeld's henchman Hans, who, after a lengthy battle, is thrown into a pond of piranhas as Bond quips, "Bon appetite."[19]

With Blofeld managing to escape, Bond blows up the facility, prevents the anticipated war, and finds himself in a dingy with Kissy where he says, "Now, how about that honeymoon…"[20] to which she responds, "Why not? But they'll never let you stay."[21] As they kiss, the dingy is lifted on top on top of a submarine, as the camera cuts to M telling Moneypenny to "Tell him to come below and report"[22] and the song "You Only Live Twice begins as the final credits begin to roll.

--------◆--------

EVEN THOUGH THE *YOU ONLY LIVE TWICE* NOVEL PROVIDES THE opportunity for Bond to address the issue of killing for good, evil, or revenge, Roald completely ignores the topic in his adaptation. As a result, it became a non-issue in the Bond film series with the escape of Blofeld appearing to be an acceptable opportunity to keep the film storyline going.

One year after the *You Only Live Twice* film release, Cubby asked Roald to write the screen adaptation of Ian Fleming's last book, *Chitty Chitty Bang Bang* (1968). Instead of his previous high salary, Roald was offered $125,000 and a percentage of the profits that were to be paid into an offshore account, thereby reducing his income taxes. The script was written in collaboration with the director Ken Hughes and Bond veteran screenwriter Richard Maibaum. The film received poor reviews in part due to the disjointed screenplay.

Although this work was not well accepted, Roald collaborated next with David Seltzer on the screenplay for *Willy Wonka & the Chocolate Factory* (1971) that was widely successful. He also wrote a CBS fourteen-episode series for *Way Out* (a predecessor to the *Twilight Zone*), six episodes of *Alfred Hitchcock Presents*, and a British series titled *Tales of the Unexpected*.

Roald continued to work until he died on November 23, 1990, at the age of seventy-four. He was buried with chocolates, burgundy, snooker cues, and a power saw at St. Peter and St Paul's cemetery in Great Missenden, Buckinghamshire.

Roald Dahl has been acclaimed as one of the best children's story-tellers of the 20th century and ranks among the highest selling fiction authors, with his work translated into almost fifty languages. Over his life, Roald developed an enormously successful collection of dichoto-mous work in the realms of action and children's fantasy stories.

In terms of his influence on James Bond, Roald's early writing may have contributed to Fleming's attempt to address the morality of assassinating people for the good of the western world. His influence on the James Bond legend continued after Fleming's death, when Roald was the only Bond inspiration trusted to write the screenplay *For Your Eyes Only*.

CHAPTER 14

*John Felix C. Bryce (991) Office of Strategic Services (OSS)
identification badge, New York (est. 1940) National
Archives at College Park, College Park, MD*

IVAR BRYCE

Field Agent & Business Partner

Sometimes a man is lucky enough to meet another male who becomes his best friend forever (BFF). Ivar Bryce[1] and Ian Fleming had such a lifetime relationship. Unlike women, who are generally better at interpersonal relationships, sometimes men may not see each other for years at a time; yet, when they find one another again, they rekindle their friendship as if it had been only days since their last meeting.

Ivar and Ian were boyhood friends, attended school together, shared adventures, met as spies during World War II, reunited after the war, and became business partners. Ivar influenced Ian in a variety of ways, from using locations in Vermont and New York state as settings for his stories, to choosing the name James Bond and naming other characters after his friends.

Ivar Felix C. Bryce (a.k.a. John Felix C. Bryce) was born in 1906. As a cousin to the British royal family, Ivar's father joined the Coldstream Guards and fought in the Boer War where, in 1914, he was captured, interned for four years, and released on Armistice Day, November 11, 1918. Unfortunately, Charles fell in love with a Dutch girl during his internment and returned to Devonshire, never to reunite with his wife or son. He divorced, married his sweetheart, maintained minimal support for his family, and died at the age of eighty-one.

Ivar's mother became an author who wrote five books under the pen name of Mrs. Charles Bryce. She played piano, painted, and became an architect later in life. She also lost the family inheritance, thousands of acres of land, and the estate at Moyns Park due to a misinterpretation of her grandparents' will. She then remarried a man with five children and minimal wealth, making her financial status respectable but meager compared to her former life.

While on holiday at a small seaside resort in North Cornwall with his mother, grandmother, and governess, eight-year-old Ivar met four boys playing by the sea. Their names were Peter, Ian, Richard, and Michael Fleming. Allowed to join the group, Ivar quickly became friends with the Fleming boys. Their meetings continued for another two or three summers, making the encounters a significantly enjoyable part of Ivar's early life.

When he was sent to school at Eton, to his surprise Ivar found Peter and Ian. Being in the same division as Peter, they became good friends, but as the years passed his friendship with Ian increased. After Eton Ivar was accepted into Oxford, while Ian was sent to Sandhurst at Christ Church College. Ivar, although above average in early scholastic records, was released by Oxford after two years.

After Oxford, Ivar lived with a family in Strasbourg to learn German. During the same period, Ian lived in Geneva to improve his French.

The two friends managed to meet once in Paris for twenty-four hours while Ian was traveling between England and Switzerland.

Soon afterward, Ivar met the sweet and talented musician Vera de Sa Innocent, who returned with her family to São Paulo a few days later. Consumed by love, Ivar returned to England and informed his mother that he needed to find a full-time job. Believing her son was becoming more mature, in November 1929 she sent Ivar to work in São Paulo, Brazil as an advertising copywriter with the General Motors Corporation. On January 23, 1930, Ivar and seventeen-year-old Vera married.

Ironically, fellow Bond inspiration Noël Coward became infatuated with Vera for her beautiful voice and mastery of the guitar while he was in Brazil finishing the show *Cavalcade*. He wanted to write a new musical that showcased her talent, but his professional advances were rejected because Ivar and Vera were still too blissfully in love. Then, after returning to England in the autumn of 1934, the light of their marriage dimmed—Ivar left to travel around the world alone in 1935, and the couple amicably divorced in 1938.

In July 1939, Ian was appointed Lieutenant in the Royal Naval Volunteer Reserve (RNVR). His new position as Personal Assistant (PA) to Admiral John Godfrey (Director of Naval Intelligence) opened a new chapter in Ian and Ivar's relationship. The two began to meet often at various places to have lunch and discuss personal matters. During one meeting, Ian suggested that Ivar travel to New York where he could be of more use to his country. Unsuitable for military duty due to a severe leg injury that had left one leg three inches shorter than the other, Ivar trusted his friend's advice.

Once in New York, he soon received a telephone call requesting a meeting with a British Passport Control Officer at 630 Fifth Avenue. Arriving at the address, he happened to see an old friend who politely requested that he go see another person in Room 320 at the Westbury Hotel at 3 p.m. that afternoon. During that meeting, a sixty-year-old man proceeded to ask questions about his life and ability to speak multiple languages, of which the most important was Spanish. It didn't take long for Ivar to realize that he was in a den of spies. After acknowledging his allegiance to His Majesty's Government (HMG), he signed a copy of *The Official Secrets Act* and was told to report to the thirty-sixth floor of Rockefeller Center at 9 a.m. the following morning, where he performed routine office duties for the next few months.

His first field assignment was to open a Special Operations Executive (SOE) office in Latin America and recruit trustworthy agents to train in espionage operations at the British Security Coordination (BSC) Camp X in Canada. Finding twenty old friends he knew from his earlier life in Brazil, he developed a network of agents—only half survived the war. During this time Ivar supplied intelligence on Nazi operations to Bill Stephenson, head of the BSC, who passed the information to Bill Donovan, head of the U.S. Office of Strategic Services (OSS). Although Brazil was a neutral country, it was believed that it would take few Nazi troops to invade and occupy the country, as well as the continent. It was also believed that wealthy Latin Americans would support the occupation in order to retain their fortunes.

Unfortunately, only the FBI was permitted to send agents into South America, and J. Edgar Hoover regarded any British interference to be an invasion of his territory. As a result, Ivar's British SOE operation functioned on a need-to-know basis. In 1941, the British discovered that a German radio communications operation in Cuba was sending messages to U-boat commanders about various non-military ships in the area. Their intent was to disrupt shipping as a preliminary diversion for an invasion. Realizing that the operation needed to be shut down, Ivar co-created a covert mission with Bill Stephenson.

As a spy in South America, Ivar predicted changes that would potentially occur if Hitler invaded Central and South America. From his conclusions, he designed a map of the continent that would suit Nazi occupation. He changed borders and countries to better accommodate the use of natural resources for Germany and Nazi fanaticism. After creating the map, he turned it over to Stephenson, who thought if the FBI could find such a document it would dramatically change the attitudes of U.S. politicians and citizens about entering the war. It is believed that a forged map was produced in the British espionage technical laboratory at Camp X, then captured by the FBI and personally pressed into President Roosevelt's hands by Donovan.

In his March 11, 1941 Navy Day address, President Roosevelt stated, "Hitler has often protested that his plans for conquest do not extend across the Atlantic Ocean...I have in my possession a secret map, made in Germany by Hitler's government – by the planners of the new world order. It is a map of South America and a part of Central America as Hitler proposes to reorganize it."[2] He described how the continent including the Panama Canal would be divided into five vassal states under Nazi German domination. From another document in his possession, he further explained how all existing religions would be abolished. "The cross and all symbols of religion are to be forbidden... In place of the churches of our civilization, there is to be set up an international Nazi church – a church which will be served by orators sent out by the Nazi government. In the place of the Bible, the words of *Mein Kampf* will be imposed and enforced as Holy Writ. And in place of the cross of Christ will be put two symbols – the swastika and the naked sword." Stirring the emotions of the American people, Roosevelt concluded by saying, "we are pledged to pull our own oar in the destruction of Hitlerism."[3]

This speech and other British maneuvers improved support for Britain. After the attack on Pearl Harbor eight months later, on December 7, 1941, the U.S. declared war on both Japan and Germany. As a result, for the remainder of the war, Ivar worked for both Britain and the U.S. on all Central and South American covert operations.

As the war progressed, in 1942 Ivar was ordered to escort a Department of Naval Intelligence officer to a five-day conference on U-boat warfare. That officer was Ian Fleming. Reunited again, the two friends traveled from Washington D.C. to Kingston, Jamaica. After German submarines sank two hundred vessels in one month, disrupted shipping lines, and depleted food rations for the Caribbean islands, the Allies managed to decipher the German communication codes, resulting in the detection and destruction of the U-boats.

In addition to teaching them about U-boat warfare, the conference also offered the opportunity for Ivar to show Ian his Jamaican home *Bellevue* in the hills just outside of Kingston. The friends had five uninterrupted days to visit with each other and enjoy the beauty of the island. On their plane ride back to Washington Ian said, "You know, Ivar, I have made a great decision. When we have won this blasted war, I am going to live in Jamaica. Just live in Jamaica and lap it up, and swim in the sea and write books. That is what I want to do, and I want your help, as you will probably get out of the war before I can. You must find the right part of Jamaica for me to buy."[4]

At the end of the war, Ivar left South America in the autumn of 1945 to become a plantation owner in Jamaica. Traveling with his second wife, Sheila Taylor-Pease Byrne of New York, whom he had married in 1939, he found the perfect home for his friend—a fourteen-acre strip of north coastland in Oracabessa that cost £2,000 with a sandy beach about the length of a cricket pitch at the base of a cliff and a bolder approximately ten feet out in the water. Ian purchased the land and built a house that cost an additional £2,000 with shutters for windows, no hot water or tub, four small bedrooms, and one extremely large room. Ian named it *Goldeneye*, and the home became a haven for creative work, friendly gatherings, and visits with Ivar and his wife. Noël Coward was so impressed with the island that he too purchased coastal land and a house he named *Firefly* in Port Maria, which was a short distance from *Goldeneye*. Today, under new ownership and remodeled with an outdoor tub, hot water, and Ian's writing desk, the home currently rents for $5,500-6,600 USD per night (See Photos).

After the war, Ian accepted a job with the Lord Kemsley newspaper corporation with the stipulation that he receive two months off each year to write a novel in Jamaica. During that period, Ivar and his third wife, Jo, would cross the Atlantic Ocean four times a year on the *Queen Elizabeth*. In May 1952 Ian wrote to Ivar, "Now here's one vital request. I am having constructed for me by the Royal Typewriter Company a golden typewriter which is to cost some 174 dollars. I will not bother for the moment to tell you why I am acquiring this machine."[5] The typewriter sold on May 5, 1995, at Christie's in London for £56,250, or $89,229.

As lucky as Ian was with his numerous affairs, Ivar seemed equally unlucky in marital relationships. Ivar and Sheila divorced in 1950. Booking passage on the *Queen Elizabeth*, he met Marie-Josephine (Jo) Hartford, whom he married that same year. She was approximately forty-six years old and had been previously married at least three times. She was also the granddaughter of George Huntington Hartford, founder of the Great Atlantic & Pacific Tea Company, later to be known as the A&P grocery store chain. Inheriting the family fortune in 1951, she became a tournament tennis player, airplane pilot, yacht sailor, musician, art collector, and philanthropist for the Hartford Foundation.

With Sheila residing at his former home in Jamaica, Ivar and Jo decided to rent the yacht *Vagrant* in Miami and sail the Caribbean to Jamaica to pay Ian a surprise visit. After reaching Oracabessa, a storm came while they were on shore and sunk the ship.

It was during this visit that Ivar and Ian discussed the use of James Bond as the name for his new protagonist. They agreed that James Bond, the name of the ornithologist and author of the *Birds of the West Indies*, was a simple and appropriate name for Ian's superspy.

Ivar was also introduced to Ian's other character names and locations for his books that were based on friends, people, and places he knew. Happily, the names started with Mr. & Mrs. Bryce signing the visitors' book in *Dr. No* and Bond and his girl using the same names to travel incognito on a train in *Live and Let Die*.

However, of greater interest was the development of James Bond's CIA agent friend Felix Leiter who appeared in six Bond novels. Fleming decided to use Ivar's middle name of Felix and Ian's friend Tommy Leiter's last name. Even the name of Ivar's elderly housekeeper, May Maxwell, was used for Bond's housekeeper at his London flat.

As Ian had opportunities to visit the Bryce's homes in the U.S., they all agreed that Ian's use of Ivar's *Black Hole Hollow Farm* in Vermont near the New York state border was an appropriate setting for "For Your Eyes Only" (1960) and *The Spy Who Loved Me* (1962). In "For Your Eyes Only" Fleming describes Ivar's home and the beautiful mountain areas around New York and Vermont that he loved to hike.

————•————

After accepting a mission to assassinate the man responsible for murdering M's friends Colonel and Mrs. Havelock, Bond travels to Ottawa, Canada where he meets Colonel Johns at the headquarters of the Royal Canadian Mounted Police. There he is briefed on a covert mission. Using directions from a local Esso map, Bond travels to Frelighsburg, Vermont, the Green Mountains, and Enosburg Falls until reaching Echo Lake, where his target currently resides. An aerial photograph shows, "a long low range of well-kept buildings made of cut stone… On the garden side was a stone flagged terrace with a flowered border and beyond this two or three acres of trim lawn stretched down to the edge of a small lake. Echo Lake looked what it was - the luxurious retreat, in deep country… of a millionaire who liked privacy."[6]

Entering the area Bond evaluates, "the endless vista of the Green Mountains stretching in every direction as far as he could see, away to the east the golden ball of the sun just coming up in glory, and below, two thousand feet down a long slope of treetops broken once by a wide band of meadow, through a thin veil of mist, the lake, the lawn, and the house."[7]

Comforted by the beautiful surroundings, Bond suddenly hears the breaking of branches. He is surprised by Judy Havelock, the daughter of the murdered couple who has come to avenge her parents' death. After trying to send her away, he attempts to rationalize her need to stay because for Bond [it] was different. "He had no personal motives against [her parents' killers]. This was merely his job – as it was the job of a pest control officer to kill rats. He was the public executioner... They had declared and waged war against British people on British soil and they were currently planning another attack,"[8] and Judy was resolved to avenge her parents' deaths.

Armed with a bow and arrow, Judy and Bond descend on the target, his three bodyguards, and two girls. Judy shoots her arrow through the target's back, as he executes a perfect dive into the lake. Bond kills the other three men in a gunfight.

After it's over she says, "that was awful. I didn't - I didn't know it would be like that."[9] Bond responds, "It had to be done. They'd have got you otherwise. Those were pro killers – the worst."[10]

IVAR SHOWED IAN THE BEAUTY OF HIS HOME IN AMERICA ONLY TO have it used as a place of fictional murder. Judy's shocking response to her actions demonstrated a normal human response to murder and revenge, while Bond used the experience to rationalize his need to kill for a just cause. The short story is yet another example of the complexity that Fleming experienced when dealing with his protagonist's conscience as an assassin.

The Bryces also owned two houses on Bay Street in Nassau, where the couple spent their winter holidays which allowed for reciprocating visits in Jamaica with Ian and his wife Anne. And,

Ian also stayed with Ivar and Jo at their New York City home on 74th Street, allowing the friends to maintain active friendship and business relations.

One major business venture shared by Ivar and Ian was in the film industry. Ivar knew Kevin McClory, who directed the film *The Boy and the Bridge*, which showed promise of being a financial success. Before seeing the results of the film, Ivar, Ian, Kevin McClory, and Jack Whittingham began collaboration on a James Bond screenplay project in 1958. However, after *The Boy and the Bridge* failed to meet financial expectations, Ian had second thoughts about the joint venture. After dissolving their business relationship, Ian was purported to use elements of a screenplay written by McClory and Whittingham in his ninth Bond novel *Thunderball*.

On November 20, 1963, Kevin McClory and Jack Whittingham initiated a plagiarism lawsuit over the writing credit and film rights for the James Bond novel/film *Thunderball*. Due to the high costs of the trial, Whittingham was forced to withdraw as co-plaintiff and received no settlement. The nine-day trial resulted in an out-of-court settlement from the defendants Ivar Bryce and Ian Fleming for the sum of £52,000, with a total of £35,000 going to McClory after the £17,000 court costs were paid. *Thunderball* was released in 1965 by Albert "Cubby" Broccoli & Harry Saltzman through EON Productions with McClory denoted as a producer and given shared credit for an "original story based on Kevin McClory, Jack Whittingham & Ian Fleming." The film grossed $141.2M from its worldwide release.

Ian suffered two heart attacks during the trial. After the trial, he convalesced in Brighton. After months of trying to rebuild his health, he suffered a final attack on August 12, 1964, that took his life at the age of fifty-six.

Ivar published his autobiography *You Only Live Once: Memories of Ian Fleming* in 1975. He died in 1985 at the age of seventy-nine and Josephine Hartford Bryce died on June 8, 1992, in New York City at the age of eighty-eight.

Throughout Ivar's life, his relationship with Ian was one of mutual respect, friendship, and support, especially during World War II when they worked for collaborating spy agencies. Ivar's work in Latin America was well known to Ian. His covert operation to further U.S. support to enter the war evidenced his win-at-any-cost attitude, which is similar to Fleming's Bond character. Elements of their lasting relationship and business interests can be found in James Bond character names as well as in story and film locations. In a letter to Ivar regarding their enduring friendship, Ian expressed a sentiment not often shared between men: "How much I owe you! I wouldn't be here and I doubt if I would have written books without you."[11]

CHAPTER 15

VALENTINE & PETER FLEMING

Introduction

L ike many writers before him, Ian Fleming found inspiration for his fictional characters in members of his own family. As a World War I military hero, Ian's father Valentine instilled the virtues of loyalty and need to serve Crown and Country in his children. As a result, Ian and his brother Peter worked in the field of intelligence during World War II.

Major Valentine Fleming (1882-1917), MP, photograph published (9 June 1917) following his death in the First World War

Valentine Fleming
Nickname: Mokie

VALENTINE "MOKIE" FLEMING[1] WAS THE SON OF WEALTHY SCOTtish-American Investment Trust president Robert Fleming. Educated at Eton and Oxford, Valentine studied for the bar but never practiced law. Instead, he lived the life of a country gentleman funded with £250,000 from his father's estate. At twenty-four years old, Valentine married Evelyn St. Croix Rose, who gave birth to their sons Robert Peter (1907), Ian (1908), Richard (1911), and Michael (1913).

As children, the boys gave Valentine the pet name of "Mokie" as he was often seen s"moki"ng a pipe. They also named Evelyn "Mi," which was later shortened to "M." Desiring to raise his children in a comfortable home, Valentine purchased Pitt House, a Georgian mansion overlooking Hampstead Heath. There he raised hounds for hunting and entertained notable visitors like Winston Churchill.

As a popular candidate, in 1910 Valentine was elected Member of Parliament (MP) for South Oxfordshire, where he dedicated his life to his district and country. At the outset of World War I, in August 1914, Valentine enlisted in the army as a captain and was given command of the C Squadron of Oxfordshire Hussars. By December 1914, he was promoted to major with his brother Phil as second-in-command.

As an MP, over the next three years, Valentine was often called back to Westminster to debate critical issues in Parliament. While his military service kept him away from family, these trips gave him opportunities to return home. Valentine last saw his family at Easter time.

In the early hours of the morning on May 20, 1917, Valentine's squadron was showered with German gas and explosive shells while holding a dangerous position at Gillemont Farm near Picardy, France. Within half an hour he and his second lieutenant Silvertop were killed instantly when traveling between two trenches. Shortly after the incident, Philip wrote his mother and father:

"My Darling Mum… I couldn't realize it first of all, but now, after an hour, oh, it is too awful. But it's fine too… what held that position against the Germans… was Val's absolutely extraordinary example of sticking to duty. It was outstanding

and helped the men... It was a hero's death he died... Val could not have died a more noble death. It makes it easier... From, your loving PHIL"[2]

Upon hearing the news, Evelyn mourned by withdrawing from social interaction for the rest of her life. Depending on their ages, the boys had mixed methods of coping with the tragedy. With their mother's strong love for Valentine, "She evoked him as an example, an ideal to look up to... Before and for long after he was killed, we always ended our prayers: 'And please God make me grow up like Mokie.'"[3]

At nine, Peter became the new male head of the household. Ian, Richard, and Michael struggled to accept the loss of their father and adapt to the new circumstances under which they had to live. Valentine was posthumously awarded the Distinguished Service Order (DSO) with his friend Winston Churchill penning his epitaph in *The Times*.

When Bond was believed killed during a mission at the end of Ian Fleming's eleventh novel *You Only Live Twice* (1964), M penned his obituary with a writer only known as "M.G." concluding the obituary with the following addendum:

"I was happy and proud to serve Commander Bond in a close capacity during the past three years at the Ministry of Defense. If indeed our fears for him are justified, may I suggest these simple words for his epitaph? Many of the junior staff here feel they represent his philosophy: 'I shall not waste my days in trying to prolong them. I shall use my time.'"[4]

THESE WORDS PENNED BY "M.G" ARE TO BE BELIEVED WRITTEN BY Mary Goodnight who was the secretary for James Bond and the

Double 0 Section in many of Fleming's stories. They also seem appropriate for Ian who always effectively used his time to further his writing career until his death in 1964 at age fifty-six.

On November 7, 1917, Valentine's estate totaling £265,596 was given to his thirty-two-year-old wife with the stipulation that she remains a widow. He further stipulated that if she remarried, she would receive a fixed income of £3,000 per year and his children would receive equal shares of the remaining estate. To enhance his unmarried wife's power, Valentine gave her the right to disinherit any of her children in the hopes of keeping the family together in the same form that he had known and loved.

Since Valentine died eight days before Ian's ninth birthday, it is difficult to determine how he influenced his young son. However, the larger-than-life legacy of his father's memory may have contributed to Ian's development of James Bond as a patriotic servant who always placed Crown and Country before his own life

Peter Fleming in uniform, (c. 1940) © The Fleming Family.
Courtesy of Ian Fleming Images.

Peter Fleming
Field Agent & Intelligence Supervisor

PETER FLEMING,[5] THE OLDEST OF THE FOUR FLEMING BROTHERS, was an explorer and spy, evidencing that adventure and espionage run in the family. At the outset of World War II, Peter developed the first British civilian resistance organization in the event of an eventual German attack on England. He additionally served in Norway, Greece, and Southeast Asia working in the areas of resistance recruitment, commando raids, and military deception.

Peter's world travels inspired his own publications. His one and only spy novel is believed to have inspired Ian to begin his own writing career. And during the many conversations between the brothers, Peter may have contributed significant elements to Ian's Bond stories such as changing the name of M's secretary from Miss Pettaval to Miss Moneypenny.

On May 31, 1907, Robert Peter was born to Valentine and Evelyn Fleming. During his early life, Peter had numerous physical problems that stunted his growth. He was the only Fleming son to be less than six feet tall with minimal senses of taste and smell. He also developed a stutter that was eventually corrected. These recurrent problems caused him to withdraw from people. He stated about his early life, "I suspect that my childhood ailments, and the semi-convalescence that followed them, helped to make me a rather solitary person."[6] As a chronically sick child, he spent a lot of time by himself. "One did not go to children's parties because one was on a diet, one might get overtired or overexcited; one had a *tête-à-tête* (and at Christmas-time a box of crackers) with Nanny."[7]

Peter even had an unnecessary appendectomy at the insistence of his grandmother. Held back for a year at the age of nine, Peter was sent to Durnford School in Dorset with his younger brother Ian where he matured intellectually and socially.

During World War I, Peter maintained written communication with his father and enjoyed his visits home on military business. After Mokie was killed on May 20, 1917, the then ten-year-old Peter would spend the remainder of his life trying to be a father figure to his younger brothers.

William Mast

By age twelve, Peter had developed into a young scholar with a penchant for languages. On the day before his scholarship exams, he fell ill with measles. Unable to obtain a well-deserved scholarship, Peter was still accepted at Eton College where he studied from 1920-26. Placed one level below the scholarship form, he was awarded the Oppidan Scholarship for quality academic achievement. Peter's love for writing helped him to become the editor of the *Eton College Chronicle*. Concurrent with Peter's academic awards, Ian, who also attended Eton, won seven of the ten sports events in the junior year competition. As a result, the Fleming brothers asserted a significant presence at the school. Peter continued to amass honors and distinctions throughout his academic career until he was finally awarded a scholarship to Oxford.

In the fall of 1926, Peter entered Oxford at the age of nineteen to study English. As a handsome, friendly fellow with a supposed wealth that made him a highly desirable catch, Peter was quite successful with the ladies. Although he possessed little talent as an actor, he developed a deep love of the theatre, and in January 1929 he met a "commoner" named Celia Johnson—a rising actress on the London stage who was eventually to become his wife.

In an effort to keep common women away from her son, Evelyn sent Peter to New York City after he graduated from Oxford in September 1929 to work as an apprentice stockbroker at his grandfather's merchant banking business, Robert Fleming & Co. The experience was a complete failure. Peter hated banking and ended his career in the family business. He next attempted to join the writing staff of the British Broadcasting Corporation (BBC) but failed. The *Spectator* finally hired him, where for the next two years he wrote stories about his travels to China and Russia.

In April 1932 Peter replied to an advertisement in *The Times* seeking explorers to travel to the Brazilian jungle for six months in search of Lt. Colonel Percy Harrison Fawcett, an "Indiana Jones" inspiration who went missing in 1925 while searching for the ancient city of "Z." The legend of this archaeologist was so popular that no fewer than thirteen expeditions were sent on this same mission. One group said that cannibals killed him. Another said he went crazy and lived with an isolated tribe as a babbling fool for the remainder of his natural life. This trip became the foundation for Peter's first and most popular book *Brazilian Adventure,* published in August 1933. Failing to stay long enough to appreciate his success, he set off for the Far East where he wrote the travelogues *One's Company* (1934) and *News from Tartary* (1936) that described his journey from Manchuria and Peking to Srinagar.

Finally, after a six-year intermittent courtship, Peter returned home and married Celia Johnson in the Old Church in Chelsea in the presence of a few family members and friends. There was no official engagement announcement. Evelyn ignored Peter's fiancée before the wedding, and a short statement was printed in *The Times* the following day.

After a honeymoon of skiing in Austria, Peter officially joined *The Times* as a part-time staff writer, permitting him to continue writing books while engaging in travel assignments for the paper. After his grandmother's death in March 1937, Peter had little concern about losing any family inheritance as his books made for a financially successful life. Unfortunately for Ian, his modest life made him financially dependent on his mother.

Two years later Peter was moved to a war correspondent position at *The Times* requiring him to make a fourth trip to the Orient, where he reported on the Japanese acquisition of Eastern Chinese lands. Celia traveled with him to share the adventure.

On September 3, 1939, when Lord Chamberlain announced Britain's entrance into the war, the thirty-two-year-old Peter was too old to fight in the infantry. So, for the next five years, he engaged in special intelligence assignments for the War Office.

He was first assigned to work with the Chinese in covert military operations against the Japanese who were occupying their territories. Then in April 1940, Peter was sent to observe and report on the destruction of the Norwegian town of Namsos by invading

German military. Originally reported dead by a Swedish radio broadcast station, his alleged death made headlines in the *Daily Sketch* London tabloid the following day. Unbeknownst to Peter, he shocked the family on his return home. Using quips and witticisms later made famous in Bond novels and films, he described to his family how he had managed to avoid death by Hitler.

Approximately two months later, Peter was assigned to organize OPERATION SEA LION to protect the homeland against an expected German invasion. He created "Auxiliary Units" that were comprised of four to eight men. Should the Germans invade, these units were trained to engage in covert mercenary operations mostly in Scotland and Northern and Southern England. In May 1940 these resistance fighters were prepared to live in underground Operational Bases (OB)[8] found in the woodland areas of the countryside. These hideouts contained food, water, ammunition, and explosives. Observation Posts (OP) were also designed for surveillance, early detection, and combat with enemy forces. Their orders were to hide during the day and fight at night.

Similar to the Auxiliary Unit underground hideouts, Ian Fleming depicts a sealed enemy base for covert operations performed by Soviet agents to kill and steal documents from Special Services motorcycle dispatchers in "From a View to a Kill," which appears in the first *For Your Eyes Only* (1960) collection of Bond short stories.

<hr />

Bond is given the mission at the Paris Station F to find out how a Royal Corps of Signals motorcycle dispatcher was murdered. Bond stakes out a location among the shrubs near to where the rider was found. Slowly a single thorny stem begins "rising until it was a clear foot above the bush. Then it stops. There is a solitary pink rose at the tip of the stem… Now, silently the petals of the rose seemed to swivel and expand… The lens seemed to be looking straight at Bond."[9] After Bond surveys the area, "two halves of the bush were opening like double doors."[10] *Three men emerge from the underground structure, with two stepping into snowshoes as they exit and the third walking out dressed in a Royal Corps of Signals uniform.*

The three men manhandle the BSA M20 motorcycle out of the shaft, "leaving no footprints, for the grass flattened only momentarily under the wide mesh."[11] The rider leaves and the two men return to the shaft, closing the rose bush over them. After a short time, the man returns to the shaft that opens and the men carry the motorcycle back underground. Realizing that the rider had been out seeking another dispatcher to kill, Bond formulates a plan.

Wanting to capture the men before they have a chance to destroy the bunker and its contents, Bond dresses as a dispatcher the next day. Riding his motorcycle to the hidden structure, he lures and shoots the enemy agent. After the rider is dead, he moves to the bush and sounds the rider's bird whistle to open the doors. It opens and, after a scuffle, Bond and his agents are in control of the underground hideout.

NUMEROUS UNDERGROUND HIDEOUTS WERE CONSTRUCTED WITH Peter's help, and many still remain today as evidence of Britain's effort to protect itself from enemy attack. Fleming's depiction of the use of snowshoes in "From a View to a Kill" mirrors that of real resistance hideouts, where the soldiers' footsteps were expected to go unnoticed until the winter snows when their impressions would easily lead the enemy back to the bunkers.

The Auxiliary Unit recruits were trained in hand-to-hand combat, pistol and small weapons operation, and plastic explosive demolition. Much of their early work was in booby trap construction, the mining of houses that might be used as enemy headquarters, and the preparation of bridge demolition to impede and destroy German advancing armies. One concept came right out of Sherwood Forest: the men were trained to use bows and arrows in the traditional manner and with arrows fitted with incendiary heads that could be used to set fire to specific targets. Additional heads with explosives and detonators were designed to create explosions that might destroy munitions or confuse the enemy.

Since the recruits had no official military status, they would have been shot as spies if captured. Therefore, Captain Peter Fleming needed individuals he could trust. Although a number of volunteers came from privileged backgrounds, most were gamekeepers, foresters, and others familiar with outdoor life. By October 1940, over three thousand recruits had been instructed at the Garth resistance training facility at Bilting to man the assorted hideouts that would defend the country.

Although OPERATION SEA LION was never carried out, Britain was the Allied country best prepared to initiate civilian resistance warfare. Peter believed that the initial resistance in killing the enemy and slowing down troop movement would have a good initial impact on the war effort until the winter leaf and snow cover would reveal their hideouts. Fortunately, this operation was never tested. Unfortunately, during this time, Peter was informed that his brother Michael had been captured after a battle in France and later died from his wounds while in prison.

Hearing about the Auxiliary Units in England, the Special Operations Executive (SOE) in Cairo requested that Peter put together a team of six officers and six commandos to engage in special covert operations in Northern Africa and Southern Europe. After receiving commando training in the Western Highlands, the team known as the Yak Mission was first sent to Egypt to raise an army to fight the Germans. The endeavor was unsuccessful. Next, they were sent to northern Greece to train a resistance army. With a faster than expected German occupation in that area, the team didn't have enough time to succeed. However, during their retreat, the team managed to blow an important bridge as well as destroy twenty locomotives. They also saved an Allied ammunition train transporting 120 tons of gasoline and 150 tons of ammunition from an enemy plane attack.

From 1942-45, the War Office sent Peter to the South West Pacific to oversee "D Division" operations. This unit was in charge of military deception for the Far East. Peter described his new duties as "to make your enemy take – or refrain from taking – a particular course of action… to improve your chances of defeating him."[12]

In Burma, Peter first worked on OPERATION ERROR. This mission sought to buy time to build a sufficient defense in India by leaving false intelligence of overinflated locally stationed Allied troop numbers for the Japanese to find. To lay the trap, Peter wrecked and abandoned a car that contained documents with personal letters, photos, war medals, and ribbons belonging to Field Marshall Wavell. Like many covert operations, it was hard to determine if the plan worked. But later a 1944 Chinese intelligence report acknowledged that the Japanese found the information and delayed an early attack on India, which confirmed that the operation had been a success.

A second operation was a variation of OPERATION MINCE-MEAT. The mission planted a dead soldier with sensitive false intelligence in a location accessible to the enemy. The hope was that after finding the intelligence and believing it to be real, the enemy would alter their future military operations. Unlike MINCEMEAT, which successfully planted a supposed drowned soldier near the coast of Spain, Peter's soldier was dropped out of a plane over Burma with twisted parachute lines causing him to crash land. Unfortunately, the radio he was carrying broke on impact with the ground, making the planted codes of no use to the Japanese.

One of the last major operations was called OPERATION PURPLE WHALES. This plan was to sell false stolen minutes from a Joint Military Council meeting to the Japanese evidencing that the Allies were preparing to invade the continent and begin bombing Tokyo. Using a Chinese double agent, the documents were sold for ten thousand Chinese dollars with the bombing of Hiroshima and Nagasaki negating any need for further evaluation.

In addition to these operations, double agents who first worked for the Germans or Japanese and later transferred their allegiance to the Allied Forces were used to successfully send deceptive communication. One such agent called "Silver" transmitted false intelligence prepared by D Division to Tokyo and later to Berlin as a confidence scam. He became so adept at his work that he was given the Iron Cross by Germany for his dedicated service to the Third Reich.

Peter's D Division also had its own "Q" figure named André Bicat. Coming from an art background where he produced theatre sets, André became a master of visual deception. He designed dummy paratroopers to deceive the enemy into believing that invasion forces were frighteningly large. And by dropping bombs that would burst into gunshots, his dummy troopers appeared to take part in actual combat. His dummy battles were so successful that they enabled the Allies to capture potential battleground areas in Rangoon, Malaya, and Meilktila.

At the end of the war in 1945, Colonel Peter Fleming was awarded the Most Excellent Award of the British Empire (OBE) and the Chinese military honor of the Order of the Cloud and Banner.

Returning home for the last time, Peter took up residence at his estate and, like his father, lived as a country gentleman. Although Celia continued to live in the spotlight, even winning the Best Actress Oscar in 1946 for her work on the film *Brief Encounter,* Peter chose to remain out of the social city life. Together they had two daughters who were raised in the countryside.

In 1951 Peter published his first and only suspense novel, *The Sixth Sense.* The story deals with the adventures of a former commando called Archie Strume and was dedicated to his brother Ian.

After his brother died on August 12, 1964, Peter became Director of Gildrose Ltd., a company that controlled all of the rights for Ian's publications, where he fought anyone who maligned Ian's name or tried to plagiarize his work. In memory of his brother, Peter kept all of the Bond books, with a photograph of Ian on top, in a small bookcase in his study for the remainder of his life.

On August 9, 1971, sixty-four-year-old Peter set off with friends on his annual hunting trip to Scotland. After a number of successful shooting days, Peter collapsed during the hunt on August 18, 1971. He died of a heart attack before hitting the ground. After the group carried his body to a safe area and sent one member to call for help, they continued the hunt because they believed that Peter would have preferred it that way.

Peter was buried at the churchyard of St. Bartholomew's Church in Nettlebed. His casket was hewn and finished from a beech tree found on his estate. According to his wishes, his dog was in attendance, no flowers were present, no mourning was permitted, and everyone who attended the ceremony later enjoyed a good, strong drink.

Peter was more than a brother to Ian. Robert Ryan described him in his 2009 *Telegraph* article as one of "Bond's unsung heroes."[13] As a Bond inspiration, he worked as an organizer for Britain's defense, a field agent for resistance operations, a head of deception operations that mirrored those of his brother, and a writer who is believed to have inspired Ian to begin his writing career.

CHAPTER 16

OTHER INSPIRATIONS

Commander Wilfred "Biffy" Dunderdale
Paris (SIS/MI6) Station Chief

ommander Wilfred "Biffy" Dunderdale was a 5'6" tall flamboyant agent who headed the Secret Intelligence Service (SIS/MI6) in Paris. Nicknamed "Biffy" for his reputation as an accomplished boxer in the Royal Navy, he made friends with Ian Fleming in 1940 and thereafter shared stories of his experiences that were used in numerous Bond books and films.

Wilfred Dunderdale was born on Christmas Eve in 1899 to British parents in Odessa, where he learned to speak Russian like a native. His father, Richard Allen Dunderdale, was a British Naval Engineer and shipping magnate. In 1919, Wilfred began working undercover in Sevastopol, collecting intelligence for England.

Because he came from a wealthy family, Wilfred was given a job as a clerk in the Passport Control Office (PCO) that was a cover for the SIS. After joining Naval Intelligence in 1924, he first worked in Constantinople. From 1925-29 he worked in Paris as the SIS Station Chief. During the 1920s-30s secret agents, like Biffy, monitored foreign espionage operations. His wife, Jane (whom he divorced at the end of the war) was the granddaughter of Samuel Morse, inventor of the Morse code. Also working as a spy, she was often believed to be a better agent than her husband.

The Dunderdales lived an extravagant life of parties until dawn. Wilfred had a passion for fast cars and pretty women. Decked out in handmade suits, solid gold custom Cartier cufflinks, and a black ebony cigarette holder for the same Balkan cigarettes preferred by James Bond, he was known for driving an armor-protected Rolls-Royce.

During his stay in Paris as a member of the Diplomatic Service, Biffy first met the 007 inspiration Fitzroy Mclean, to whom he taught the finer subtleties of diplomacy espionage. Continuing to work in the city until it was invaded, Wilfred booby-trapped his personal safe to explode when opened by German military personnel. As an individual who always lived on the edge, he had no problem using his spy skills to dismantle or destroy anyone who tried to get in his way.

After the invasion of France in May 1940, Biffy escaped to London. Working with Section A4, he sent fifty-seven agents back into French-occupied areas. Although not sent by Dunderdale, the Dutch agent Pieter Tazelaar[1] personified James Bond by landing "at 4.35am on November 23, 1940, at Scheveningen in the Netherlands, near the seafront casino, dressed in a specially designed rubber oversuit which he stripped off to reveal full evening dress."[2] And after sprinkling a few drops of Hennessy XO brandy on him to strengthen his partying image, he began his mission. Although Wilfred was not directly involved in the wetsuit story, he did later describe it to Ian Fleming who possibly inspired it to be the opening scene in the third Bond film *Goldfinger* (1964).

The story begins with an exterior shot of the Ramirez warehouse at night. A close-up of a seagull decoy "rises out of the water revealing Bond in a black diving suit."[3] After scaling a wall and rendering a guard unconscious, he enters a storage tank and places white jelly from a plastic tubular belt on three storage tanks labeled "NITRO."[4] After leaving and jumping back over the wall, "He pulls off his diving suit to reveal him wearing a white tuxedo and black bow-tie. He takes a red carnation from his back pocket, puts it in his lapel and exits."[5]

Moving into the El Scorpio Café amidst a crowd of customers admiring a dancer, Bond lights a cigarette as the storage tanks explode. Following the chaos and after receiving a covert acknowledgment of congratulations from a man sitting at the bar, Bond follows the dancer into her dressing room. Finding her in the bath scrubbing, he throws her a towel and takes off his jacket and gun. As he prepares to kiss her, he sees an assailant in the reflection of her left eye. Turning her around quickly, she receives the blow meant for him. As a battle between the men begins, the assailant is thrown into the tub where he reaches for James' gun. Then trying to save his own life, Bond throws a small electric fan into the tub that results in sparks and smoke, as the man is electrocuted in the water.

The camera "PAN[S] him as he walks through smoke to the tub, takes his gun, puts it in his holster, takes his holster from the hook, puts it on,"[6] and departs, transitioning to the "MAIN TITLE SEQUENCE."[7]

WILFRED LATER TRAVELED TO LISBON, UNDER THE COVER NAME John Green, where he worked with the Vichy French in assorted underground movements. He worked extensively with the Polish intelligence from 1939-45, and during this time he helped to smuggle two Polish Enigma cipher machines to the communications experts at Bletchley Park in England.

At the end of the war, Wilfred was awarded the Most Excellent Order of the British Empire (OBE), the Legion d'Honneur as well as the U.S. Legion of Merit. He died in 1990 at the age of ninety, but it is unclear whether he passed away in Surry, England or New York, where he had recently moved with his third wife.

Michael Mason
Field Agent

SINCE THEY ALL WORKED WITH NAVAL INTELLIGENCE, MICHAEL Mason knew Biffy Dunderdale and Ian Fleming. During one of his field assignments, Michael was targeted for assassination in Bucharest, where two German agents attacked him in a lavatory railway car. Cornered, he broke both their necks in a fight and threw their bodies out the window. A modified version of the story was later used by Fleming in *From Russia with Love*.

Michael Mason was born in Oxfordshire to a wealthy family. He attended Eton and later went to Canada where he worked as a fur trapper. His advanced fighting skills helped him to become a professional boxer.

During World War II, he worked in Rumania as a field agent. In one of his missions, he swam to a German vessel and placed magnetic explosives around the hull. After killing thirty enemy sailors in the explosion, he shot the remaining three as they swam toward shore.

Michael was wanted by the German government, which tried numerous times to kill him. On two occasions, agents followed him and tried to run him down in the street. Michael always managed to get away. His agent reports reveal that he lived according to an ethical code that allowed him (with the exception of the ship he sunk) to kill the enemy only when his own life was threatened. Fleming chose to replicate Michael's beliefs in *The Spy Who Loved Me* (1962), where Bond states that he is unable to kill in cold blood.

------------◆------------

Vivienne Michel is a French-Canadian who was "born just outside Quebec."[8] Similar to Bond's early life, her parents died tragically, making her a ward of her aunt. At the age of twenty-three, after two failed love affairs, she leaves England with the intent of traveling by scooter from Canada to Florida, where she will seek employment at a newspaper. "And then [she] would think again"[9] about her direction in life. Upon reaching the Adirondacks, she finds her first temporary job as a manager of the Dreamy Pines Motor Court that is preparing to close for the winter season. There she is abducted and held against her will by two thugs hired to burn the resort down for the insurance claim.

After Vivienne makes a failed attempt to escape, Bond unexpectedly shows up at the door. Initially unaware of the circumstances, he is allowed to stay the night as a guest, during which time he quickly recognizes the problem. However, he doesn't seem worried as he "weigh[s] them up like a chess player. There [is] a certitude of power, of superiority, in his eyes."[10] After the men set the place ablaze, Bond saves the girl from perishing in the flames and says to Vivienne, "These are killers. They'll be off killing someone else tomorrow."[11]

After failing to shoot the thugs when "They were sitting ducks with those [television] sets in their hands,"[12] Bond curtly says, "Never been able to in cold blood."[13] He finishes the job when the thugs attempt to mow him down with their car by shooting the driver and watching the out-of-control vehicle roll into the lake and sink.

<hr />

THIS INABILITY TO KILL IN COLD BLOOD BEGAN WITH FLEMING WHO, after being trained in spy skills at Camp X in Canada, was unable to kill a mark during a mock mission. This issue which Fleming shared with Michael, significantly impacted the ethical development of the Bond character throughout his entire writing career.

Promotional photograph of composer Hoagy Charmichael (1947)

Hoagy Carmichael
Musician & Actor

PHYSICAL DESCRIPTIONS OF JAMES BOND ARE FOUND IN NO FEWER than twelve of Ian Fleming's Bond novels and short stories. However, Hoagy Carmichael,[14] the musician and actor, is the only public figure cited in Ian Fleming's novels *Casino Royale* and *Moonraker* as resembling James Bond—without the scar that ran down the secret agent's face. In *Casino Royale*, Vesper Lynd states, "[Bond] is very good-looking. He reminds me rather of Hoagy Carmichael, but there is something cold and ruthless"[15] about him.

This is the first physical description of the Bond fictional character. Fleming gave him a taste for coffee, alcohol, and cigarettes that reflected his own personal habits. However, he always envisioned Bond's physicality as more like Carmichael than himself.

In *Moonraker*, Special Branch officer Gala Brand considers Bond, "certainly good-looking… Rather like Hoagy Carmichael in a way. That black hair falling down over the right eyebrow. Much the same bones. But there [is] something a bit cruel in the mouth, and the eyes [a]re cold."[16] From this description, Fleming presents Bond as a loner, capable of ruthless behavior, yet still attractive to women.

Moving beyond these descriptions, it is only in Fleming's fifth novel *From Russia with Love* (1957) that Bond's physical description is officially recorded in print.

———————◆———————

In a meeting to research James Bond and determine if he is a threat to the Soviet Union, General Vozdvishensky contacts the Central Index. From a preliminary discussion, information emerges that Bond is the British agent who disrupted SMERSH operations led by Le Chiffre, Mr. Big, and Hugo Drax. They also discover that "he was involved in some diamond smuggling affair… between Africa and America."[17] General Grubozaboyschikov concludes that Bond "appears to be a dangerous enemy of the State,"[18] whose liquidation will benefit all of their intelligence departments.

In a collection of four photographs in Bond's file from 1946, '50, '51, and '53, the most recent one shows a three-inch white scar stretching "down the sunburned skin of the right cheek. The eyes [are] wide and level under straight rather long black brows."[19] His hair is black, parted on the left and falling over the right eyebrow. He has a rather long nose, with a wide, finely drawn, cruel looking mouth above a straight and firm jaw.

His height is 183 centimeters and weight 76 kilograms, resulting in a slim build. His eyes are blue and he shows "signs of plastic surgery on back of right hand."[20] He speaks French and German, smokes and drinks heavily, enjoys women, and carries a .25 Beretta in a holster under his left arm.

After analyzing the file, General G sends out a "Death Warrant… made out in the name of James Bond."[21]

But why did Fleming give Bond a scar? In a January 2009 *Personality and Individual Differences* publication, psychologists from the universities of Liverpool and Stirling found that men with scars were found to be 5.7 percentage points more attractive than men with undamaged skin. Robert Burriss, who headed the study, said, "A large scar is unlikely to make you more attractive, but there are some scars that women do seem to find appealing. There's the whole James Bond thing, where a person is attractive but probably not the best marriage material."[22]

Yet, in the Bond films, only a few of the Bond characters were given scars. Instead, they mostly had well defined and physically appealing faces. And this may be the reason why Fleming chose Hoagy Carmichael to represent his spy. Hoagy epitomized male features that women found attractive and the addition of a scar gave Bond a "bad boy" edge that made him even more irresistible.

Hoagland "Hoagy" Carmichael was born to Howard Clyde Carmichael, of Scottish ancestry, and Lina Mary (Robison) in

Bloomington, Indiana on November 22, 1899. Hoagy began playing the piano at six years old, following in his mother's footsteps, as she was known to play piano for silent films and parties.

As a teenager, he began playing ragtime and improvisational jazz. From 1920-26, he attended Indiana University, graduating with a degree in law. Finding law unsatisfying, he returned to his love of music. In 1927, he recorded one of his most beloved songs, "Stardust," with lyrics added in 1929.

Hoagy acted in fourteen motion pictures and hosted numerous radio musical variety shows. He also starred in *The Hoagy Carmichael Show* for two years on CBS television. In 1960, his song "Georgia on My Mind," performed by Ray Charles, won two Grammys for Best Male Vocal and Best Popular Single. Physically, he was a handsome man who was meticulous in his grooming and dress, thus making him a widely recognized popular music and movie star. As a result, Fleming appears to have chosen Hoagy's physical appearance to make James Bond more appealing to women.

In 1971, Hoagy was inducted into the Songwriters Hall of Fame. On December 27, 1981, in Rancho Mirage, California, he died of heart failure, at the age of eighty-two. His body was sent to Bloomington, Indiana, where he was buried at Rose Hill Cemetery.

Although Hoagy Carmichael was the only popular figure to be associated with Bond in the novels, other actors were considered for the film role due to their similar looks:

- David Niven was a popular first choice of Ian Fleming but not the producers.
- Cary Grant was offered the role but only agreed to one film. Cubby Broccoli wanted a minimum of three.
- James Mason was offered the part after Cary Grant but turned it down because he would only do two films.
- Burt Reynolds was offered the role after Sean Connery quit. He refused the part, believing it couldn't be played by an American actor. He rued his decision for years.

- James Brolin was considered before Roger Moore was hired for the eighth Bond movie *Live and Let Die* in 1973.
- Patrick McGoohan was considered but felt the role lacked a serious story.
- Mel Gibson turned down the role a number of times in the 1980s.
- Adam West was considered after Roger Moore left the role.

Of all the celebrity figures known to Fleming, Hoagy Carmichael is the only one to achieve 007-inspiration status due to his reference in two Bond novels.

Forest Frederick Edward Yeo-Thomas
Codename: White Rabbit & Shelley

"TOMMY" YEO-THOMAS WAS A BRITISH SPECIAL OPERATIONS EXECutive (SOE) agent who paralleled James Bond through his work as a field agent for the French resistance. He was captured by the Gestapo, tortured, sentenced to death, and sent to the Buchenwald concentration camp from which he escaped.

Forest Frederick Edward Yeo-Thomas was born to John and Daisy Yeo-Thomas on June 17, 1901. Born in England and educated in northern France, he developed French language diction equal to the local residents. In 1920, while fighting for the Polish Army against Bolshevik Russia, he was captured by the Red Army and sentenced to death. Shortly before his execution, he strangled a drunken guard and fled.

After working as an apprentice mechanic and banking accountant, at the outbreak of World War II he was declared too old to fight in the British Army. At the age of forty in February 1942, he joined the Air Ministry Intelligence Section (AI 10) of the Special Office Executive (SOE) as a citizen spy who would work closely with the Free French movement.

After completing parachute and cipher radio instruction at the Special Training School 36 in Southampton, in February 1943 he jumped into Normandy, France, where under the codename "Shelley" he spent approximately six weeks developing relations and overseeing British supplies air-dropped to the French resistance. During his second eight-week mission in Paris, he lured an enemy agent who was following him to the river, where he shot him at point-blank range with his .32 Colt pistol. As a result of this mission, Tommy built a name for himself as an important resistance agent. In February 1944 he returned to France, where approximately four weeks later he was captured by the Gestapo and taken to their interrogation headquarters.

Trying to persuade them that he was not Shelley but rather the RAF Squadron Leader Kenneth Dodkin, Tommy was taken to a German interrogation center where he experienced general beatings, icy water torture (precursor to water-boarding), solitary confinement, sleep deprivation, hanging by handcuffs from the ceiling, and genital beating. Tommy described how five men lifted him on a table and tied his ankles to its legs. "While two held his shoulders, 'the others, armed with rubber coshes, proceeded to rain blows all over me … Then they concentrated on the most vulnerable part of my anatomy. I could not restrain a scream, the agony was so intense and they continued to slam away.'"[23] They continued to beat him until he passed out.

A collection of espionage papers that was released by the SOE British National Archives in the new millennium contained a document Ian Fleming wrote on May 9, 1945, that evidences his knowledge about Tommy's work as a spy. As one of the numerous spies familiar to Fleming during World War II, Tommy's "torture held all the dark torments that Fleming would inflict on his personal spy. The beating of Bond's genitals in *Casino Royale* (1953) is all too familiar of the Gestapo techniques that Forest endured."[24]

After Bond beats LeChiffre at baccarat and enjoys a celebration dinner with Vesper Lynd, Vesper is kidnapped and pushed into a fleeing car. Running to his car, Bond follows in hot pursuit only to run over "a small carpet of glinting steel spikes right under his off-side wing... an adaptation of the nail-studded devices used by the Resistance against German staff-cars."[25]

With his tires blown, Bond loses control of his steering, crashes the car, and loses consciousness. Removed from the vehicle, Bond is transported to an unknown location where he is stripped of his clothes, strapped to an open-bottom cane chair with his naked buttocks protruding, and struck with a carpet-beater against his genitals. "Bond's whole body arche[s] in an involuntary spasm. His face contract[s] with a soundless scream and his lips [draw] right away from his teeth."[26] His head jerks backward, his muscles tighten throughout his body, and his toes and fingers begin to turn a pale white. As his body begins to sag and perspiration beads all over his body, he lets out a deep groan. "He had been told by colleagues who had survived torture by the Germans and the Japanese that towards the end there came a wonderful period of warmth and languor leading into a sort of a sexual twilight where pain turned into pleasure and where hatred and fear of the torturers turned into a masochistic infatuation."[27]

LIKE TOMMY, BOND WAS BEATEN UNTIL HE PASSED OUT. HOWEVER, his torture was interpreted in a different manner for the *Casino Royale* (1954) USA CLIMAX live broadcast kinescope production.

The American Jimmy Bond wins 87 million francs from Le Chiffre (played by Peter Lorre) at the baccarat table. Le Chiffre captures Bond and demands that the cheque for his losses be returned. With

Bond held down in a hotel room bathtub, Le Chiffre produces a pair of pliers and says, "Alright! See this tool Mr. Bond, it's a very handy little tool, it serves all sorts of purposes,"[28] at which time Le Chiffre clamps Bond's toes, resulting in excruciating pain. Unable to allow the torture to continue, Valerie [the Vesper character] divulges the information needed to find Bond's cheque.

After the henchmen leave to find the money, Bond frees himself from his bindings, confronts Le Chiffre, and shoots him dead when Le Chiffre attacks him with a razor blade hidden in his hatband.

--------------------◆--------------------

ALTHOUGH THE SCRIPT [OR, THE STORY] INDICATES THAT LE CHIFfre is supposed to die, he didn't die in the live television program, and Peter Lorre continued acting until the broadcast show ended. This was either because the writers made a mistake, or because Lorre refused to allow his character to die.

Similar to other tortured individuals who survived the war, Tommy fought through physical and psychological problems until his death on February 26, 1964, after experiencing a massive hemorrhage. He was sixty-four-years-old.

Having been overlooked as a Bond inspiration for many years, Forest Frederick Edward Yeo-Thomas is a good example of an espionage agent whose background was found to be directly known by Ian Fleming and possibly used as inspiration for the descriptions of the German torture techniques found in the first Bond novel, *Casino Royale.* The recent discovery of Tommy as a Bond inspiration suggests that other correlations may emerge from future espionage classified documents released by the British government.

CHAPTER 17

Ian Fleming in publicity pose (1960s)
Courtesy of Everett Collection

IAN FLEMING

Codename: F and 17F

Like many authors, Ian Fleming[1] created his most famous fictional character from a myriad of sources—his own personal experiences, individuals who he knew, people who he met indirectly, and others whose adventures became known through reports and research.

Born into a wealthy family, Ian's millionaire Scottish grandfather was president of his own London bank, and his father was a Member of Parliament (MP) who died at Ypres during World War I. Living in the shadow of his older brother Peter, Ian was dismissed early from Eton College due to an embarrassing sexual experience with a school maid (an experience he later attributed to James Bond in his eleventh novel *You Only Live Twice*). He was then sent to the Royal Military Academy at Sandhurst, which he left in 1927 after an encounter with a female caused him to contract gonorrhea. Lastly, his mother sent him to a private Austrian village school in Kitzbühel, where he studied for the Foreign Office (FO) examination which he failed in 1931.

With no other career options, through his mother's influence, the Reuters News Agency hired Ian to perform routine jobs in the newsroom where he began showing promise as a reporter. From April 6-23, 1933, he was sent to Moscow to cover a trial of six British engineers from the Metropolitan-Vickers Electrical Company arrested on the charge of espionage by the Russian All Union State Political Administration (OGPU). Reuters circulated his early trial reports and although he never scooped the final verdicts before his fellow journalists, his attempt at shutting down their phones was acknowledged as a humorous valiant attempt. From this early experience, Ian became known as a young specialist in the fields of Russia, international politics, and espionage. Shortly thereafter, he was offered a Far-Eastern correspondent position in Shanghai.

During the same year, the death of his grandfather, the absence of any inheritance from his estate, and the control of his father's inheritance by his mother left Ian personally insulted, depressed, and financially insolvent. In response, he rejected the lower paying correspondent offer and accepted a new position with the merchant bankers Cull and Co., with the intention of developing a financially independent future. The new position didn't work out and, two years later, Ian became a junior partner stockbroker with Rowe and Pittman in London. Earning £2,000 per year, he finally achieved financial independence from his family and moved into his first home at the age of twenty-seven.

While still at Rowe and Pittman, in 1939 Ian was sent to Moscow as both a stockbroker and reporter for *The Times* where he worked on a Chamberlain Government Anglo-Soviet trade mission. During this time, the smell of war was in the air. In reality, the project was believed to be a ruse for a real mission to seek information relating to Russian military strength and morale that was of interest to British Intelligence. There he observed Soviet leaders and their political strategies in heavily guarded bomb-proofed rooms.

After five days in Moscow, his final report gave little information about the Soviet movement. However, it did contain imaginative, very readable descriptions of military life that were to become his future writing style. The document headed with the words "Russia's Strength" was accepted with a favorable review, placing him in the thicket of political espionage.

During his trip, Ian also spent an evening with an Odessa girl whom he left the bottom half of his silk pajamas as a farewell present. This sexual encounter and other amorous adventures further paralleled Ian's lifestyle with that of his future fictional character. Like Bond, Ian's ability to seduce women in multiple languages was also enhanced by his comely appearance.

Ian continued to develop a name for himself in espionage, and in May 1939 the M inspiration Rear Admiral John Henry Godfrey requested a meeting with him at the Carlton Grill. Recently appointed Director of the Naval Intelligence (DNI) and unknown to Ian, the Admiral was in search of a Personal Assistant (PA). During the course of the meeting, Godfrey intimated that Ian was a possible candidate for that position.

Recommended as the top candidate for the job by a number of behind-the-scenes individuals, after a second meeting he was offered a part-time position to clandestinely learn the developing operations of the newly reorganized Department of Naval Intelligence (DNI). And, for the next month, he worked in his stockbroker position each morning, followed by afternoon meetings on DNI administration activities that resulted in Ian's commission as a Lieutenant in the Royal Naval Volunteer Reserve (RNVR) and PA to Admiral Godfrey, on July 26, 1939.

With the imminent entrance of Great Britain into World War II, he found himself in the central administration of British Navy intelligence. He further found himself in the infamous Room 39 of the War Office (WO), which was the central hub for all transmitted communication between the WO and field spies used by MI5, MI6, and the SOE. "At the peak of the war one captain, seven commanders, two lieutenants, two male civilian assistants and four female secretaries worked there."[2] Situated in this central location, Ian interacted with numerous Bond, M, Q, and Moneypenny inspirations. At the age of thirty-one, he was positioned to work on real espionage missions that would someday be the foundation of his future novels.

Although classified as a PA, Admiral Godfrey's confidence in him extended well beyond his position. Ian represented the DNI on numerous committees resulting in significant military strategic actions, in which he became an integral element. Godfrey recognized his assistant's abilities and used his power to advance him to Lieutenant Commander, and ultimately Commander, as rapidly as possible, making Ian a central figure in many WO strategies and decisions. Years later after Fleming's death, Godfrey stated, "Ian should be the DNI and I his naval advisor."[3] He further described that if he had been ten years older and Godfrey ten years younger, this might have been a workable proposition. As a result of his new status, recent British National Archive records find that Ian used the codename "F" or "17F" to sign many DNI and WO top-secret memos.

So what specific experiences led Ian to his greater understanding of espionage? Early in his first year, he was permitted to travel to France to work with the French Resistance. However, as his position of importance increased, he was rarely permitted to go to dangerous areas due to the potential of being captured, which could have resulted in the leakage of classified information. As a result, with his growing exposure to numerous WO operations, Ian became intimately knowledgeable of espionage missions by not only the DNI but other espionage agencies including MI5, SOE, BSC, OSS, and other numerous international groups.

In June 1941 he flew to the U.S.A., where, with Godfrey, he tried to establish cooperative clandestine communications between the two countries. Unfortunately, just months before the attack on Pearl Harbor, no international espionage organization existed in the U.S. The director of the FBI, J. Edgar Hoover, was found to be an obstreperous individual who believed that the FBI was the only secret service organization in the country, with no desire for international relations with Britain.

It wasn't until President Roosevelt supported Godfrey's recommendation that "Wild Bill" Donovan was appointed Coordinator of the Office of Information (on June 18, 1941), later to become the Office of Strategic Operations (OSS) and finally the Central Intelligence Agency (CIA), which was given power over all international operations. After Ian assisted Donovan by writing the OSS initial charter, Donovan gave him a .38 Police Positive Colt pistol inscribed with the words "For Special Services." This interest in pistols was to follow Ian into James Bond's future, through his character's use of the Beretta and, later, the Walther PPK.

Ian's interest in spy equipment and paraphernalia continued. He was given a commando knife (that he had his name and rank engraved onto the blade), a fountain pen that carried a tear gas cartridge to get out of tight situations, and a cyanide cartridge to ensure a quick and certain death if caught during a dangerous mission. In 1941, Ian once used this equipment during a short mission to Tangier. Inspecting intelligence personnel and procedures in North Africa, he traveled with his commando knife and cyanide cartridge. Although they weren't needed, this marked the closest encounter with danger that the young author faced.

As Ian had limited espionage field experiences, it is well known that he had direct, indirect, or researched knowledge of all of the Bond inspirations reported in the earlier chapters.

For example, Sir William Stephenson may be credited in part for Bond's attainment of the Double O license. In order for Bond to achieve Double O status, he has to assassinate a Japanese cipher expert in the Rockefeller Center Building. In reality, in 1941 Stephenson had an office on the thirty-sixth floor of the Rockefeller Center where he found a Japanese cipher expert sending short-wave coded information to the enemy from two floors below. One morning at three a.m., William, Ian, and two other agents broke into the cipher's office, microfilmed the codebooks, and sent the intelligence to the appropriate authorities the next day. Although nobody was killed, Ian created a similar experience in his first novel Casino Royale to initiate his mythical character's career.

To learn more about the field of espionage, Ian traveled to the village of Oshawa near Toronto on Lake Ontario where Stephenson had developed a training facility for saboteurs and spies called "Camp X." There, Ian received training in marksmanship with assorted weapons, hand-to-hand combat, lock-picking, safecracking, cipher radio transmission, underwater survival, and explosives training for use above and below the water. In the end, he received outstanding marks in underwater demolition and extremely favorable marks in all other areas.

However, when Ian was given a final test in which he had to successfully kill a mark, he was unable to complete the mission. He found that he was simply unable to kill anyone in cold blood—a problem that would plague James Bond throughout his entire career. Fortunately, Ian attended the school more for a practical understanding of the work than actual application. The experience increased his understanding of the dangerous fieldwork he needed to supervise and develop a greater understanding of the men he sent on those missions.

From his first novel (*Casino Royale* (1953)) to his last (*The Man with the Golden Gun* (1965)), Bond is as resistant to the idea of committing murder as his creator. And it was his friend and colleague Renee Mathis who tried to keep Bond on the narrow path of accepting the life of an assassin in *Casino Royale*.

———•———

After assisting Bond to beat Le Chiffre at baccarat, Mathis visits the hospital room where Bond is recovering three days later from his ordeal of being tortured.

Telling Renee that he plans to resign from the service, Bond explains "in order to tell the difference between the good and evil, we have manufactured two images representing the extremes – representing the deepest black and the purest white – and we call them God and the Devil."[4] Having difficulty philosophically distinguishing between the two, it is Renee who tells James, "Surround yourself with human beings…But don't let me down and become human yourself. We would lose such a wonderful machine."[5]

HOWEVER, IT WAS ALSO FELIX WHO ALWAYS STOOD BY HIS FRIEND and tried to keep him psychologically stable as an assassin. Working together again in Fleming's second novel *Live and Let Die* (1954) Felix loses his arm and half a leg from a shark attack and returns two novels later in *Diamonds are Forever* (1956) with a prosthetic leg and hook for his hand. He later helps Bond to foil a plot of Auric Goldfinger to steal the gold reserves from Fort Knox in *Goldfinger* (1959) and Emilio Largo to blackmail western countries with nuclear bombs in *Thunderball* (1961).

However, it's not until Ian's last novel *The Man with the Golden Gun* that Felix comes full circle (at the end of their careers) in rationalizing the need for Bond to continue accepting his life as a Double O agent.

After Bond tries to kill M with a cyanide gun, he is sent to special MI6 doctors to reverse the brainwashing he has experienced over the past year. After undergoing shock treatment, Bond's hatred of the KGB returns. M states that Bond has accused MI6 "of using him as a tool… The problem at hand could only be solved by a killing… Bond must prove himself at his old skills."[6] If he succeeds, he will regain his previous status, but if he fails, it will be an honorable death.

Given a mission to find and kill the assassin Francisco Scaramanga (also known as the "Man with the Golden Gun"), Bond travels to Jamaica. Working undercover, he becomes Scaramanga's personal assistant, helping him to host a group of American gangsters interested in investing in a new local hotel.

As he enters a car behind Scaramanga he wonders "whether to shoot the man now, in the back of the head–the old Gestapo-KGB point of puncture,"[7] but instead chooses not to kill him in cold blood. When Scaramanga discovers his true identity, Bond manages to shoot him in the right side of his chest near the lung. Now controlling the situation, Bond says, "Fraid you haven't got much time, Scaramanga. This is the end of the road. You've killed too many of my friends. I have a license to kill you and I'm going to kill you. But I'll make it quick."[8]

Bond gives Scaramanga time to say a last prayer. After covering his face and speaking Latin, Scaramanga suddenly jumps up and shoots Bond with a gold Derringer. Bond shoots back five times, killing his enemy.

When Bond wakes up in a hospital a week later, he receives a visit from his old friend and colleague Felix Leiter who tells him, "You did a good job. Pest control. It's got to be done by someone. Going back to it…Of course you are… It's what you were put into the world for. Pest control."[9]

BOND'S KILLING OF SACRAMANGA IS ACCEPTABLE BECAUSE HIS Double O power to kill was given to him by the government with administrative control to assure that he will never abuse it. And, in this case, with Scaramanga having killed other British agents, his death is acceptable to the government without need of being investigated and tried by a jury.

During Ian's time, the operational procedures for MI6 agents remained rather unclear. Finally, thirty years after Ian's death, the Parliament passed the 1994 Intelligence Services Act[10], which stated, "the Secret Intelligence Service, colloquially known as MI6 exists, '(a) to obtain and provide information relating to the actions or intentions of persons out-side the British Islands; and (b) to perform other tasks relating to the actions or intentions of such persons.'" This open-ended wording that can include assassinating such persons is in direct opposition to MI5's assertion, "It is claimed from time to time that we have been responsible for murdering individuals who have become 'inconvenient' in some way. We do not kill people or arrange their assassination. We are subject to the rule of law in just the same way as other bodies." In other words, MI6's open-ended accountability allowed for the creation of a Double O section while MI5's emphasis that it is illegal for any of their agents to assassinate individuals became the philosophy that Ian found growingly acceptable for Bond at the end of his career.

Following the thought that good spies may not have to assassinate individuals, in 1941 Ian created the No. 30 Assault Unit (30AU) that was modeled after a similar German unit designed to seek out and capture British intelligence including maps, codebooks, orders, and equipment that could help the Third Reich to better understand their enemy's operations. In contrast, Ian's units were designed to seize and bring back intelligence that could assist the Allied war effort.

These commandos, in part inspired by Patrick Dalzel-Job, were specially trained soldiers who operated from 1941-46. Originally designed to include Marine, Army, Air Force, and Navy recruits, the units ultimately comprised of a Naval Commander, Royale Marine Officer and six Marine Commandos, with one or two scientists or specialists occasionally included for special operations.

Like Ian and Bond, the commandos were trained in martial arts, demolition, small arms weapons, SCUBA diving, parachuting, glider flying, car and motorcycle riding, safecracking, and other assorted skills necessary for a Double O agent, with the goal of merging field fighting and intelligence gathering.

His units began working in North Africa, Sicily, Italy, and Greece. By the D-Day invasion, Ian's personal army was approximately one hundred fifty strong. By the end of the war, his Red Indians had amassed numerous accomplishments that included finding defense and minefield locations prior to the invasion of Sicily, capturing new German radar equipment and weapons in Cherbourg, obtaining coding machines and charts of the German Navy fleet advancements in Paris, unearthing a newly developed state-of-the-art acoustic homing torpedo in a Houilles concealed laboratory, discovering the first German one-man submarine in southern Holland, and finding design plans for submarines in Hamburg and torpedoes in Eckernforder.

Near the end of the war, they also captured the entire German Naval archives dating back to 1870 in Tambach. When they were sent back to London, an old admiral also came for a few months to help Ian organize the tons of collected information.

As the war and Ian's job in espionage neared an end, he began to search for a home where he could transition into his new writing career. In the autumn of 1944, he was sent to a meeting in Kingston, Jamaica with his old friend Ivar Bryce, who was working for the U.S. Navy Office of Intelligence, to discuss a German U-boat threat in the Caribbean. Bryce had a home on the island and, after seeing his house and a little of the surrounding area, Ian decided to live in Jamaica.

Ivar helped him find a fourteen-acre plot of land near the sea cliffs. He named his new home Goldeneye, believed to be named after either OPERATION GOLDENEYE (a project to protect Gibraltar that Ian worked on in 1940), a Carson McCullers book titled *Reflections in a Golden Eye*, a print of a goldeneye duck Ian purchased, or a Spanish tomb with a golden eye in a gold head that Ian had in his garden.

After six and a half years, Ian was released from his commission at the Admiralty and left His Majesty's Service on November 10, 1945. Like many other British servicemen, he received no awards from his own country but was awarded the Commander's Cross of the Order of the Dannebrog from Denmark.

His next job as the foreign news manager for the Kensley newspapers paid a salary of £5,000 per year plus expenses. Granted in the contract was a minimum two-month paid vacation each year—a guarantee that began Ian's annual hiatus to Goldeneye to work on his future books. The practice started January-February 1946 and continued for the remainder of his life.

By 1949, at the age of forty, Ian's attachment to the newspaper industry had begun to unravel. By this time his long-term habit of smoking seventy cigarettes and drinking a quart of gin each day began to take a toll on his body. His cigarette abuse resulted in a tightness of his chest that began in 1946, and his alcohol abuse resulted in kidney stones by 1948. Although he tried to reduce his additional wine, port, brandy, and after dinner liquors, his alcohol consumption and habit of smoking three hundred (Morland Specials) handmade cigarettes per week began to wreak havoc on his life.

On March 24, 1952, at the age of forty-three, Ian married Lady Anne Rothermere, who he first met in 1936. Their continued encounters at social occasions resulted in a non-committal sexual relationship during the war. After the death of her husband Lord O'Neill in 1944, Anne had received no commitment from Ian, so in June 1945 she married Lord (Viscount) Rothermere, Esmond Harmsworth, proprietor of the Daily Mail. Unable to accept their separation, Ian and Anne began an open affair that resulted in them falling passionately in love. After divorcing Rothermere in 1951, she married Ian in 1952.

Before their marriage, Ian said, "I can promise you nothing. I have no admirable character. I have no money. I have no title. Marriage will be entirely what you can make it." Anne responded saying, "I think any other man would be a frightful bore after you, I should miss the infinite variety of wall-gazing, pointless bullying so harsh and then so gentle if I cry."[11]

Shortly after their marriage, Ian began writing *Casino Royale*. He wrote every morning between 9 a.m. to 12 noon and every afternoon from 2 to 6:30 p.m., at a rate of 2,000 words a day, learning to complete an entire novel in two months. This regimen continued for the next fourteen years, at a rate of one novel or book of short stories per year, until his death.

As the books evolved, Bond's life became a mirror image of Ian's. Their high tolerance for alcohol, habit of smoking seventy cigarettes a day, and proclivity for numerous sexual relationships became foundational to their lives. While Ian never engaged in field espionage, Bond became his alter ego as the agent for all the dangerous assignments that Ian used to design in his office during the war. And Bond became, "what every man would like to be, and every woman would like between her sheets."[12]

Casino Royale was published on April 13, 1953. The first printing sold 4,750 copies and earned him £218, which was deemed successful for a first novel. It was reprinted twice selling 8,000 copies in the UK and another 4,000 copies in America.

In 1954, the book rights to *Casino Royale* were sold to the USA Columbia Broadcasting System for $1,000 to produce a one-hour dramatic version of the story. This business venture launched the television career of James a.k.a. "Card Shark Jimmy" Bond as an American secret agent. Barry Nelson, who maintained a successful career as a movie, television, and Broadway actor, played the part.

Ian spent £3,000 of his earnings on a new 190 hp. Ford Thunderbird. Subsequent novels were produced with increasingly higher book sales, film options, and full film rights. These successes began to lead to a small feeling of financial solvency. As time passed, Ian traveled to numerous locations that were later described in his books. These locations, in addition to the local ones found in Jamaica, supplied the background for his fictional character's adventures. Additionally, the secondary characters were named after many of his friends and acquaintances.

As his health declined, Ian visited the Eaton Hall health clinic where, like Bond, he was to rebuild his body through proper diet, massages, exercise, and sitz baths. Unfortunately, it did little good for his sciatica. Ian's continual smoking and drinking of gin (and later bourbon) continued to debilitate his body. With growing kidney problems, he began to give up and accept his inevitable fate.

The continuing success of Ian's books and films prompted the British Daily Express to produce an ongoing James Bond cartoon strip. Then in a March 1961 *Life* magazine article,[13] *From Russia with Love* was cited as the ninth of President John Kennedy's ten favorite books, which led to Ian being invited to dinner with President Kennedy and his wife, where he entertained them with methods of discrediting Fidel Castro.

Unfortunately, around this same time, a plagiarism lawsuit regarding his ninth novel and screenplay *Thunderball* was filed by the writer Kevin McClory. In 1963, the suit lost Ian considerable respect in the book and film industry. His friend and financial collaborator, Ivar Bryce, lost £80,000 over novel and film screen copyrights. Fortunately, however, Canadian film producer Harry Saltzman bought an option on all available Bond novels. Together with Warwick Films producer Albert "Cubby" Broccoli, they collaborated on the first film production of *Dr. No* through United Arts studio. Ian was guaranteed a minimum payment of £100,000 plus five percent of all producer profits. This venture mitigated the effects of the *Thunderball* lawsuit, and the legend of the cinematic icon began.

As a gift to himself from the *Dr. No* profits, Ian purchased a new supercharged Avanti car. From 1960 to 1964, profits increased tenfold with his book profits reaching approximately £250,000.

On August 11, 1964, sixteen days after the death of his mother, Ian attended a golf club meeting, ate lunch, and returned home. That night he had a hemorrhage, was taken to Canterbury Hospital, and died, the following morning, at the age of fifty-six. Although he sold 40 million books prior to his death, the amount of Ian

Fleming's estate was inconclusive due to the actualization of ongoing books, films, and merchandising profits. His cash estate left £302,147 and approximately £22,000 of Jamaican property to his wife as the primary beneficiary.

Not long before his death, Ian wrote a short story in which he indicates a shift in Bond's thinking regarding assassination. "The Living Daylights" is a short story in Ian's fourteenth and final book *Octopussy & The Living Daylights* (1966). In it, Bond is sent on a mission to assassinate a KGB sniper on a mission to assassinate an MI6 agent.

-----------◆-----------

"[Bond's] final rendezvous on one of the next three nights in Berlin [is] with a man. He [has] to see this man. He [has] to see this man and infallibly shoot him dead."[14] *M sends Bond to kill a KGB assassin named "Trigger" who is planning to assassinate a double Agent 272 working for the British. M says, "You know where you come in. You've got to kill this sniper. And you've got to kill him before he gets 272. That's all. Is it understood?"*[15]

After traveling to a fourth floor West Berlin apartment building that overlooks the border from East to West Berlin, Bond spends two nights with a sniper rifle and scope surveilling the field of weeds that 272 is expected to run across. Bond is positioned to kill Trigger before he can shoot 272 when on the third and final night, the target begins his run to freedom. As the KGB assassin takes aim, Bond realizes that it's a woman he has seen each evening carrying a cello case. Sparing her life, Bond shoots the butt of the rifle, possibly hitting her left hand and preventing completion of the mission.

The British agent reaches safety and Bond now expects to be reported by his associate as intentionally failing to complete his mission. Bond says, "Okay. With any luck it'll cost me my Double-O number... Scared the living daylights out of her. In my book, that was enough. Let's go."[16]

SHOOTING THE ASSASSIN'S HAND AND RIFLE BUTT ELIMINATES THE threat of death to anyone and allows Bond to avoid murdering Trigger in cold blood, which evidences that Bond has decided to stop being the "blunt instrument" of M to commit murder for his country without proper cause. This behavior illustrates a moral side of Bond that is similar to Ian's inability to kill his mark while training at Camp X.

Bond's decision further compliments "the Universal Declaration of Human Rights adopted by the General Assembly of the United Nations in 1948, which guarantees to all persons the right to a fair public hearing… [and] the United States' official blanket prohibition on assassination, enacted by President Ford in 1976 under Executive Order 11905 and affirmed by President Regan in 1981 under Executive Order 12333."[17]

Essentially, at the end of his career, Ian decided to make Bond a more moral Double O agent in defiance of British MI6 policy. With these similarities between Ian and his fictional character, perhaps we can view Bond as the man Ian himself wanted to be. I like to think that this sense of Bond's morality also makes him more appealing than other fictional spies in print and on screen because he is an assassin who refuses to shoot anyone who doesn't deserve to die.

It is fitting to summarize Ian Fleming's life with the James Bond epitaph from his twelfth novel, *You Only Live Twice*. It reads, "I shall not waste my days in trying to prolong them. I shall use my time."[18] Always drawing from other inspirational work, in typical Ian Fleming style, the epitaph is believed to have come from a "Jack London Credo" published in a 1956 collection of London stories. The credo reads: "I would rather be ashes than dust! I would rather that my spark should burn out in a brilliant blaze than it should be stifled by dry-rot. I would rather be a superb meteor, every atom of me in magnificent glow, than a sleepy and permanent planet. The function of man is to live, not to exist. 'I shall not waste my days in trying to prolong them. I shall use my time.'"[19] Regardless of the origin of Ian's epitaph, the sentiment appropriately eulogizes the life of James Bond as well as Ian Fleming, two men who seized every moment of their full and thrilling lives.

Conclusion

In Fleming's eleventh (and second-to-last) novel, *You Only Live Twice* (1964), Bond is committed to avenging the death of his wife Tracy, who he was married to for less than a day. Nine months after the wedding, he finds a castle in Japan where her murderers Ernst Stavro Blofeld and Irma Bunt are living. Working as a rich Swiss botanist under the cover name of Doctor Shatterhand, Blofeld collects and raises rare plants that are used to help Japanese citizens commit suicide—the mode of death in which their country ranks the highest in the world.

Bond is sent on a mission to murder his nemesis. With the help of Tiger Tanaka, Head of the Japanese Secret Service working undercover as a Japanese miner named Taro Todoroki, Bond meets Kissy Suzuki on Kuro Island. After swimming to the castle, he completes his mission. And while escaping the burning building, the helium balloon that Bond holds is punctured by a bullet, causing it to deflate and send him plummeting into the sea below. Unconscious from the fall, he is rescued by Kissy, who helps him back to the island.

Left with a case of amnesia, Bond is hidden at Kissy's home from Tiger and an Australian visitor from MI6. The Shinto priest says, "The spawn of the devil is dead. So is his wife. The Castle of Death has been totally destroyed."[1] Kissy replies, "I love him. I wish to keep him and care for him. He remembers nothing of the past. I wish it to remain so, so that we may marry and he may become a son of Kuro for all time."[2]

As time passes, Bond and Kissy begin an intimate relationship resulting in a pregnancy. "Kissy wonder[s] what moment to choose

*to tell Bond that she [i]s going to have a baby and whether he [will]
propose marriage to her."[3] But, after Bond finds a crumpled piece of
newspaper with the word "Vladivostok," she reluctantly allows him
to leave the island to find his memory in the city that brings back a
slight remembrance of his past. Realizing that Bond is entering into
a potentially dangerous situation, Kissy tells him before he departs,
"take care, for the Russians are not friendly people."[4]*

IN THE 1967 FILM ADAPTATION OF *YOU ONLY LIVE TWICE*, BOND
marries Kissy in a mock wedding to conceal his undercover identity and does not pursue romantic involvement with her after he
successfully completes his mission.

But Fleming left no definitive answer as to whether Bond has
or will have any descendants. Did Kissy die before childbirth? Did
she possibly have a miscarriage? Or did she have a child whom she
chose to keep away from Bond?

Despite the dangers of his chosen profession, after a fifteen year
career as an MI6 assassin (evidenced by fifteen consecutive years
of Ian Fleming's published novels, short stories, and the first five
films from 1953-67), Bond emerges as a man who has lost a child
he never knew, the mother of his only child who never shared her
life with him, a wife (Tracy) who was murdered a few hours after
taking their marriage vows, and a lost love (Vesper) who he wanted
to marry but who committed suicide to spare his life.

Then, in Fleming's twelfth (and final) novel *The Man with the
Golden Gun* (1965), a brainwashed Bond returns to MI6, attempts
to murder M, regains his memory, and completes a mission to
assassinate the assassin Francisco Scaramanga, who he kills in
self-defense by firing five bullets into the villain's chest.

And it is only in the short story "The Living Daylights" (published in *The Octopussy* & *The Living Daylights* short stories collection) that Bond finally rationalizes a moral method of dealing

with killing in cold blood. After shooting a female KGB assassin in the hand, causing her to drop her rifle before she can kill her target, he says, "She'd certainly be court-martialed for muffing this job. Probably be kicked out of the KGB… At least they'd stop short of killing her – as he himself had done."[5]

Through these two encounters at the end of the spy's fictional life, Ian Fleming leaves Bond with a moral rationale for when to kill in cold blood that is more compliant with MI5 and other western world espionage organizations than that of MI6, Renee Mathis, and Felix Leiter. He will no longer assassinate under orders from M. He will try to capture criminals and follow the due process of law that allows them to face their accusers with legal representation and no fear of cruel and unusual punishment. But, when placed in a life-threatening circumstance, Bond will kill in self-defense.

However, this decision leaves the reader with further questions. Would Bond be fired by M for insubordination if he refuses again to kill in cold blood, or could M recognize a need to end the Double O section? Either scenario would end Bond's career as we know it.

Epilogue

A number of the Bond inspirations cited in this book are well known and supported by Bond-related historians and writers.

For the novice reader, I hope that this work will be recognized as a definitive account of James Bond's life as characterized by Ian Fleming before and shortly after his death. For the seasoned Bond reader, I wish that the diverse research may reveal limited unique information of personal interest. And, for the critical reviewers of Bond books, I pray that this alternative respectful approach to Ian Fleming's body of work may find modest acceptance into the James Bond iconography.

However, regardless of the desired perceptions, I sincerely hope that the alternative writing style of making direct correlations between the factual history of Bond inspirations with associated passages of Fleming's works may be modestly found to be informative, insightful, and entertaining.

William Mast

List of Acronyms

Abwehr	Defense (Nazi German Intelligence Agency)
ASRL	Air Sea Rescue Launch
BBC	British Broadcasting Corporation
BOI	Bureau of Investigation
BSC	British Security Coordination (Baker Street Irregulars Club)
BSS	British Secret Service
C	Chief of MI6
CBE	Commander of the Most Excellence Award of the British Empire
CD	"Chief" Director
Cheka	The Extraordinary Commission for the Suppression of Counter-Revolution and Sabotage (Bolshevik Secret Police)
CIA	Central Intelligence Agency
CID	Committee of Imperial Defense
CIG	Central Intelligence Group
CIWC	Co-ordinator of Intelligence to the War Cabinet
COI	U.S. Office of Coordinator of Information
CMG	Companion Most Distinguished Order of Saint Michael and Saint George
DMI	Directorate of Military Intelligence
DNI	Department or Director of Naval Intelligence

DoS	U.S Department of State
DSO	Distinguished Service Order
Enigma	German covert communication system
FBI	Federal Investigation of Investigation
FO	Foreign Office
GC&CS	Government Code and Cipher School
GCHQ	Government Communications Headquarters
GPU	State Political Directorate (Russia)
GURK-NKO	People's Commissariat of Defense Chief Counterintelligence Directorate (earlier version of SMERSH)
HMG	His Majesty's Government
ISLD	Inter-Services Liaison Department
KCMG	Knight Commander Most Distinguished Order of Saint Michael & Saint George
KGB	Ministry of State Security
MC	Military Cross
MI5	Military Intelligence 5 (Security Service/SS)
MI6	Military Intelligence 6 (Secret Intelligence Service/ SIS)
MI(R)	Military Intelligence (Research)
MP	Member of Parliament
NCO	Non-Commissioned Officers
NID	Naval Intelligence Department
NKVD	People's Commissariat for International Affairs (НКВД)

OBE	Order of the British Empire
OGPU	All-Union State Political Administration
Okhrana	Administration for the Protection of the State (SMERSH)
OP	Observation Posts
OSS	Office of Strategic Services
OUN	Organization of Ukrainian Nationalists
PA	Personal Assistant
PCO	Passport Control Officer
PURPLE	Japanese covert communication system
PWE	Political War Executive
RAF	Royal Air Force
RCFC	Royal Canadian Flying Corps
RNVR	Royal Navy Volunteer Reserve
RSHA	Reichssicherheitshauptamt (Nazi - Reich Main Security Office)
SAS	Special Air Service
S&T	Schools and Training
SBO	Senior British Officer
SD	Sicherheitsdienst (Nazi - SS Intelligence Division)
SIS	Secret Intelligence Service (MI6)
SOE	Special Operations Executive
SMERSH	Smert Shpionam ("Death to Spies" - Soviet Secret Service)

SS	Security Service (MI5)
SS	Schutzstaffe (Nazi – Defense Corps) (Secret Service)
SSB	Secret Service Bureau
30AU	30 Assault Unit Commando (AKA Red Indians)
T & S	Topographical and Statistical Department
TeleX	Anglo/American covert communication system
ULTRA	British covert communication deciphering system
Ustase	Croatian Revolutionary Movement
WO	War Office
WRNS	Women's Royal Naval Service
XX	Double Cross (Agent) Committee

Notes on Sources

Preface

1. The Guardian. Kennedy, 2011.
2. The Times. The Times, 2008.
3. Amazon Publications. The Deadline team, 2012.
4. "a legend'" MacDonald, 2001, p.8.

Introduction

1. "November 11, 1920..." Pearson, 2008, p. 21.
2. M sends an obituary... Fleming, 1964, p. 256-60.
3. "uninteresting man..." Hellman, (Ian Fleming Interview) 1962, p. 32.

Chapter 1: John Dee

1. Dr. John Dee image. Wikimedia Commons.
2. "intelligencer" Woolsey, 2001, p. 56.
3. "that devastating storms..." Cooper & Gerald.
4. "glyph." Cooper & Gerald.
5. "He [i]s mildly intrigued ..." Fleming, 1960, p. 052.
6. "full of bullets" Ibid, p. 055.
7. 'These people..."' Ibid, p.059.
8. "The red sanserif letters..." Ibid, p. 060.
9. "all the top-secret signals..." Macintyre, 2008, p. 65.
10. "largest philosophical and scientific library collection in Elizabethan England." McDowall, 2015.
11. 'The Boneyard' ..." Fleming, 1954, p. 060.
12. "a frenzy of applause." Ibid p. 063.
13. "a single black G-string." Ibid, p. 066.
14. "Whom have you been sent over to kill here..." Ibid, p. 076.
15. "Edward IV Rose Nobles" Ibid, p. 076.
16. "She stood just inside the room ..." Ibid, p. 077.
17. "inquisitor." Ibid, p. 078.

18. "Torture is messy..." Ibid. p. 078.
19. "He speaks the truth." Ibid, p.081.
20. "came to rely heavily on codes." Woolsey, p. 71.
21. "'Language'..." Fleming, 1954, p. 039.
22. Enochian language. Enochian.
23. Rosicrucian. Rosicrucian Order.

Chapter 2: Four Bonds

1. "lifted the author's name" Bond, 1966. p. 17.
2. James Bond image. Wikimedia Commons.
3. "I wanted the simplest..." Pryor, 2010.
4. "When I wrote my first book..." Bond, 1966. p. 24.
5. Dear Mr. Fleming... Ibid. p. 18-19.
6. Dear Mrs. James Bond... Ibid p. 20-22.
7. "To the *real* James Bond..." Ibid p. 40.
8. "interested in birds." Fleming, 1958, p. 108.
9. "I was entertained..." Ibid, p. 220.
10. Agatha Christie image. Wikimedia Commons.
11. "a rather Agatha Christie-style little Englishwoman" Ibid, p. 026.
12. "the little old English lady" Ibid, p. 028.
13. "bancoe[s] him at the tenth turn" Ibid, p. 028.
14. "three kings, making zero." Ibid, p. 028.
15. *Climax Casino Royale* (spoof version) DVD. Brown 1967.
16. Barry Nelson image. Wikimedia Commons.
17. "Card Sense Jimmy Bond," Brown, 1988.
18. "A chunky Malacca cane ..." Fleming, 1953, p. 073.
19. 'softly, urgently,...'" Ibid, p. 081.
20. "Non Suffict Orbis" (The World Is Not Enough) also just happens... Fleming, 1963, p.070-4.
21. "we have some ten different families..." Ibid, p. 070.
22. "The World is not Enough" Ibid, p.074.
23. 'It's an excellent motto...' Ibid, p. 074.
24. "Fleming once said..." Britton, 2008.

Chapter 3: Sir Robert Bruce Lockhart

1. Robert H. Bruce Lockhart image. Wikimedia Commons.
2. "of blue and red squares…" Lockhart, 1985, p. 18.
3. "Every day at five o'clock…" Ibid, p. 20.
4. "Do anything you like…" Fleming, 1963, p. 038.
5. "He had an instinct…" Ibid, p. 005.
6. "Bond quickened his step…" Ibid, p. 008.
7. "had come to Corsica…" Ibid, p. 052.
8. "I wish you to pay court…" Ibid, p. 059.
9. "Bond suddenly thought…" Ibid, p. 230.
10. "Tracy. I love you…." Ibid, p. 231.
11. "It will be better…" Lockhart, 1985, p, 319.
12. "The note-book… Ibid, p. 319.
13. "I asked permission…" Ibid, p.319.
14. "As calmly as I could…" Ibid, p. 320.
15. "Say nothing – all will be well." Ibid, p. 337.
16. "From the moment…" Fleming, 1954, p. 001-2.
17. "there won't be any strong arm stuff…" Fleming, 1964, p. 031.
18. "You are to enter this Castle of Death…" Ibid, p. 105.

Chapter 4: Sidney Reilly

1. Sidney Reilly image. Wikimedia Commons.
2. "Sidney Reilly was the most successful…" Kettle, p. 11.
3. "May your soul rot in hell…" Lockhart 1984, p. 25.
4. "You can look for me…" Ibid, p. 25.
5. "He found her companionship easy…" Fleming, 1953, p. 158.
6. "That day he would ask Vesper to marry him…" Ibid, p. 164.
7. "Tell me what's hurting you." Ibid, p. 172.
8. "I love you with all my heart…" Ibid, p. 177.
9. 'Yes, dammit…' Ibid, p. 181.
10. Lenin survived. World Assassinations video. 2008.
11. "the small granite cross…" Fleming, 1963, p.018.
12. "25th Sept. 1925…" Reilly, 1986, p. 200-202.
13. Reilly: Ace of Spades Campbell & Goddard, 1983.

14. "Reilly lived on for at least twenty years..." Lockhart, 1987, p. 28-32.
15. "Four GPU officers..." Smith, 2002.
16. "James Bond is just a piece of nonsense..." Lockhart, 1984, p. 11.

Chapter 5: Sir Fitzroy Maclean

1. Sir Fitzroy Maclean. Rayner, Erina. 1990, YouTube. Wikimedia Commons.
2. "Children were denouncing their parents..." Mclean, 1999, p. 19.
3. "There were thousands ..." Ibid, p. 19.
4. "anything one said..." Ibid, p. 19.
5. "He then t[akes] out a pocket knife..." Fleming, 1964, p. 081-2.
6. "He screw[s] back the plate..." Ibid, p. 082.
7. "say very devout prayers ..." Ibid, p. 082.
8. "For tonight..." Ibid, p. 084.
9. "Bond verified that his room..." Ibid, p. 094.
10. "The handle of a safety razor..." Ibid, p. 095.
11. "None of the other little traps..." Ibid, p. 095.
12. Montague Grover. Reuters online article, 1987.
13. "I do wish I could meet the nice Mr. [Ian] Fleming ..." McLynn, 1992, p. 50.
14. "he's very busy." Ibid. p. 50.
15. "him time to get on with a project..." Fleming, 1959, p. 059.
16. "presented to M..." Ibid, p. 060.
17. "a translation of a manual..." Ibid, p. 060.
18. "Come-along and Restraint Holds..." Ibid, p. 060.
19. "Bond read again the passage..." Ibid. p. 060-061.
20. "a jaw-breaking dissertation..." Fleming, 1967, p. 051.
21. "Fitzroy was a good delegator..." McLynn 1992, p. 149.
22. "Seeing that capture was inevitable..." Maclean, 1999, p. 338.
23. "he had destroyed himself..." Ibid, p.338.

24. "None of the girls…" McLynn, 1992, p. 213
25. "[H]e preferred…" Ibid, p.213.
26. " My initial feeling …" McLynn, p. 270.
27. Fitzroy Maclean died, at the age of 85… McLynn, 1996.

Chapter 6: Patrick Dalzel-Job

1. Patrick Dalzel-Job image. Imperial War Musuem.
2. "Her name was Bjorg…" Dalzel-Job (1991) p. 23.
3. "He's a bachelor…" Fleming, 1964, p. 018-19.
4. "just shock," Ibid, p.019.
5. "Castle of Death." Ibid, p.099.
6. "to enter this Castle of Death…" Ibid, p.105.
7. "deaf and dumb…" Ibid p. 118.
8. "The Japanese Garbo," Ibid p.158.
9. "You are very beautiful …" Ibid, p. 194.
10. "tonight I have to swim…" Ibid, p. 196.
11. "Our boss in Admiralty was Ian Fleming…" Dalzel-Job (1991), p. 115.
12. "My accelerated promotion…" Ibid, p. 116.
13. "someone said that I gave him…" Ibid, p. 116.
14. "THE BEARER OF THIS CARD…" Ibid. p. 116.
15. "At nineteen she was taller…" Ibid. p. 181.
16. "She had brought…" Fleming, 1964, p 222.
17. "It's Kissy…" Ibid, p. 261.
18. "put her arms under his armpits…" Ibid, p.262.
19. "she had got her man back…" Ibid, p.263.
20. "Real-life model for James Bond without the martinis." van der Vat.
21. "only ever loved one woman and was not a drinking man." Obituary of Patrick Dalzel-Job, 2003.

Chapter 7: Eddie Chapman

1. Eddie Chapman image. Wikimedia Commons.
2. "There are hundreds of secret inks…" Fleming, 1963, p.194.
3. "Held in front of a flame…" Ibid, p. 195.
4. De Havilland Aircraft Company factory. Security Service MI5.,

5. "Admiral Sir Miles Messervy..." Fleming, 1965, p.004.
6. "They gave me VIP treatment..." Ibid, p.017.
7. "need for East and West..." Ibid, p.17.
8. "across the table..." Ibid, p. 18.
9. "great sheet of Armourplate glass hurtled down..." Ibid, p. 019.
10. "The story of Chapman is different..." Stephens, 1942.

Chapter 8: Merlin Minshall

1. Merlin Minshall image. Wikimedia Commons.
2. "At the age of eighteen..." Fleming, 1961, p. 109.
3. "He had told a highly coloured story..." Ibid, p, 110.
4. "He didn't mind..." Ibid, p. 111.
5. "Stay on the bus..." Minshall, 1971, p. 25.
6. "You do realize, *mein Liebe*..." Minshall p. 29.
7. "would let no torturing take place..." Fleming, 1957, p.094-5.
8. "The State is pleased with you." Ibid, p. 099.
9. "Your body belongs to the State...." Ibid, p.108.
10. "Did you miss me very much..." Minshall, p. 107.
11. "What do you think?" Ibid, p. 107.
12. "But now I think we are wasting time..." Ibid, p. 107.
13. "Now that you have seen..." Minshall p. 134.
14. "pulls a pistol from a holster..." Maibaum, 1963, p. 112.
15. "keeping you alive..." Ibid, p. 115.
16. "a gale of smoke..." Ibid, p. 119-21.
17. "Grant's head slumps back..." Ibid, p. 122.
18. "Bond follows carrying the Lektor..." Maibaum, p. 131.
19. "Heave to! Heave to!" Ibid, p. 135-6.
20. "Bond glances back at the fuel drum..." Ibid, p. 138-9.
21. "Why are you giving up?..." Ibid, p. 139.
22. "There's a saying in England...." Ibid, p. 139.
23. with his fourth wife Christina Majorie Zambra. RNVR Officers 1939-1945.
24. Merlin Minshall died. Obituary, 1987.

Chapter 9: Conrad O'Brien-ffrench

1. Conrad O'Brien-ffrench image. Wikimedia Commons.
2. Conrad Fulke Thomond O"Brien-ffrench Video interview with Conrad and short article about his life. Atkinson, 2007.
3. "I met a nineteen-year-old American..." O"Brien-ffrench, 1979, p. 85.
4. "Despite many previous warnings..." Fleming, 1961, p. 003-4.
5. "JAMES BOND, face down..." Maibaum & Hopkins, 1965, p.13.
6. "Funny looking bruise..." Ibid, p. 15.
7. "A poker..." Ibid, p.15.
8. "Whine of the motor builds..." Ibid. p. 21.
9. "Steam billows around the camera..." Ibid. p. 23.
10. "We will spend the day climbing..." Fleming, 1966, p. 020.
11. "It was a small glacier..." Ibid, p. 038.
12. "'Oberhauser was a friend of mine...'" Ibid, p. 038.
13. "To the average individual..." O"Brien-ffrench, 1979, p. 222.
14. "Censorship makes a minute study..." Ibid, p. 222.
15. "I had been a secret agent..." Ibid, p. 258.

Chapter 10: Dusko Popov

1. Duško Popov mage. Wikimedia Commons.
2. "If you want to destroy a team..." Popov, 1974, p. 34.
3. "You are honest without scruples..." Ibid, pg. 74-75.
4. "The top gangsters..." Fleming, 1962, p. 196.
5. "The scars of my terror had been healed..." Ibid, p. 198.
6. "There was only one appropriate codename..." Hills, 2002.
7. "It's much the same as any other gambling..." Fleming, 1953, p. 060-61.
8. "time to explain the mechanics..." Ibid, p. 062.
9. "If I haven't got a natural..." Ibid, 063..
10. "But although Agent Tricycle..." Hills, 2002.

Chapter 11: Sir William Stephenson

1. William Stephenson image. Wikimedia Commons.
2. "'If she could come over to us…" Fleming, 1957, p. 141.
3. "Top Secret traffic of all…" Ibid, p. 141.
4. "Every day, at eighteen-thirty local time" Fleming, 1958, p. 005.
5. "the weight of each pulse…" Ibid, p. 010.
6. "And, if an agent had been captured…" Ibid, p. 010-11.
7. "You know what you must do…." Hyde, 1983, p. Xv.
8. "THE AMERICAN GOVERNMENT IS DEBATING …" Stevenson, 1976, p. 117.
9. *Dear Lord*…. Stevenson, 1976, p. 14-115.
10. "Well, I think it's all a pack of nonsense." Fleming, 1963, p. 089.
11. "Miss Moneypenny…" Ibid, p. 089.
12. "dressed in tails…" Ibid, p. 234.
13. "And this is James…" Ibid p. 235.
14. 'M PERSONAL FOR 007 EYES ONLY…" Fleming. 1965, p. 193&5.
15. "I'd like all those things…." Ibid p. 199.
16. "*I was delighted to hear* …'" Macdonald, 2001, p. 113-14.
17. *The Intrepid Society* Stephenson Honorary Society website.
18. *The True Intrepid* McEvoy, 2004.
19. *A Man Called Intrepid* Bernews, 2011.

Chapter 12: Noël Coward

1. Noël Coward image. Wikimedia Commons.
2. "During the last war …." Day, 2007, p. 374-75.
3. I can honestly assure that…" Ibid, p. 389.
4. I am an Englishman…" Ibid, p.390.
5. "It was a great privilege to be with you…" Ibid, p. 397.
6. "A dry Martini…" Fleming, 1953, p. 045.
7. "as the deep glass became frosted…" Ibid, p. 045.
8. "I think it's a fine name…" Ibid, p. 053.
9. "a pinch of black pepper…" Fleming, 1955, p. 056.
10. "It's a trick the Russians taught me…" Ibid, p. 056-7.

11. "a medium dry Martini…." Fleming, 1956, p. 080.
12. "Made with Cresta Blanca…" Ibid, p. 080.
13. "I was to go as an entertainer…" Day, p.403.
14. "I was a perfect silly ass…" Ibid, p. 403.
15. "I ridiculed the whole business…" Ibid, p. 403-4.
16. *Blithe Spirit* original trailer. Lean. 1945.
17. *In Which We Serve.* Coward & Lean 1942.
18. "The King and Queen kept their promise …" Day, 2007, p. 469.
19. *Don't let's be beastly to the Germans…* Coward HMV Recordings, 1943.
20. "conferment of Knighthood…" Day, 2007, p. 471.
21. "*rognon de veau…*" Fleming, 1953, p. 054.
22. "The trouble always is…" Ibid, p. 054.
23. "the Blanc de Blanc Brut 1943…" Ibid, p. 054.
24. "I've taken the chance…" Fleming, 1956. P. 080.

Chapter 13: Roald Dahl

1. Roald Dahl image. Library of Congress.
2. "Shot Down Over Libya," Dahl, 1942.
3. "'Rather dazed…" Sturrock, 2010 p. 74.
4. "Of course you're our heroes" Fleming, 1953, p.058.
5. "'It's not difficult…" Ibid, p. 058.
6. "It's a confusing business…" Ibid, p.059.
7. "The first was in New York…" Ibid, p. 134.
8. "For various reasons…" Ibid, p.134.
9. "when you get back to London…" Ibid, p. 138-9.
10. "the most breathless and exhilarating time …. ' Sturrock, 2010, p.146.
11. "whose Hurricane was in flames…" Ibid, p. 146.
12. "A Piece of Cake" video documentary describes how Roald started his writing career. Lane, YouTube.
13. "The man buzzed off…" Sturrock, 2010, p. 216.
14. "But then he thought of Kissy…" Fleming, 1964, p. 222.
15. "is a public service…" Ibid, p. 249.
16. whisper[s] through his gritted teeth…" Ibid, p. 252.

17. "That's what you've got to find out..." Dahl & Bloom, June, 1967, p. 2/3-4.
18. "She's dead..." Ibid, p. 8/7.
19. "Bon appetit." Ibid, p. 12/11.
20. "Now, how about that honeymoon." Ibid, p. 12/17
21. "Why not?" Ibid, p. 12/17.
22. "Tell him to come..." p. 12/18.

Chapter 14: Ivar Bryce

1. Ivar Bryce image. www.archives.gov.
2. "Hitler has often protested...." Weber 1985.
3. "we are pledged to pull our own oar..." Ibid.
4. "You know, Ivar..." Bryce, 1984 p. 74.
5. "Now here's one vital request..." Ibid p. 103.
6. "a long low range of well-kept buildings..." Fleming, 1960, p. 065-6.
7. "the endless vista of the Green Mountains..." Ibid, p. 070-1.
8. "He had no personal motives ..." Ibid, p.088.
9. "'that was awful..." Ibid, p. 095.
10. "It had to be done...." Ibid, p. 095.
11. "How much I owe you..." Bryce, 1984, p. 139.

Chapter 15: Valentine & Peter Fleming

1. Valentine "Mookie" Fleming image. Wikimedia Commons.
2. "My Darling Mum..." Hart-Davis, 1987, p, p. 29.
3. "She evoked him as an example..." Ibid, p. 20.
4. "I was happy and proud to serve...'" Fleming, 1964, p. 259-60.
5. Peter Fleming image. The Fleming Family. Ian Fleming images.
6. "I suspect that my childhood ailments..." Hart-Davis, 1987, p. 15.
7. "One did not go..." Ibid, p. 15.
8. Operational Bases (OB). Angell, Subterranea Britannica.
9. "rising until it was a clear foot..." Fleming, 1960, p. 029.
10. "two halves of the bush..." Ibid, p. 030.

11. "leaving no footprints …" Ibid, p. 031.
12. "to make your enemy take…" Hart-Davis, 1987, p. 265.
13. "Bond's unsung heroes." Ryan, 2009

Chapter 16: Other Inspirations

1. Pieter Tazelaar. Gardham, 21, Nov. 2010.
2. "at 4.35am…" Ibid.
3. "rises out of the water…" Maibaum & Dehn, p. 1.
4. "NITRO." Ibid, p. 2.
5. 'He pulls off his diving suit…" Ibid, p. 3.
6. "PAN[S] on him…" Ibid, p. 7.
7. "MAIN TITLE SEQUENCE." Ibid. p. 8.
8. "born just outside Quebec." Fleming, 1962, p. 017.
9. "And then [she] would think again" Ibid, p.070.
10. weigh[s] them up…" Ibid, p.131.
11. "These are killers…" Ibid, p. 156.
12. "They were sitting ducks…" Ibid, p. 164.
13. "Never been able to kill in cold blood." Ibid, p.164.
14. Hoagy Carmichael image. Wikimedia Commons.
15. "[Bond] is very good-looking…." Fleming, 1953, p. 034.
16. "certainly good-looking…" Fleming, 1955, p. 161.
17. "he was involved…" Fleming, 1957, p. 62.
18. "appears to be a dangerous enemy…" Ibid, p. 63.
19. "down the sunburned skin…" Ibid, p. 66.
20. "signs of plastic surgery…" Ibid, p.67.
21. "Death Warrant…" Ibid, p. 68.
22. "A large scar…" Burriss, Rowland & Little.
23. "While two held his shoulders…" Seaman, 1997, p. 147.
24. "torture held all the dark torments …" Jackson, p. 207.
25. "a small carpet of glinting steel spikes …" Fleming, 1953, p. 101 & 106.
26. "Bond's whole body arched…" Ibid, p. 113.
27. "He had been told by colleagues…" Ibid, p. 115.
28. "Alright! See this tool…" Brown, 1988, Act III, p. 2.

Chapter 17: Ian Fleming

1. Ian Fleming image. www.everettcollection.com
2. "At the peak..." Pearson, 1966, p. 89.
3. " Ian should be the DNI" Macintyre, Summer 2008.
4. "in order to tell the difference..." Fleming, 1953, p. 136.
5. "Surround yourself with human beings..." Ibid, p.139.
6. "of using him as a tool..." Fleming, 1965, p. 026-7.
7. "whether to shoot..." Ibid, p. 078.
8. "Fraid you haven't got much time..." Ibid, p. 175.
9. "You did a good job...." Ibid, p. 190-1.
10. 1994 Intelligence Services Act... Held & South, p.129.
11. "I can promise you nothing..." Pearson, October 1966.
12. "what every man would like to be..." Mortimer, 1963.
13. March 1961 *Life* magazine article ... James Bond Museum.
14. "[Bond's] final rendezvous..." Fleming, 1966, p. 092.
15. "You know where you come in..." Ibid, p. 94.
16. "Okay. With any luck..." Ibid, p. 118.
17. "the Universal Declaration of Human Rights ..." Held & South, 2006, p. 114-15.
18. "I shall not waste my days..." Fleming, 1964, p. 260.
19. "I would rather be ashes than dust! ...'" Mr. Blofeld, 2011.

CONCLUSION

1. "The spawn of the devil is dead..." Fleming, 1964, p 264.
2. "I love him..." Ibid, p. 264.
3. "Kissy wonder[s]..." Ibid, p.272.
4. "take care..." Ibid, p. 274.
5. "She'd certainly be courtmartialled for muffing this job..." Fleming, 1966 p. 118.

Sources for Further Investigation

Angell, Stewert. *Site Name: Hurstpierpoint Patrol (Auxiliary Units)*. Subterranea Britannica. http://www.subbrit.org.uk/sb-sites/sites/h/hurstpierpoint_au_hideout/index.shtml

Atkinson, Paul. *Conrad Fulke O'Brien-ffrench. Artist and Spy: The real James Bond*. 2007. http://00brien.com.

BBC. *Could you be a spy like us?* BBC News. September 24, 2008. http://news.bbc.co.uk/2/hi/uk_news/magazine/7112814.stm

BBC. *Spies like us*. BBC News. November 26, 2007. http://news.bbc.co.uk/2/hi/uk_news/magazine/7112814.stm

BBC. IMI6 agents give first interviews. BBC News. November 15, 2006.

Bernews. *Bermuda's WWII Espionage Role*. Bermuda's News & Culture Source. November 11, 2011. http://bernews.com/2011/11/bermudas-second-world-war-espionage-role/

Bond, Mary Wickham. *How 007 Got His Name*. London: Collins, 1966.

Blacklock, Mark. *Was a 16th British spy called John Bond the inspiration for 007?* The Daily and Sunday Express, Britton, Nick. UK News. October 31, 2008. http://www.express.co.uk/posts/view/68782

Brown, William. *Casino Royale*. USA: Climax, CBS, 007 Magazine, Issue #18. Autumn, 1988. http://www.007magazine.co.uk/

Brown, William. *Casino Royale*. MGM DVD, 1967.

Byrce, Ivar. *You Only Live Once: Memories of Ian Fleming*. Maryland: University Publications of America, Inc. 1984.

Burriss, R. P., Rowland, H. M., & Little, A. C. (2009). Facial scarring enhances men's attractiveness for short-term relationships. *Personality and Individual Differences, 46*(2), 213-217. http://dx.doi.org/10.1016/j.paid.2008.09.029

Campbell, Martin & Goddard, Jim. *Reilly: Ace of Spades*. BBC mini-series, 1983. http://video.search.yahoo.com/video/play?p=sidney+reilly+youtube&tnr=21&vid=&turl=http%3A%2F%2Fts3.mm.bing.net%2Fth%3Fid%3DU.5055314702106774%26pid%3D15.1&tit=Reilly%3A+Assassinate+Stalin&back=http%3A%2F%2Fus.yhs4.search.yahoo.com%2Fyhs%2Fsearch%3Fei%3DUTF-8%26p%3Dsidney%2Breilly%2Byoutube%26type%3DW3i_IA%252C206%252C6434_01%252CStartPage%252C20120105%252C18674%252C0%252C0%252C6434%26hsimp%3Dyhs-geneiotransfer%26hspart%3Dw3i&sigb=15plbsgf4

Cooper, D. W. & Gerald, Lawrence. *A Bond for All the Ages: Sir Francis Bacon and John Dee: The Original 007*. Sir Francis Bacon's New Advancement of Learning. http://www.sirbacon.org/links/dblohseven.html

Coward, Noel. *Don't Let's Be Beastly to the Germans*. HMV Recordings 1928-1953. 1943. http://www.youtube.com/watch?v=wve-W9Tw2JKE

Coward, Noel & Lean, David. *In Which We Serve*. UK: British Lion Film Corp Ltd., 1942. http://www.youtube.com/watch?v=pTNscjQ_Hgc

Dahl, Roald. "Shot Down Over Libya." Saturday Evening Post, August 1, 1942.

Dahl, Roald & Bloom, Harold Jack for "additional story material." *You Only Live Twice*. Loosely based on the novel by Ian Fleming. Produced by Ion Productions, June, 1967.

Dalzel-Job, Patrick. *Arctic Snow to Dust of Normandy: The Extraordinary Wartime Exploits of a Naval Special Agent*. South Yorkshire: Pen & Sword Books Ltd., 2005.

Day, Barry. *THE LETTERS OF NOËL COWARD*. New York: Alfred A. Knopf, 2007.

The Deadline Team. *Amazon Acquires License to James Bond Novels for Digital and Print*. Amazon Publications. April 17, 2012.

https://deadline.com/2012/04/amazon-acquires-license-to-james-bond-novels-for-digital-and-print-257931/

Enochian. Enochian Language. http://enochian.com.

Favorite Books of President Kennedy. Boston: John F. Kennedy Presidential Library and Museum. http://www.jfklibrary.org/Research/Ready-Reference/JFK-Miscellaneous-Information/Favorite-Books.aspx

Fleming, Ian. *The Property of a Lady.* London: Pan Books Ltd., 1967.

Fleming, Ian. *Octopussy and The Living Daylights.* London: Jonathan Cape Ltd., 1966.

Fleming, Ian. *The Man with the Golden Gun.* London: Jonathan Cape Ltd., 1965.

Fleming, Ian. *You Only Live Twice.* London: Jonathan Cape Ltd., 1964.

Fleming, Ian. *On Her Majesty's Secret Service.* London: Jonathan Cape Ltd., 1963.

Fleming, Ian. *The Spy Who Loved Me.* London: Jonathan Cape Ltd., 1962.

Fleming, Ian. *Thunderball.* London: Jonathan Cape Ltd., 1961.

Fleming, Ian. *For Your Eyes Only.* London: Jonathan Cape Ltd., 1960.

Fleming, Ian. *Goldfinger.* London: Jonathan Cape Ltd., 1959.

Fleming, Ian. *Dr. No.* London: Jonathan Cape Ltd., 1958.

Fleming, Ian. *From Russia with Love.* London: Jonathan Cape Ltd., 1957.

Fleming, Ian. *Diamonds are Forever.* London: Jonathan Cape Ltd., 1956.

Fleming, Ian. *Moonraker.* London: Jonathan Cape Ltd., 1955.

Fleming. Ian. *Live and Let Die.* London: Jonathan Cape Ltd., 1954.

Fleming, Ian. *Casino Royale.* London: Jonathan Cape Ltd., 1953.

Gardham, Duncan. *Real 'James Bond' revealed in MI6 archives.* The Telegraph: London, 21, September, 2010. http://www.telegraph. co.uk/news/uknews/defence/8017038/Real-James-Bond-revealed-in-MI6-archives.html

Hart-Davis, Duff. *PETER FLEMING: A Biography.* Oxford: Oxford University Press, 1987.

Held, Jacob & South, James. *James Bond and Philosophy: Questions are Forever* (Editors). Peru, Ill.: Open Court Publishing Div. of Carus Publishing Company, 2006.

Hellman, Geoffrey. *Bond's Creator.* The New Yorker, April 21, 1962.

Hills, Claire. *The name's Tricycle, Agent Tricycle.* BBC News. May 9, 2002. http://news.bbc.co.uk/2/hi/uk_news/1973962.stm.

Hyde, H. Montgomery. *Secret Intelligence Agent.* New York: St. Martin's, 1983.

Jackson, Sophie. *Churchill's White Rabbit: The True Story of a Real-Life James Bond.* Stroud: The History Press, 2012.

Kennedy, Maev. *Ian Fleming and Agatha Christie lead list of UK's top-earning crimewriters.* The Guardian, 2011. https://www. theguardian.com/books/2011/apr/10/top-earning-crime-writers-uk

Kettle, Michael. *Sidney Reilly: The True Story of the World's Greatest Spy.* New York: St Martin's Press. 1983.

Lane, Terry. *Rare Roald Dahl Interview from 1990 – How he became a writer.* YouTube.com. by notasissy. http://www.youtube.com/watch?v=vDbHEGEtiOc

Lean, David. *Blithe Spirit original 1945 film trailer.* YouTube.com November 19, 2007. http://www.youtube.com/watch?v=-jIiCtxXtVXY

Lockhart, Robin Bruce. *Reilly: The First Man.* New York: Penguin Books, 1987.

Lockhart, R. H. Bruce. *Memoires of a British Agent*. London: Macmillan Publishers Ltd., 1985.

Lockhart, Robin Bruce. *Reilly: Ace of Spies*. New York: Penguin Books Ltd., 1984.

Macdonald, Bill. *The True Intrepid: Sir William Stephenson and the Unknown Agents*. Vancouver: Raincoat Books, 2001.

Macintyre, Ben. *007 For Your Eyes Only: Ian Fleming & James Bond*. London: Bloomsbury Publishing, 2008.

Macintyre, Ben. *James Bond: Fact and fiction*. Despatches. Summer 2008. www.iwm.org.uk/upload/pdf/8-11_fleming.pdf

Macintyre, Ben. *Was Ian Fleming the real 007?: The war heroes, spymasters and beautiful women who inspired Ian Fleming to create James Bond*. London: The Sunday Times, April 5, 2008.

Maclean, Fitzroy. *Eastern Approaches* (reprint ed.). Penguin Global, 1999.

Maibaum, Richard & Hopkins, John. *Thunderball* screenplay based on the Original Story by Kevin McClory, Jack Whittingham and Ian Fleming. Produced by Eon Productions, 1965.

Maibaum, Richard & Dehn, Paul. *Goldfinger* screenplay based on the novel by Ian Fleming. Produced by Eon Productions, 1964.

Maibaum, Richard. Adapted by Harwood, Johanna. *From Russia with Love* screenplay based on the novel by Ian Fleming. Produced by Ion Productions, 1963.

McEvoy, Terry. *The True Intrepid*. Winnipeg: Quiet Canadian Inc./ MidCanada Entertainment., 2004. http://www.youtube.com/ watch?v=cQbOsi8vEP0&feature=player_embedded

McDowall, Carolyn.*ScholarCourtier Majician: The Lost Library of John Dee*. The cultureconcept circle, Nov. 11, 2015. https:// www.thecultureconcept.com/scholar-courtier-magician-the-lost-library-of-john-dee

McLynn, Frank. *Sir Fitzroy Maclean Bt: Obituary.* The INDPEN-DENT. June 19, 1996. http://www.independent.co.uk/news/obituaries/sir-fitzroy-maclean-bt-obituary-1337837.html

McLynn, Frank. *Fitzroy Maclean.* London: John Murray Publishers Ltd. 1992.

Minshall, Merlin. *Guilt-Edged.* London: Panther Books Ltd., 1977.

Moogheer. How Ian Fleming created James Bond. D.A. Confidential, YouTube, July 20, 2010. http://daconfidential.blogspot.com/2010/07/carruthers-peregrine-carruthers-no-not.html

Mr. Blofeld. *"I shall not waste my days..."* The Jack London Connection. CommanderBond.net forums. May 5, 2011. http://debrief.commanderbond.net/topic/59859-i-shall-not-waste-my-days/

Obituary of Merlin Minshall. London: The Times, September 23, 1987. http://www.broadscapeproductions.info/Broadscape_Website_August_2008/Merlin_Minshall_Times_Obituary.html

Obituary of *Patrick Dalzel-Job; War Hero Inspired Ian Fleming's Bond.* Los Angeles Times, October 18, 2003. http://articles.latimes.com/2003/oct/18/local/me-passings18.4

O"Brien-ffrench, Conrad. *Delicate Mission: Autobiography of a Secret Agent.* London: Skilton & Shaw, 1979.

Official Secrets Act 1989 (c.6). Statute Law Database. The United Kingdom National Archives. http://www.legislation.gov.uk/ukpga/1989/6/section/1.

Pearson, John. *The Life of Ian Fleming.* New York: McGraw-Hill Book Company, 1966.

Pearson, John. *Rough Rise of a Dream Hero.* Life Magazine vol. 61. October 14, 1966.

Popov, Dusko. SPY/COUNTERSPY: The autobiography of Dusko Popov. New York: Grosset & Dunlap Publishers, 1974.

Rayner, Erina. *Off the Page: Fitzroy Maclean.* STVPEOPLE. Scottish

Television Production. 1990. YouTube. http://www.youtube. com/watch?v=j2bR6T2kilE

Reilly, Sidney. *Britain's Master Spy: The Adventures of Sidney Reilly.* New York: Carroll & Graf Publishers. Inc., 1986.

Reuters. *Stalin Showed Mercy in 1938 and Lovelorn Pilot Won a Bride.* Los Angeles Times, June 1,1987. http://articles.latimes. com/1987-06-01/news/mn-5373_1_briton

Rosicrucian Order. *The Key to Universal Wisdom.* Rosicrucian.org. http://rosicrucian.org/home.html

Royal Navel Volunteers Reserve (RNVR) Officers 1939-1945. *Minshall, Merlin Theodore.* http://www.unithistories.com/officers/ RNVR_officersM3.html

Ryan, Robert. *Bond's unsung heroes: Peter Fleming, adventurer.* London: The Telegraph, May 21, 2009. http://www.telegraph. co.uk/culture/film/jamesbond/5297115/Bonds-unsung-heroes-Peter-Fleming-adventurer.html

Scripts.com, STANDS4 LLC, 2019. *"You Only Live Twice"* Accessed March 13, 2019. https://www.scripts.com/script/you_only_ live_twice_23868

Seaman, Mark. *Bravest of the Brave: The True Story of Wing Commander 'Tommy' Yeo-Thomas SOE Secret Agent-Codename 'White Rabbit.'* London: Michael O'Mara, 1997.

Security Service MI5. *Documents from the Chapman Case.* MI5.gov. uk. https://www.mi5.gov.uk/home/mi5-history/world-war-ii/ eddie-chapman---agent-zigzag/documents-from-the-chapman-case.html

Smith, Michael. *Stalin had Britain's Ace of Spies killed* London: The Telegraph, May 9, 2002. https://www.telegraph.co.uk/news/ uknews/.../Stalin-had-Britains-Ace-of-Spies-killed.htm...

Stephens, R. *MI5 report v2 437.* January 7, 1942.

Stevenson, William. *A Man Called Intrepid: The Incredible WWII*

Narrative of the Hero Whose Spy Network and Secret Diplomacy Changed the Course of History. Guilford, CT: Globe Pequot Press, 1976.

Sturrock, Donald. *Storyteller: The Authorized Biography of Roald Dahl*. New York: Simon & Schuster, 2010.

The Times. *The 50 greatest British writers since 1945*. The Times, January 5, 2008. http://www.thetimes.co.uk/article/the-50-greatest-british-writers-since-1945-ws3g69xrf90

van der Vat, Dan. *Patrick Dalzel-Job: Real-life model for James Bond without the martinis*. The Guardian. October 23, 2003. http://www.guardian.co.uk/news/2003/oct/24/guardianobituaries

Weber, Mark. *Roosevelt's 'Secret Map' Speech*. Originally published in The Journal of Historical Review (vol. 6, no. 1) Spring 1985. Institute for Historical Review. http://www.ihr.org/jhr/v06/v06p125_Weber.html

Woolsey, Benjamin. *The Queen's Conjurer: The Science and Magic of Dr. John Dee, Advisor to Queen Elizabeth I*. New York: Henry Holt & Company, LLC, 2001.

World Assassinations. *The Attempted Assassination of Vladimir Lenin*. YouTube. November 17, 2008. http://www.youtube.com/watch?v=9eiNPsFkl_E

Sources for Further Investigation IMAGES:

Bond, James (ornithologist). https://commons.wikimedia.org/wiki/File:James_Bond_1974.jpg

Bryce, John Felix C. https://www.archives.gov/contact

Chapman, Eddie. https://commons.wikimedia.org/wiki/File:Eddie_Chapman_(Agent_ZigZag).jpg

Charmichael, Hoagy.

https://en.wikipedia.org/wiki/File:Hoagy_Carmichael_-_1947.jpg

Christie, Agatha. https://commons.wikimedia.org/wiki/File:Agatha_Christie.png

Coward, Noel. https://commons.wikimedia.org/wiki/File:Noel_Coward_(1963)_by_Erling_Mandelmann_-_2.jpg

Coward, Noel. Firefly statue & house. https://commons.wikimedia.org/wiki/File:NoelCowardFirefly.jpg

Dahl, Roald. http://hdl.loc.gov/loc.pnp/van.5a51869

Dalzel-Job, Patrick. https://www.iwm.org.uk/collections/item/object/205160640

Dee, John. https://commons.wikimedia.org/wiki/File:John_Dee.jpg

Dee, John glyph. https://commons.wikimedia.org/wiki/File:John_Dee%27s_-Eyes_Only-_signature.svg

Fleming, Ian. https://www.everettcollection.com/#/sign-up

Fleming, Peter. http://www.ianfleming.com/ian-fleming-images/

Fleming, Valentine. https://commons.wikimedia.org/wiki/File:Major_Valentine_Fleming.png

Lockhart, Robert Bruce. https://commons.wikimedia.org/wiki/File:%2BR._H._Bruce-Lockhart_in_Malaya.jpg

Maclean, Fitzroy. https://commons.wikimedia.org/wiki/File:Yugo-slav-leader-marsal-tito-talking-with-itzroy-maclean.jpg

Minshall, Merlin. https://commons.wikimedia.org/wiki/File:Mer-lin_Minshall.jpg

Nelson, Barry. https://commons.wikimedia.org/wiki/File:Barry_Nelson_1962.jpg

O'Brien-ffrench, Conrad. https://commons.wikimedia.org/wiki/File:Conrad_obrien-french_military_200x290.jpg

Popov, Dusko. https://commons.wikimedia.org/wiki/File:Dusko_Popov.jpg.

Reilly, Sidney. https://commons.wikimedia.org/wiki/File:Sidney_Reilly_German_Passport_September_1918.jpg

Stephenson, William. https://commons.wikimedia.org/wiki/File:-Sir_William_Stephenson_from_1942_passport.jpg

Made in the USA
Columbia, SC
19 January 2020

86906103R00152